EXPLORE THE WORLD ALONE
By MARY McCLURE GOULDING

HOW TO TRAVEL SPLENDIDLY
A MEMOIR OF PEOPLE AND PLACES

CHANDRA BOOKS
P.O. BOX 650
AROMAS, CALIFORNIA
95004

first published: March 2005
second edition: July   2005

Library of Congress Cataloging-in-Publication Data
EXPLORING THE WORLD ALONE
1.   Goulding, Mary 2. Travel 3. Solo Travel
4. Older Women 5. Seniors 6. Politics

cover design:
Kenneth Small at Digital Book Designs, Blue Springs, MO

photographs by:
William Kreger, Claudia Pagano, Brian Ward

printed in the U.S.A. by:
Total Printing Systems, Inc, Newton, IL

computer expert and general organizer:
David Edwards, DAE

also by :

Mary McClure Goulding, MSW:

WHO'S BEEN LIVING IN YOUR HEAD?

SWEET LOVE REMEMBERED

A TIME TO SAY GOOD-BYE

Mary McClure Goulding, MSW and Robert L. Goulding, MD:

CHANGING LIVES THROUGH REDECISION THERAPY

THE POWER IS IN THE PATIENT

NOT TO WORRY

Claudia Pagano, RN and Mary McClure, Goulding MSW:

LUPUS, WHAT'S IT ALL ABOUT?

To

Claudia Pagano,

my favorite nurse, with thanks

INTRODUCTION

This book is dedicated to my friends, not all of them still alive, and to me on my eightieth birthday, whether I am alive for it or not.

There once was a Mrs. Winchester in San Jose, California, who believed that so long as she was building her house she could not die. She kept adding rooms, stairs going nowhere, strange little alcoves, until at last she died. Now tourists traipse around the Winchester House and pay for guided tours.

Of course I am not really that silly. Yet there may be some part of me that thinks I cannot die so long as I still have more places to visit and write about in this world. So, this memoir may keep on growing until I die, and be published posthumously. Or it may keep on growing until I die, but never find its way to a publisher. Either way, I won't know.

My story begins officially on January 15, 2002, two months before my 77th birthday. 9 - 11 has happened. We have a war-loving president. I want out. So I give my furniture and art to my son and daughters, my professional books to friends, miscellany to goodwill, and am ready to vacate my apartment. My apartment is on the twentieth floor, with a glorious view of San Francisco Bay and an astronomical rent which has just risen again. The carpets are scrubbed, all traces of my ten years in San Francisco are erased from walls and closets, I turn in the keys. I am homeless.

My first stop will be Cuba, then my old favorite, Isla Mujeres, Mexico. Then wherever I choose.

My grandson Brian thinks every chapter should have a map. Instead. I am assuming that everyone who loves to travel owns an atlas.

EXPLORE THE WORLD ALONE

HOW TO TRAVEL SPLENDIDLY
A MEMOIR OF PEOPLE AND PLACES

INDEX

2002

2003

2004

2005

GOOD-BYE, SAN FRANCISCO

Back up a week. It is a stunning day in this finest of all cities, so clear that the Richmond Bridge sparkles silver its entire length. Though this is January, the weather is mild and sailboats are out. Coit Tower shines concrete-bright against the sky. Sitting in my apartment, I feel premature homesickness for this almost empty apartment I am leaving.

Today, as I pack, my apartment doorbell is being rung hard. I open the door to a very fat Moslem woman, my age perhaps, surrounded by bags of food from Safeway, more than a month's supply for the largest possible family. She is screaming a rapid-fire non-English and is close to tears. I phone downstairs to Safeway and to the doorman to come help her. They do. The doorman knows where she belongs. I continue packing. And then I begin to feel quite ill. Scratchy throat, followed by four days of flu, 102 degree fever that Tylenol can't break, diarrhea, and high sugar count even though I eat almost nothing and use insulin as before. My favorite doctor, who is also a best friend, lives in Watsonville, so I phone her rather than my local physician.

Like any good psychotherapist, I am sure this is simply ambivalence about leaving the land of (hopefully) eternal Medicare. But she says to taxi to a hospital emergency room, so I do. On the way to the hospital I feel my fever break, so wonder if I should check in. I am sweaty, cool, and quite weak. A cute young male doctor greets me; young male physicians are a delight to this old female. I tell him my fever has broken, so probably I don't need his services. "Please stick around," he says. "You may not need me, but I need your money." Because my blood pressure is 70/50, he prescribes an IV.

A nurse arrives to insert the IV needle in my arm, jabs and misses my vein, jabs again and again, until a huge dark bruise grows on my arm. "Let's try the other arm," she says casually. She doesn't even apologize. I tell her to get out of the room. "No more needles. I mean it. No IV." I am furious. Finally she leaves.

The doctor returns. "I hear there are problems."

I tell him it is disgraceful to have an incompetent nurse in the

1

emergency room. He tests my blood pressure again and says it is approaching normal, so no IV is necessary. "Nothing like a good tantrum to get the body going," he says.

"I hope you get paid anyway."

I am putting this in my diary, to prove that my leaving home is not 100% problem free. Mostly, however, I am excited. I'm not a novice. I've dreamed of traveling all my life, planned trips around the world since I was twelve, and taken many of them. But this is the first time I am about to be homeless. If I find out I do not like being homeless, I am one of the lucky people. I can change my mind. I put my US government-issued permission to teach in Cuba in my wallet, and take off.

CUBA

La Habana. I am staying in what was once a mansion owned by one of the Batista crowd but now used by CIMEQ, a large hospital complex, as a home for visiting physicians and teachers. Next week four Canadian transactional analysts and I will teach Cuban psychotherapists our methods. Today I am ambling alone in the old part of the city. I love what I have found so far:

Music everywhere.

Beautifully polished and cared for vintage cars, which I am told drive their owners mad because they are constantly breaking down and needing new parts. Cuba has learned to manufacture these parts, so presumably the cars can go on forever.

No accidents, honking of horns, squealing of sudden stops. Traffic is safe here, because people are driving carefully and defensively. No one risks losing a car to an accident.

Mansions and grand hotels, some restored to rent to tourists for badly-needed dollars, and some still rotting grandly away, like old bag ladies in once-beautiful gowns.

People laugh and hug when they greet each other. Blacks and Whites stroll hand in hand.

On Malecon boulevard high waves splash over the seawall into the street in sparkling cascades. I feel more air in my lungs, lightness in my spirit. If I were young, I would run fast and twirl in the cascades.

I talk with people in my inadequate Spanish. One man volunteers that he is sixty-eight, "poor but peaceful like my country." He is being sincere, not sarcastic. A woman asks if I have hand lotion to share. Unfortunately, I don't. "We can't buy it and I love it so much."

The Museo de Arqueologia, in a sixteenth century building, displays broken pottery and glass dug up some years ago from the garbage dump that had been beneath it. Garbage four centuries old is no longer garbage. One plate dates back to ninth century Spain. The newest are from the eighteenth and nineteenth century Spain and England. A guide, as elderly and myopic as is fitting in this tourist-

3

empty museum, tells me the history of every shard. We chat up a storm in broken (like the plates) English and Spanish. She relishes my interest. A lone and silent Japanese man enters, and now there are two visitors, but he isn't able to communicate with us or perhaps he is not interested in our in-depth study of ex-garbage.

I walk the length of the Paseo de Prado along a wide sidewalk with shade trees and benches. I meet friendly people, especially among the older ones. Today is Sunday, so artists are exhibiting paintings and ceramics. The stereotype paintings of Old Habana are in too-brilliant colors, changing reality. Families stroll by. The benches are filled with people watching the scene, reading, and chatting with friends. Teenagers are plastered against each other, making a big show of their passion, as teenagers do almost everywhere. People look festive, with bright clothing in wild colors. Pinks and oranges, reds and purples. Women wear skin-tight latex, even those whose abdomens are as fat as mine. I am happy in this crowd.

Then I tense, as I hear loud shouts from a corner of the paseo. A group of men are yelling and gesturing angrily. I worry that a riot is beginning, until I recognize the word "beisbol." I ask a young man what is going on. He explains that the men meet here in the park almost every day to discuss baseball àt top volume.

The Museum of the Revolution is in the old government palace, a grand pre-revolution building. The exhibits begin with the early, futile attempts to bring about a democratic government after the United States defeated Spain and considered Cuba a colony to exploit. (Thomas Jefferson was the first of our presidents to suggest we grab Cuba.) The major exhibits are of the Revolution, photos of Castro and his followers. There are heartbreaking letters and memorabilia of men who died during the fighting. I watch the seventy-fifth birthday video of Castro, made in 2000. It begins with the triumphant parades; the cheering, adoring, happy crowds; Castro's early speeches; his first visit to New York and the welcome given him by the city; the recent visit from an older Castro, when he is welcomed by noisy, affirmative crowds in Spanish Harlem. I listen to a desperately sad Castro, talking to millions of mourners at the funeral of Che Guevara. (Our CIA arranged his murder.)

I go to the Bellas Artes museum of Cuban paintings and enjoy a few, but modern art has never excited me nor has anyone's

4

revolutionary art. Someday I must study modern art. After the museum, I search for a book store that exchanges used English-language books. There are none. Where in Cuba are the books the tourists discard? I never find out, though I imagine they are hidden away in the major hotels for the use of their guests. I read titles in the immense book market, but the only English language books are those about Cuba since 1960, and old classics, vintage Charles Dickens. Fortunately, I have met a Canadian resident of Cuba and will exchange books with her.

The next day I visit Coppella park, where Cubans sit at tables under the trees, eating dishes of ice cream that cost less than four cents. It's a shady park, full of wonderful yaguey trees whose roots grow from all the branches, making vines that Tarzan would adore. Even on weekdays people are standing in long lines, waiting their turn to enter. "Is the ice cream really that good?" I ask three teenagers in line. "Oh, yes, it's the best!" It is featured in the first scene of the movie, "FRESA Y CHOCOLATE" (Strawberry and Chocolate). The film was made in Cuba with the approval of Castro, as an apology for the governments' earlier homophobia. However, homophobia dies slowly everywhere. Because the gay young man in the movie chooses strawberry, teenage boys here ostentatiously choose chocolate.

Pinar Del Rio. Five of us therapists and our host Dr. Rivas drive to this small city to see its spectacular, conical limestone hills and caves, and to visit a farming family. The drive is spectacular. The slate-gray hills emerge suddenly from the green landscape, each separate and unique, like the hills in paintings from the Guilin and River Li area of China, which I am planning to visit this year. We pass tobacco farms, then stop at the farm owned by Rivas' friend. It is poor by our standards, with little furniture. Chickens and pigs are running on the tamped dirt beside the home, and children play with them as if they are pets. There seem to be several families living together and very few rooms. A son, about forty, hugs Rivas and says "If you'd told me you were coming, I'd have put on shoes." (It makes a nice verse: "If I'd known you were comin, I'd a worn my shoes.") His wife serves us very sweet Cuban coffee I can't drink because of diabetes, while the children stare at us and giggle at my Spanish.

The patriarch of the family shows us the stack of planed wood he and his sons have readied for a new house that they will start to build

5

on the property this week. To get this lumber: they made a small, steep path from their property to the top of the mountain (half a mile away), cut down the necessary pine trees with an ordinary saw, carried them one by one down the mountain, sawed them into boards, planed them by hand, and sawed the boards into the correct lengths for the ceiling and walls. Climb, saw, carry, saw, plane, saw, and repeat again and again. They also planted new trees to replace those they cut down. The man was a carpenter at Rivas' hospital, but now has retired to this hard work on his farm. He's very excited about the new house, which will belong to his two oldest sons and their families.

Lots of hikers come to Pinar Del Rio to explore the caves and to climb. We have coffee at a restaurant next to one of the famous caves, walk inside to admire its intricate twists and turns, and then drive back to La Habana. (We opted out of visiting a tobacco factory that makes the famous Cuban cigars.)

Veradero. We are driven here by bus to attend the annual meeting of the Canadian Psychiatric Association. While the others, including the Cuban psychiatrists, attend the sessions, I alternate between the beautiful beach and the swimming pool. This is an area of expensive resorts, for people who are primarily interested in sun, sand, and sea. It is indistinguishable from plush hotels in Miami, Honolulu, Cancun, or any other such resort area. The only Cubans here are those employed in the tourist trade. On the way back we stop in the city of **Matanzas** to visit Ediciones Vigia, a book store that makes its own special paper for first editions of poetry and children's books.

Curtis Steele, Canadian psychiatrist and photographer, and I rent a car to go to villages a short distance from Havana, which his guidebook says are "off the beaten path." When we announce our plan to Rivas he insists we take a guide, and finds us Pepe. We soon see why Rivas was concerned. There are no road signs and the maps in the guide book are ludicrous in their lack of detail. It is a splendid drive. The roads wind around farmland where farmers are plowing by hand and with oxen. Many people walk along the roads, seemingly for miles. Others ride in horse-driven carriages. In the fields, men and women use short hoes, the kind finally banned in California after so many migratory workers were crippled by their use.

In one small town, while Curtis and Pepe look for photo opportunities, I ask a man about my age, "What is interesting here?"

He grins, takes my hand, and leads me to a ceiba tree that grants wishes. He urges me to wish for something secret and special, so that I can discover that he speaks the truth. I hug the tree, according to his instructions, and silently wish for continued peace for this lovely land. As he and I walk back to the car, he greets everyone he passes with hugs and kisses. To me he explains, "I've lived here thirty years. I know everyone and they all love me. There are good people and bad people in the world. We in Cuba are mostly good people. When you are good, you have friends."

There is a saying in Cuba, "Los amigos multiplican las alegrias y dividen las penas." Friends multiply happiness and divide troubles.

We set out for the next town. Pepe, our guide, doesn't know the way. Our routine: Pepe tells me to tell Curtis to stop the car. I do. Pepe asks directions from someone walking along the road. The answer, accompanied by great, sweeping gestures, "Straight ahead for maybe 300 meters, then left, and after awhile double back and go right. Pepe says, "Derecho - derecho;" I say, "Straight ahead, Curtis." "Ya a la izquierda;" "Quick, go left here." "Ya, doble a la derecha;" "You're supposed to double back on that road to our right." and then Pepe tells me to tell Curtis to stop again, and he asks another walker. If Curtis were not exclusively interested in old towns, we could simply stop right here on the road, where he could get splendid shots of carts, oxen, horses, and the passing pedestrians. Or he could shoot beautiful panoramas of the sugar cane and rice fields.

When we arrive at the second village, Curtis photographs while Pepe and I have a beer together. We speak in slow, over-simplified Spanish and even then I don't always understand him. This is a real problem in getting to know people. I do learn that he was a high school history teacher and gave up teaching to switch to janitorial work. Now he is a head janitor at the hospital and likes the job. He's with us today as a favor to Rivas, who is on call. Because all salaries are about the same in Cuba, Pepe didn't either gain or lose money by switching careers. We have a second beer, Curtis comes back, happy about his photos, and we return to La Habana in time for dinner.

I don't like Cuban food. It is free to us and beautifully served at the hours of our choice. The problem: meals consist of meat, day after day for lunch and dinner, plus sugary stuff which I can't eat. Cubans, forced into meatless days during the desperate years in the early '90s, call meatless meals "starvation food." So they consider it a favor to give us meat, plus potatoes, too-dry rice with only a few frijoles sprinkled into it, and over-cooked root vegetables. For those of us who are vegetarians, this is dreary. Even in the Paladares (family-owned restaurants) and tourist hotels, the focus is on meat. No Cuban seems to know how to make a tasty salad dressing. Their only cheese is process cheese. In other words, it's the same food we had to eat in Illinois when I was young. My Canadian friends like it.

The workshop is a success, with excellent translators and participants who are eager to learn. It reminds me of the enthusiasm in the US in the seventies and eighties, when Bob Goulding and I taught transactional analysis and our redecision therapy. At that time Cuba was developing superb schools of medicine, but for political reasons their psychotherapy was mostly confined to Pavlovian theory and psychoanalysis. Now they are bringing in a variety of fine teachers and catching up fast.

Though knowledge of modern psychotherapy techniques has lagged, Cuban physicians have established one of the finest medical systems in the Americas, in many ways better than our own. They are acknowledged experts in both Western and Eastern medicine. Foreigners, including US citizens, are brought to CIMEQ for their world-famous post-stroke treatment. All medical services and medicines are available to Cubans without charge.

They have sent many teams of physicians and nurses to Africa and South America to treat the poor, and have established a large medical school in Cuba that pays all expenses for poor, bright students to come to Cuba to study medicine. There is a Chenobyl village for Ukrainians who need protracted care. When a Ukrainian child needs extensive surgery or physical therapy, the family comes with the child. All receive free food and housing, and free education is provided for the children as well as any adults who wish it.

I am deeply grateful for the laserpuncture treatment I am receiving. I have arterial disease as a result of diabetes, with nightly leg cramps, numbness, "restless feet," and inability to walk distances. In San Francisco acupuncture helped a great deal. My acupuncturist there advised me, "When you get to Cuba, let them work with you. The Cubans are the best in the world." He explained that Cuban physicians, treating Vietnamese war-injured in China, saw what

8

acupuncture could accomplish and reported this to Castro, who then sent them back to China to learn the skill. "The Chinese tend to stick with their traditional methods, but the Cubans are innovative," my acupuncture physician said.

At CIMEQ I am having daily treatments from professor Hecheverria, who has taught laserpuncture at medical centers in many countries of the non-hostile (to Cuba) world. He is a very formal man, with a beautiful vowel-laden Caribbean-Spanish that is almost impossible for me to understand. I do let him know that the treatment is wonderful and I appreciate it. It seems to be more effective than acupuncture, and it doesn't hurt.

The final evening before the Canadians leave, we go to a fine and funky night club, where strong rum drinks are $1.50 and the music exciting. People dance with magnificent sensuality. Men of all ages ask me to dance; I don't because I can't. I watch in awe, wishing that the genetic code from my Scot and German ancestors included the ability to gyrate hips. I can't even keep time to music. (Che Guevara, an Argentinian, couldn't carry a tune or dance. Castro doesn't dance much either.) A handsome young Cuban singer arrives, goes down the line kissing each of us, grabs the mike, and belts out in English, "I Do It My Way." Everybody cheers. In this night club, in the hospital, on the streets, people of all races mingle easily. There are not blacks at one table and whites at another, as in our night clubs, schools, and colleges. Castro said, "In Cuba we are all mulattos" and "If we don't have mixed blood in our veins, we have mixed blood in our souls." I appreciate many aspects of Cuban life and this I appreciate most of all.

I move out of CIMEQ housing and rent an apartment from Celeste, a retired professor who lives in the adjoining apartment. We become friends. I visit other new friends, walk around town, and often go to the beach, Playa Santa Maria, to sit in a deck chair, read, eat wonderful fresh fish and shrimp, and get a massage for ten dollars.

Three social workers come to my apartment to ask me to give a course to their rehabilitation staff next year. I speak slowly, but, hurrah for me, I arrange all this without a word of English. We set the date for February, 2003.

I see Dr. Hecheverria for the last time. My symptoms have disappeared and my legs feel healthier than at any time in the past fifteen years. I am walking everywhere and have had no leg cramps for a week. I hate to say good-bye, because I know that only consistent treatment will keep my legs healthy, but I assure him I will see him next year. He says, "I'll be here." He is retirement age and no longer travels.

Celeste tells me that there is a monument to the Rosenbergs in a small park just a few streets away, so I go to see it. It is modern, very stark, with these words written on it:

> Por la paz, el pan, y las rosas,
> enfrentemos al verdugo.
>> Julius and Ethel Rosenberg
>> Enero, 1953

(For peace, bread, and roses,
we face the executioner)

Celeste fixes us a spaghetti dinner. I provide beer. Both a bit drunk, we talk loudly at the same time about the US stance against Cuba, and she tells me of her Revolutionary years. I am leaving tomorrow. I don't wonder why I came. I wonder why I stayed away so long. I don't want to leave.

CELESTE

Celeste is seventy years old, good looking and vivacious. She is retired now and earns a little money renting rooms to foreign visitors. Forty-four years have passed since the triumph of the revolution; she was one of the thousands of pro-Castro supporters who helped bring it about. Judging from photos and a fine painting by her famous husband, I'd say she was movie-star gorgeous back then. She'll tell you about her life if you ask.

She was born in Santiago de Cuba, the youngest of ten. Her mother was a teacher in a one-room grade school, her father an unemployed lawyer. Before Celeste was born, her father was imprisoned for opposing the dictator, Gerardo Machado. While in prison he was falsely told by the police captain that the police shot to death his oldest son. The father suffered an immediate, severe heart attack. He was taken to the hospital, seemingly near death. When he recovered, he was released from the hospital to his home and charges were dropped, but he was never the same after that. He remained withdrawn, a hypochondriac, and severely depressed. Sometimes, when her mother had to go months before receiving her salary, they were destitute. Her mother somehow remained cheerful, as she figured out how they could survive.

She had wisely chosen for each of her children well-to-do godparents who had few or no children. The children would visit them during weekends, in order to eat well and get needed clothing and school supplies. Their father hated this procedure and argued angrily with their mother, but she insisted that the children deserved healthy, happy lives. Celeste remembers that he would sit around sourly, and sometimes he would try to be friends with her by asking her to read passages of Victor Hugo and discuss them with him. Her mother played, sang, and danced with the children.

Celeste's godparents, a childless physician and his wife, wanted to adopt her. When Celeste was five years old, Celeste's mother, tears on her face, suggested that it was a good idea. "You'll have a better life." Celeste sobbed and screamed "No, Mama, never!" until her mother relented.

Though she loved her godparents and wouldn't have minded leaving her father, there was no way she would allow herself to be parted from her mother. She continued to spend weekends with her godparents and weekdays at school with her mother.

Celeste relishes her stubbornness. She tells with joy how she fought successfully against the attempts of everyone to change her from left- to right-handed. The same stubbornness kept her in the family home, and later helped her focus single-mindedly on the revolution.

Her father died when she was ten and the family moved to Havana. Celeste graduated from a teacher's college at seventeen, worked briefly in a "terrible clothing store," then in a "terrible private school with rowdy, untamed boys," and finally returned to Santiago to teach adults in a government-sponsored night school. She lived in a rooming house and for the first time in her life was totally free. She signed up for day classes at the university, learned to speak French and English well, and met Mariano through his brother, who was one of her professors. Mariano was already an internationally known artist. He had studied in Mexico, his painting El Gallo already hung in the Museum of Modern Art in New York, and he was considered one of the leaders of the modern school of Cuban painters. He lived in Havana, but began visiting Celeste often in Santiago, bringing art books, and talking art and politics. He was a communist during his entire adult life.

On March 10, 1952, Batista seized power in a military coup that stunned a nation preparing for general elections. Celeste immediately got a fraudulent "sick leave" and went to Havana to join the university students who were protesting under the leadership of Fidel Castro.

In December, 1952, she and Mariano were married; she was nineteen and he was forty. She began teaching school in Havana and stepped up her underground activities. During the next few years, when many of the leaders had been killed, and others, including Castro, were in prison, women met secretly, often in the churches of sympathetic priests. They disseminated news, and kept up national and international pressure to free their imprisoned comrades. When Fidel and Raul Castro were freed and went to Mexico to train men and women to re-enter Cuba to fight Batista, the people in Cuba were preparing themselves as well.

December 2, 1956, Fidel Castro and eighty-two others landed in Cuba, and were almost wiped out by Batista's forces. Only twelve men survived, reaching safety in the Sierra Maestra mountains.

The work to support this tiny army began. A group unknown to Celeste (for security reasons) rented a car in her name, to use in transporting weapons. Some days the car would be missing, so she'd simply take the bus to work. Other days she would drive the car, filled with arms, to her place of work and leave it to be unloaded. One day in a very heavy rain, she was driving the car loaded with arms, when the car swerved on the Malecon (the boulevard along the ocean), and spun around. A policeman came up immediately to help her. "Are you all right? Let me inspect your car to be sure nothing's wrong." Hurriedly she turned on the engine and told him it was fine, but he was insistent. "You look nervous." She said she was, a little, and let him take her across the street to headquarters for a cup of tea. Afterwards, she thanked him profusely, told him, "I feel just fine now," and drove on.

An apartment was also rented in her name, for the leaders to use in secret meetings. She was an assigned lookout. Once, when the meeting was over and she had signaled that the coast was clear, a police patrol car began to follow her. She tried to walk calmly, but she expected to be arrested any moment. That would mean terrible torture and probably death. The car stopped in front of her, blocking her way, and in that instant she felt her urine and feces seeping through her underpants.

A policeman opened the patrol car door. "Hey, beautiful, we're on our way to a party. How about joining us?" She pretended anger, "I'm married and I'm on my way home to my husband. So get lost!" They drove off. When she got to her home she was "a total mess, shaking so hard I could barely stand up." Mariano washed her body, put her to bed, and brought her cookies and tea.

In 1957 Celeste went alone to New York, ostensibly to find a gallery to exhibit Mariano's work, but primarily to make contact with the anti-Batista Cubans there. She was given an assignment to smuggle arms to Cuba. With a special trunk filled with hidden arms, she was escorted by fellow Cubans through customs in New York. A man in the Havana airport took the trunk from her and disappeared. This happened so quickly after her arrival in New York that she hadn't had time to contact galleries.

Celeste and thousands of others continued working "like little hidden ants, everywhere." Everyone had a task. Some, including Celeste's mother, stayed home, making uniforms for those who would need them when the revolution started. Many workers were discovered and tortured to death. Police dragged suspects, including innocent adults and older children, from their homes and beat them to death in the streets in front of their families in an attempt at intimidation, but from inside homes on all sides, people shouted back defiantly. At night revolutionary slogans appeared on walls everywhere.

Because they worked underground, Celeste and Mariano were not able to let the people on their own block know their true feelings. They continued a public life as artists, going to operas, night clubs and fancy parties, where messages, documents, and many thousands of dollars were secretly passed to the right people.

Mariano sold his paintings to the Cuban rich for $50 or $100 to get money for the revolution. The buyers took the paintings with them to Florida when they fled Cuba, and sold them abroad for up to $350,000 each. Celeste believes that these same people, living opulently in Florida, still collect US welfare money, which the US lavishes on anti-Castro Cubans. Many people in Cuba agree with her about this.

December 31, in the middle of the night, Batista fled Cuba, and January 1st, 1959 was the day of triumph. Everywhere people were shouting and dancing in the streets. Celeste and Mariano awakened to the celebration, but they couldn't celebrate in their own area, where no one knew they were pro-Castro. They rushed to her mother's street, where they danced and shouted their joy. Then, almost immediately, they went to work. Along with other known pro-Castro Cubans, they were given armbands and guns to protect the city against reprisals and looting. Castro had declared that everyone would be safe. Celeste was posted at a very wealthy home, wearing her armband and holding a rifle she hadn't the slightest idea how to use. Inside, women and children were screaming that they were going to be killed. Celeste told them, "I am here to protect you. Open the door," and she stayed on duty inside that home. (I have heard that some Cubans used their guns for vengeance against those who had tortured or killed their friends and families. Celeste says she doesn't believe this happened in La Habana.)

Afterwards, she helped organize literacy programs and served as a translator for the foreign press. Mariano was appointed cultural attaché to India, so she spent a year there with him and their infant son. She was flying back to Cuba with their son when the Bay of Pigs invasion occurred. The plane was forced to land in the Bahamas. Because no official would tell her when the plane would be allowed to continue to Cuba, she phoned the press and gave an angry interview. The full interview was printed, concluding with: "The Americans have lost a battle and now they are doing this to us." The next day a plane left for Cuba with her son and her aboard.

Many Cubans, including family members and friends from the revolutionary days, have left Cuba. Some were not in favor of communism and the alignment with Russia. Some simply wanted a chance to earn more money and live an easier life. She is sorry to lose the friendships, but on the whole she believes Cuba is better off without them. The finest people remain in Cuba, she insists.

By 1980 she and Mariano were separated, and their son grown. Celeste decided to go to Nicaragua on her own, hoping to set up literacy programs there, and was able to do that to a small extent, but the Sandanistas needed her to interpret for the French- and English-speaking press. She went by jeep with the reporters to the battle lines, saw the war on all fronts, and talked with communists and anti-communists. Once she had four reporters in her jeep, including one passionate anti-communist. When they got to an anti-communist village he was so excited he leaped from the jeep in spite of her warning to stay put. He raced up to the villagers, who screamed, "Down with the communists!" and beat him up. She stayed nine years in Nicaragua, leaving only when the Sandanistas were overthrown.

In Cuba she worked as a professor of languages, and is now retired. Mariano has been dead for some time. She loves her government. Her biggest joy today is her son, his wife, and especially her two-year-old grand-daughter. She lives simply, buying cheap food, as I do, at the market, and accepting the free lunches which the government makes available to all retired people. She attends the ballet, symphonies, operas, movies, and public lectures with her friends, for less than ten cents admission.

She could be a very wealthy woman if she sold the rest of Mariano's paintings, but she is keeping them for the family. "What do I need money for?" she asks. "In Cuba my life is beautiful." Her favorite song, which she sings often, is "Gracias a la vida, que me ha dado tanto." (Thanks to life, that has given me so much.)

ISLA MUJERES

women's workshop and solo

Isla Mujeres is half an hour from Cancun, Mexico, by boat. Friar Diego de Landa wrote in 1566 that it was named the Island of Women because the explorer Hernandez de Cordova and his men found small stone figures of women, the flat kind that look as if they were made by cookie cutters. From this one fact comes the myth that once upon a time the island was ruled by women, or was the home of the famous Ixchel, goddess of the moon, the seas, and fertility.

Until the tourists discovered it, the island was inhabited primarily by fishermen and their families. They, too, had their romantic stories:

The large statue of the Virgin on top of the local church was brought to the island with two other Virgins by Cuban fishermen in the 1700s. They are lovely statues and, after all, this is the Isle of Women, so why not three? Somebody, however, decided one was enough, and the Virgins were separated. The other two were taken to churches on the mainland. The Isla Madonna is lonesome for her sisters, some villagers say, and has been seen walking on the water, searching for them. Each time someone sees her on the water, always early on a foggy morning or at twilight, the person and her friends rush to the church. So far, the Madonna has always beaten them back, but supposedly she is sometimes damp from the water, and has a bit of seaweed clinging to her stone vestments.

The second story is about a pirate who fell in love with an island girl. In 1860, this pirate (who was also a slave trader) brought all his gold and silver to Isla Mujeres, purchased a huge piece of property, planted trees to make it beautiful, and began to build a mansion for an Island woman he loved. She shrugged him off and married an Island fisherman. The pirate, brokenhearted, hung around for a while, but never completed the building of the mansion. Instead, he carved his own headstone, then left to die and be buried on the mainland. His headstone remains, as does his property, which is now a rather uninteresting park. From time to time people dig in vain for the treasure they are sure he buried somewhere.

Isla Mujeres is my favorite vacation place for just hanging out. Lots of sun, warm sea, and good people. It's about five miles long and a quarter mile wide, except where it bulges at the middle to almost half a mile. The south side is for snorkelers; the west and north sides for people who like white sand and warm, shallow water; the east side, with its sharp rocks and high waves, is for those who like to sit and look at the Caribbean. In the middle are funky, fun tourist shops and restaurants, and the two small towns where Islanders live. Everyone rides mopeds and golf carts around the island; the tourists stop at all the little beaches, drink margaritas, and watch spectacular sunsets. Sunrises are equally grand, but they come early. They are best seen from the eastern rocks along the Caribbean.

I've been visiting Isla Mujeres every year since the early 1980s, to give or attend psychotherapy workshops, and always stay at the Garrafon de Castilla hotel beside the national underwater park named for the Garrafon reef. By now the hotel people and I are family. The people who work in the park also know me well. I am the old lady who refuses to wear a life jacket and doesn't give a damn that it is illegal to swim in national park waters without one. I wouldn't have worn one when I was five years old! I tell the men this, and they smile and look at the ground. They are paid to enforce the law. So I swim the park waters at 7:00 A.M. (guards don't arrive until 8:30 A.M.) and again at 5:30 P.M. when they are supposed to have left. To avoid confronting me, they are now leaving work on time.

The swimming is equally fine off the hotel beach, and that is where I swim between nine and five. The dividing line is a long pier, where tour boats dock. On the park side of the pier, jackets are required; on the hotel side you are on your own. Under the pier between the park and the hotel waters, fish congregate, waiting for the tourists to bring them fish food. There are also hundreds of fish along the reef, around pilings, everywhere, singly and in huge schools. Unless there is a storm at sea, the water is so clear it seems as if you can see forever.

The fish: *Cowfish with huge round heads and dark, cow-like eyes; bright parrotfish; hundreds of snappers; schools of grunts and yellow jacks; an occasional black and gold angelfish; sergeant majors; sting rays; a large resident barracuda and his family whose numbers increase every year; my favorites, the black and white, spotted trunkfish with their triangular bodies, pouting mouths and tiny yellow*

18

*fins that whirl in frantic, inefficient circles; and many others whose
names I keep forgetting.*

*Once I saw a dozen squid in flowing white, like brides, bobbing
vertically in the water around me and then switching to horizontal
swimming.*

The finest swim, when I am not alone, is north one and a half
kilometers with the current, over bright green sea grass, dozens of
barracudas, shells, and brilliant gold starfish, to the Playa Paraiso
beach, where we have a beer and take a taxi back. When the current is
really strong, we go so fast I feel like an Olympic athlete instead of an
old woman.

Now I am here alone for a month. My bedroom, as always, is on
the third floor, with a balcony overlooking the sea and, in the distance,
Cancun. The grounds are filled with palm and banana trees, and
masses of Bougainvillea. Small birds, yellow/black and orange/black,
fly from tree to tree. Iridescent black birds with long tails sit in the
palms. A grayish bird with a soft yellow breast sings soprano in a
three-note trill. Frigate birds soar overhead. Pelicans sit on the pilings
and flop into the water to grab their dinner. On land they are funny; in
the air they, too, are elegant.

The Garrafon Park is both public and private. The grounds are
managed privately and are worth seeing. A path runs along the water
to an area of shale rock and limestone in fascinating designs. At the
southern tip there is a lighthouse and an old Mayan ruin, a beautiful
place to sit and look out to sea or read a book. The park also has a
swimming pool, lots of lounge chairs, a restaurant, two shops, and
hordes of tourists who come by boat from Cancun. On a flat area
overlooking the sea there is a modern sculpture park with an outdoor
restaurant beside it.

The manager of the hotel is Ismael, a retired Captain in the
Mexican Navy. He has a Kewpie doll smile and is almost always
smiling. We chat in Spanish every day over breakfast. I was in
Acapulco first in 1944, and he lived there in 1977 in the Navy, so we
talk about the old days in Acapulco. I tell him that on our honeymoon
in 1970, Bob Goulding and I rented the hotel room where Augustin
Lara lived and wrote several of his most famous love songs. We talk
about Lara and I tell him I attended Lara's funeral, along with all the
residents of Mexico City. He tells me about Acapulco, Puerto Vallarta,

and Mazatlan, and clucks disgustedly over the current contamination of the city beaches. He says the oil companies wrecked the Guaymus beaches before Guaymus could become a tourist resort. It remains Mexican, so is his favorite.

Every day he and I plot how to improve this hotel and bring in more customers, even though we know the owner will continue to veto all our ideas. Ismael wants a new bar, better beach chairs, and fancy awnings to attract the tourists who arrive at the National Park by boat from Cancun. He wants to change the signs, enlarge the gift shop, have a more exotic lunch menu, and add even more flowering bushes. He wants a big slide into the water, perhaps so tall that it will be visible from Cancun, just as the huge Mexican flag flying in Cancun is visible here.

I remind him over and over that all good hotels have swimming pools, and that should be top priority. I don't think he ever swims, but he says that he can if he chooses. After each of his happy sentences about the changes he would like, I say the one word, "Piscina" (swimming pool). Finally, he takes me to the perfect spot for a large, luxurious swimming pool. It can be seen both from the road and from the tourist boats. He is right! We are exuberant at our astuteness. His smile is more radiant than ever. We high five! Our conversation will change nothing, as we both know, but it is fun. When we finish discussing how to spruce up the hotel, we talk about how to fix the politics of the island, and on some days we solve together Mexico's difficulties with the US. We both agree that the debt must be canceled, but we have as much chance of influencing the US government as we have of influencing Don Manuel, the owner of Garrafon de Castilla.

Through the years many locals have become my friends. Sometimes in the early evening I go to the north beach for "two-for-one" drinks and a glorious sunset. The waiter is Ernesto. If I am the only customer, he sits with me. He is handsome, bright, and desperately angry. He works for tips seven days a week and earns very little. He detests the owner of the bar, who is a member of one of the five rich families on the island. That is why that man is an owner rather than a waiter. He is the most stupid man Ernesto knows. Ernesto says the owner is continuously suspicious that the waiters are cheating him, which they would do gladly if they could. I ask why he doesn't look for other work. He glares. There is no work on this island, only slave labor, he insists. All bosses are like his. There are not nearly enough jobs to go around; therefore all workers are exploited.

He is only twenty-two and looks older. He started out differently. He went to school for eight years and studied English on the side. He had dreams of getting to the United States and owning a famous night club. Of course, like most of his friends, he met a girl, she had their baby, and he is trapped. He blames Fate. Like many men here, he wants me to appreciate how hard he works and how little he gets out of life. Probably his father and his grandfather had similar run-ins with Fate.

When the sun has set, I walk through town, sometimes to exchange books at the only book store, which is owned by a group trying hard to keep all dogs and cats on the island well-fed, happy, and non-reproductive. They are fine people, but I do not linger to talk with them, because the store smells of cat piss. I rush in and try to find books at top speed, breathing as little as possible.

Often I eat dinner at Manolo's, which has the best fresh seafood, or at one of the outdoor cafes along the pedestrians-only street. May is my favorite month on the Island, because there are fewer tourists. Tonight children are playing hopscotch and a kind of field soccer with small rocks and whatever they have found for hockey sticks. The younger children are trying out the puppets and the bouncing rubber iguanas that their parents sell to tourists. The parents sit in front of their shops, chatting and watching the children play. After dinner, I go to the super mercado to stock the refrigerator in my room with cheese, crackers, fruit, peanut butter, and beer for supper on my balcony tomorrow.

Lots of people talk very seriously to me. They believe I understand everything they say, which is not true, and they enjoy talking to an outsider, someone who hasn't known them their entire lives. One friend is an illiterate Mayan woman less than five feet tall, round and squishy as a marshmallow, dressed in the white embroidered skirt and blouse that Mayan women on the Island have always worn, except that nowadays the embroidery is done quickly by machine. She walks the beach, selling small embroidered purses, and each year I buy one or two. They are pretty, but pull apart in about three months. Her face lights up when she sees me. "Dona Mari, you have returned!" She is a delight to hug, because no bones get in the way. She tells me she may need surgery this year, because her stomach still hurts. Sometimes, she says, she is pain-free, "Gracias a Dios," but mostly she hurts. The Red Cross doctor, the adored "Doctor Greta" from England, whom she idolizes, has taken blood samples, X-rayed her, and prescribed various remedies which have not worked. She describes all this in great detail. I think that she has very few people who are still interested in her pain.

The hotel gardener is exactly my age and is known all over the island as "El Viejo" (the old man.) His real name is Aristeo (Aristotle), a fine name for someone who is illiterate. He tells me he is the father of over a dozen children. He has no idea how many grandchildren and great grandchildren he has. His first two wives died, and he is married to a woman about twenty-five years his junior. Their youngest is ten, a happy little fat boy whom I have known since he was born. Their world has changed now that Ismael has installed a TV in the hotel office. Aristeo and his wife and son spend their evenings watching Novelas (Mexican soap opera,) the unending sagas of rich Mexicans who have more problems than he ever dreamed of.

A taxi driver talks about his family. His father died when he was eleven, and his mother supported eight children by washing clothes in a river. They rarely had enough to eat. He tells me of his wife, who runs a small gift shop, their two children, and his dreams for them. He laughs a lot, tells jokes I do not understand (jokes are impossible in another person's language), and considers himself lucky to be driving a cab. He is Catholic and earnestly espouses birth control. "If I had eight children, my family would be as hungry as I used to be."

Cora, an ex-nurse, comes to the hotel to swim and have lunch. She tells me, "I worked in Los Angeles and saved enough money to buy my own little place here on the Island before the prices went sky high. If I ever need to, I can go back to California to work, but I believe I have enough money to stay here." She says she likes the tranquility of the island and is one of the few Islanders who swim almost every day. "I have dozens of nieces and nephews and young cousins here. I don't take care of them or I would be insane and bankrupt, but they like to visit me to sit on my lap. When I want to be alone, I say, 'Time to see your mother. Tia Cora is going to rest.' I also have local women friends. This island is my home forever." Isla Mujeres is a lovely place to call home and, like all places everywhere, it can be a glory, a trap, or both.

Today the sea is full of living creatures I have never seen before, little pulsating Os that look like thousands of cheerios sprinkled on the water. Ismael tells me that they are a harmless jellyfish called "dedal," a favorite food of turtles. There are no turtles nearby, so I guess the Os are safe until the currents float them eastward. I see a sting ray eight feet across. I am not exaggerating. The next day the dedals are gone, and I never again see the ray. I think there are more birds than ever, especially the gray and yellow sopranos. The iguanas are out en masse, now that most tourists have left the hotel. A large bunch of bananas are ripe on the tree by the stairs to my room.

Once a year our Women's Workshop meets at this hotel. Twenty psychotherapists decided, about nine years ago, to form a group of outstanding women in our field. We need a time to be together, to give to ourselves what we have long been giving to clients, caring, empathy, treatment as needed, and to share new theory and methods. We come from several countries, and each woman has her own unique style. The first year, everyone knew at least one other participant. Now, of course, we are best friends, and keep in touch by email. The first year I needed help mourning the death of my husband. I wrote of that in my book, A TIME TO SAY GOOD-BYE. This year others are facing loneliness and grief from family deaths. Our lovely Flo is saying good-bye; she is dying. There are joys as well. We are all cheering that Gloria is now president of the International Transactional Analysis Association. This year's theme seems to be: What shall I do with the rest of my life?

Travel tips: *There are lots of things to do on Isla. Visit an ecologically correct turtle farm where the collected eggs are incubated and the turtles cared for until they can be put out to sea successfully. Swim with dolphin. Take a boat to a nearby reef for snorkeling or diving. Visit Contoy, a bird refuge where frigate males puff out their red chests and whoop at the females they are wooing. And, of course, shop. Tourists buy handmade clothes and crafts from all over Mexico and Guatemala at prices that are considerably cheaper than in Cancun. The trades people are friendly and do not hustle tourists.*

Hotel Garrafon de Castilla, $65 - $75 including breakfast.
Hotel Rolandi, about $250, with glorious pool and private hot tubs
There are many hotels in town for $25 - $30

AN ISLAND DEATH

Requiem For A Friend
We can so easily
slip back from what we have struggled to attain,
abruptly, into a life we never wanted;
can find that we are trapped, as in a dream,
and die there without ever waking up.
                    Rainer Maria Rilke, SELECTED POETRY

He was so good-looking and so sweet, so gay in every sense of the word. His toes danced when he smiled. He used to greet me with, "Hola, Mari, come quick! I have a scandal to tell you!" Then he'd laugh. He was a sunbeam of a man, and at the same time bleakly discontented with his life.

An interesting artist, an unknown, he took forever to complete a painting, because he worked in very tiny strokes and dots. A flower might take all day. He did angels well. One quite proper angel sits on the front steps of a brightly colored house, her wings tucked behind her and her sexy, high heeled, open slippers beside her bare feet. Another angel, that he calls "my angel without wings," is a dark, voluptuous woman in a dark, voluptuous jungle. Some of his paintings were for the commercial market, houses with flowers and crooked streets, for example, but even these have some hidden quirk, a little surprise, like the hint of an angel behind a flower or in a far-off tree, something to make a viewer smile. He says he no longer offers his paintings for sale. "I want them here with me."

We sit together in his condo on the fourth floor of a building facing the Caribbean. His windows are large, his rooms full of light, ideal for an artist. His paintings cover his walls and recently he's been hanging paper butterflies and rainbow garlands around them. His paints are laid out but there are no large empty canvasses any more. Only two small ones, one half-started, on a desk-table.

He has had AIDS for a long time, was comatose and dying before the new drugs of those days suddenly gave him back life. Now he is very ill again. His skin looks like yellow marble against the bones of

24

his beautifully shaped head, and his eyes are huge. There has been irreversible damage to his liver from side effects of the drugs, one of his women friends tells me. I am shaken by his appearance.

For something to say, I ask, "Know any scandals?"

He giggles. "I stopped paying for this condo, did you know that? I decided not to bother. The bank is having what I think you call in English a shit-fit." I see a flash of the young man I knew, joyously irresponsible, before AIDS overwhelmed him. "I'll be dead by the time they get all the legal papers they need to throw me out." He suggests that his father, who always hounded him to be a business man, should be pleased by this sign of his astuteness. "He's not pleased. He's upset, as always. I can't honestly think what I could do to please him." He sighs dramatically, wrist on forehead, a self-mocking gesture. "Anyway, *I* am pleased. I will spend the rest of my life right here, surrounded by my art. I have the best view on the Island, and it's free."

As if to emphasize the beauty of his view, five frigate birds sail past his window. I say, "You know that I'm always writing a book. May I write about you to put in my next book?"

He has no hesitation. "Begin with: All my life I have wanted to be a fine artist. Always. I had an exhibit in Valladolid once, and once in Merida. Did you know that?" He straightens his back, crosses his legs into a lotus position, and closes his eyes. He looks like what he is, a very sick man, but also like an emaciated guru.

"My father didn't approve of my becoming an artist, because he didn't think it would pay. It didn't, of course. I never planned it would." He pauses. "Did you know I once lived in Mexico City? I should have studied art there. Or gone to Paris."

He explains that he finished Preparatorio in Merida, living with relatives, and went on to the national university in Mexico City. "My father insisted I study finance. I hated it. It was difficult and boring, and I had no time to paint. I was lonely, even though there are a lot of gays in the capital. Some used drugs and some were violent, and I was afraid most of the time. I'd never been away from my family before. Or in a huge city. After the big earthquake, I quit the university and came back to Isla. My father got me a job in the tourist bureau. I hated it, too. Didn't I know you then?"

"Sure." I remind him that I'd offered him a free room in my San

25

Francisco apartment, if he wanted to study art there. At the time I felt sorry for him. I knew he needed to break away from piddling jobs, from his father's bossing and his mother's babying.

"San Francisco has more earthquakes than Mexico City." He grins like a defiant kid, and then says seriously, "Besides, I had found a lover, not openly, because my father fought against my having an apartment of my own. But we were together as often as possible. Then I found out I had AIDS. I must have gotten it in Mexico City. When I told my lover, he dropped me immediately. He won't have anything to do with me." He is not crying, but is wiping his eyes against imaginary tears. "My lover is so afraid of AIDS that he still refuses to be tested. He says he will kill himself, as one of our friends has, if he is ever diagnosed positive. When I came home from my first time in the hospital in Merida, everything had changed for me." He pauses. "Well, that's about it with my life. My life is here on the island. I never leave except to go to Merida to see my doctor." He gets up to pour us tea. "I've got cookies but you don't eat sugar."

We chat a bit about his family, and then I ask if he'd be willing to tell me about homosexuality on the island.

"People hate the very thought of it. A few gays live here openly and everyone stays away from them. Some live under the water (secretly). Most gays are as homophobic as the rest of the Island people. They lie to themselves. They say, I am not really gay because I'm married. Because I only have gay sex when I'm drunk. Because I never let anybody in my ass. Because I'm just playing around so it doesn't mean anything." He talks about homosexuals who never visit him, because of his illness or because they are 'under the water.' "Two friends still visit me, but they won't even mention the word AIDS. They are so afraid of AIDS that they sit across the room from me. No man touches me any more." His voice is tearful and again he rubs his face.

"And the families! They are worse! Have you ever heard Mexican families explain why their son isn't married? They say he hasn't found the right woman yet, even though everybody knows that he's never looked for one. They say their son was once in love with a girl who wouldn't marry him, so he never let himself love again. The favorite story is about Maria. She died here on the Island when she was only sixteen, and now the mothers of gays say their sons were in love with her. Nobody was, really. But she is blamed for half the homosexuality on this island."

We sip our tea. Then I ask, "And how is life really for you these days? I know it can't be good."

"I'm depressed, but I try not to notice. I'm still painting when I have the strength. You know my two women friends. I don't think I could go on without them. They are like sisters. We tell each other everything, and they take care of me. My only real friends have turned out to be two American women and my mother. My mother has always loved me. You know that. But she won't talk about AIDS either."

"There's something else about families. I'm dying of AIDS and my father still tells people I have cancer. Everyone on the Island knows the truth about me, I'm gay and I have AIDS, but no one says this out loud."

He shows me his assortment of medicines. "You wouldn't believe the expense! I bitch about my father, but I am truly sorry I cost him so much. My father thinks I should try to get the medicine from a government clinic. I am very afraid of that. I have a good relationship with my doctor in Merida and I don't want to be forced to go to a public clinic. If I don't die quickly, that will happen." He gives a short, unhappy laugh. "And if that happens, I will die quickly."

His final statement about his life is, "I want to paint. I haven't much strength left for painting, but I paint when I can." He pauses. "In spite of everything, I want to live."

Three months later he is dead.

PANAMA

solo

Panama is not a planned destination. I expected to go from Cancun to Belize, Honduras, and Nicaragua, then Costa Rica. Last year that route existed. This year, zilch. The only way to get to Costa Rica from Cancun is through Panama, so I scrap my plans for Central America and fly to Panama City for a few days of snorkeling at the San Blas (Kuna Yala) islands. I have no reservations, but am told at the Panama City airport that there are lots of choices, once I get to **Porvenir**. It is a short, beautiful flight in a five-person plane over dozens of tiny, palm-covered islands to Porvenir, a landing strip without an airport. My guidebook mentions a place called Wichibuale and a hotel Ainu, reached by dugout. On arrival I learn Ainu is "finished," which means that the old lady who ran it is dead and none of her relatives want to leave Panama City to live on a godforsaken island with a bunch of tourists. A German man has a reservation with a guy named Fernandez, the owner of a dugout and an island, and suggests I might find a room there. Fernandez agrees, so I jump aboard. The island turns out to be about fifty meters long, with two sleeping cabins made of cane at one end. At the other end is a tiny cane hut with a hole in the ground and a toilet seat secured to an open box over the hole. Period.

Fernandez leaves to get us food, and comes back from a neighboring isle with stale bread and the kind of undrinkable coffee made by boiling the grounds but not straining them. He does not live on this island, but says he will come each day to bring food and take us to a snorkeling reef. I decide I need an upgrade. The German man says he will stay because he has never been on a totally deserted island before, and finds it challenging. He seems pleasant, but that does not compensate for the coffee and toilet facilities. I give Fernandez a bit of money, explain in Spanish that I want an island where the owner also lives there, and he immediately assumes I am afraid of the German. Nodding wisely, he helps me aboard the dugout, and we head for Coco Blanco. Bless Fernandez, and my apologies to the anonymous German who obviously was not lusting for this seventy-seven-year-old woman.

Coco Blanco is picture-perfect, with palms, sand, and palm-roofed cottages, a bit of heaven which I barely have time to see before jumping into the owners' dugout for a trip with four other guests to a nearby reef. The water is bright and clear, with lots of tropical fish. Multicolored coral extends around the island, and to one side is an ancient, sunken ship, encrusted with coral. Inch-high "Christmas trees" (anemones) in red, white, black, blue, purple, and pink disappear when I swim over them, then pop up again one by one. I snorkel, sit on the sand and drink coconut milk from a fresh coconut, then snorkel again. We return to Coco Blanco for a late lunch of freshly-caught lobster, rice, and tomatoes.

After lunch I sit in a hammock between two palm trees and gaze at the bright blue sky and sea. Nearby are three palm-studded islands. With my binoculars I pick out four more that appear uninhabited and another two with square buildings and round casitas. Facing the other direction, I see dozens of tiny islands, little gray spots on the immense sea. Behind them are the blue-gray mountains of Panama that cut off the coast from the rest of the country.

Brief history: There are more than 400 islands in the Kula Yala group, belonging to the Kula Indians who lived in Colombia and Panama until the Spanish invasion. Since the Spaniards were uninterested in such tiny islands of sand and coconuts, the Indians were able to establish themselves here peacefully. Some of the islands were mere specks in the sea, which the Kulas laboriously enlarged by bringing sand and stone from the mainland. They developed their own government, quite apart from Panama. Every community (group of islands) has a council that meets regularly, and an elder who "runs things." Though elders are men, women are in charge of families and a husband becomes part of the wife's family on marriage.

Coco Blanco is an island about 150 by 50 meters. The four guest cottages each have a bedroom, bathroom, and porch. The floors are swept-sand with a piece of linoleum, like a throw rug, beside each bed; the walls are of cane, loosely fit together so breeze and light come through. The bathroom has a toilet, sink, and large vat of water with a dipper for giving oneself a shower. Compared to Fernandez' facilities, this is perfection, even though there are no mirrors and no towels. A person dries fast in this climate.

A large, one-room cabana is living room, bedroom, and kitchen for the owners, Beatrix and Tony, plus her brother the cook, and a young cousin who knows a bit of English and attempts to translate for them. They all sleep in hammocks in the same room. Tony is shy, almost toothless, and speaks only their native language, Tule. Beatrix talks loudly and cheerfully in Tule-accented Spanish.

In one huge cabana at the far end of the island live a small group of families related to Tony, though they seem to have little contact with Beatrix and Tony. They definitely keep to their own area. I walk over to where their ten young children, mostly naked, are playing outside the cabana. They giggle and smile at me, then go back to their games: chasing each other, wrestling with their dogs, filling cans with sand and dumping them, and cradling little dolls made of cloth stuffed with sand. It looks like a happy nursery school.

A woman inside the cabana waves me in, to show me their molas, (appliquéd and embroidered cloth to be sewn on blouses). Four or five women, one very pregnant, one with a baby, sit in hammocks, laughing and chatting as they sew molas. The cabana contains single and double hammocks, two double beds, and a stone circle for cooking. A couple of monkeys, family pets, jump about and climb the poles from which the hammocks are hung. The children follow me inside. The younger ones jump onto their mothers' laps to be petted, while the older ones watch curiously as I look through the stacks of molas. A baby screams when I smile at her, and is gently calmed by turning her so that I am not visible. I choose a mola, and all of us smile at each other as a substitute for words. The women don't understand my Spanish, and if any of them is speaking Spanish, it is so accented I don't recognize it.

Later, I learn from Beatrix that the men are away during the daytime, fishing and selling coconuts and fish on the mainland. When old enough, the children will live with relatives on the mainland so that they can attend school. It is hard to believe that any of the parents attended school, if school is taught in Spanish.

For the first two days at Coco Blanco, the other guests and I cannot communicate. One couple speaks Finnish and German, and the other speaks Italian. On the third day a Dutch couple arrives, who between them speak German, Italian, English, and Spanish, so conversation becomes quite animated. In the evening with the generator giving us light, we sit at the food table and chat. Beatrix joins in happily and

Tony sits a bit back from the table and smiles at us. The Dutch couple is under thirty, and has already been around the world several times. They work a year, then travel a year, and tell us that their life style is easy. They own no property and do not plan to have children. "Some of our friends dislike us, because we have such a fine life, while they work constantly and are always in debt. They act as if it is somehow immoral not to have children and debts." At 10:00 P.M. the generator is turned off, our world turns black, and millions of stars appear. The night is noiseless, except for the sound of the waves. We go to bed by flashlight.

Travel tips: Always carry a flashlight and extra batteries! Also pack a tiny Japanese towel, which soaks up water and takes little space in a suitcase. It doubles as a wash cloth. This trip I forgot mine.

The food is excellent, though unvaried. Breakfasts are sausages in a tomato sauce, an egg, and unleavened home-made biscuits, quite tasty with the sauce. Lunch is lobsters or fish, home-made french fries, tomatoes, cucumbers, and watermelon. Dinner is the same, except that rice substitutes for french fries. All fresh water, staples, and food except fish come from the mainland, about two hours away by motorized dugout.

We snorkel every day at a different island.

One morning at sun-up all the men from the other side of the island, plus Tony and the cook, leave in dugouts, taking with them a huge net. Beatrix reminds us it is Easter, and says her family is coming to be with them. When the fishermen return, the dugouts are filled with fish. Everyone immediately helps gut them. Around noon a large boat with over fifty people arrives from Colon, a five-hour journey. On arrival, many jump into the water without changing clothes; it must have been a hot, vastly uncomfortable trip, all wedged together on that boat. Chairs, brought yesterday by dugout from somewhere, are filled with the new arrivals, their clothes dripping. Others sit in the sand beside them. People come from nearby islands, including a minister who begins immediately to preach in Tule. As he continues, many stretch out on the sand and sleep through the sermon. As soon as the minister finishes, everyone comes to life. They talk loudly to each other, laugh, and gorge on fish. Then the boat is filled and the passengers begin their long voyage back to Colon. Others return to their nearby islands.

On my last night here, the rest of the guests have gone. An orange moon, magnificently magnified, is swallowed by a crocodile-shaped cloud, then pops out of the crocodile's stomach as the crocodile turns into a fish, a ship, a squiggle, and the moon turns to brightest white. The sea glistens in the moon's silver trail. Beatrix and I sit together, talking. She tells me of her life and is not at all curious about mine.

The next morning I fly back to Panama City.

Coco Blanco, $20 a day, with meals and dugout rides to snorkeling sites.

Travel tips: This is an example of how successful an unplanned trip can be and how easy it is to arrange at the last minute. If I had not liked Coco Blanco, I'd have found another island or gone on to Costa Rica early, as it is possible to fly stand-by without a penalty. Spontaneous travel is easy, if you adopt a "no problem" attitude.

Panama City. A happy, talkative cab driver takes me to see the canal. He is obviously proud that his country finally owns it. On the way he shows me the huge city of barracks and houses that once belonged to the US military, and is now condos, private homes, and universities. I wish that could be the fate of all our bases everywhere. How happy Cuba and Okinawa, for example, would be, if we would simply pack up and leave!

Does anyone else still remember Richard Halliburton? He was one of my favorite authors when I was young. August 14-23, 1928, he swam the Panama Canal for a thirty-six cent tonnage fee. He was the first and last person permitted to swim in the canal, and his was the lowest toll ever collected. The highest, (adjusted by weight per vessel), was over $200,000.

The canal is fascinating, with ships of all sizes lined up waiting their turn, and then rising and lowering with the changing water level, as they go through the locks. A fine movie in Spanish and English, plus a lighted three-dimensional floor map, show exactly how the canal functions and tell of the incredible task of building it.

The next day I hire the same driver to take me to the ruins of the old Spanish town, where silver from Peru was stored during its long journey to Spain. There were never more than 500 soldiers and fortune hunters living here, as they were wiped out by malaria and yellow fever almost as fast as they arrived. The area is now a slum and incredibly hot.

To get away from the city, I take a forty-minute ferry early the next morning to Taboga, a weekend vacation spot and commuters' town. Our boat sails under the famous Bridge of the Americas past more than a dozen cargo ships waiting to go through the canal.

In Panama City I found no hotel I would recommend.

Taboga is a pretty place, with pastel-colored houses overlooking the sea, and exquisitely kept gardens. Mothers bring their young children, in bright red shorts or skirts and immaculate, ironed white shirts to the grade school, deposit them, and peer through the school windows to see how the children are settling in. Men have already left on ferries for Panama City. The only men on the island in the daytime seem to be hotel employees and gardeners. After the heat and shabbiness of Panama City, living here would be paradise. I spend two days walking around town and lounging in a hammock by the sea.

I meet a retired US military couple who were once based in Panama. They live well here on their pension, and say that they like the people. They rent videos and books on their every-other-week trip to Panama City. This upper-middle class island, seemingly inhabited only by whites, is an interesting contrast to Coco Blanco.

The big hotel at Taboga is pretentious but run-down. I made the mistake of booking immediately, because I liked the grounds. If I had walked around town first, I'd have chosen one of the lovely old seaside inns.

BEATRIX

Beatrix is the owner of Coco Blanco Island. As owner, she is in charge of everything. She collects the money from her guests, chats with those who speak Spanish, orders food and staples from the mainland, serves the food, and hand-embroiders molas, place mats, napkins, and tablecloths to sell to her guests. Especially, she is in charge of her husband, Tony the fisherman, her brother, Pedro the cook, and a young female relative who cleans the cabanas. "I tell them what to do and they do it," she says. The two men do not speak Spanish, only the Kula language, Tule. The young woman speaks Spanish and Tule, studies English, and hopes to leave soon to live in Panama City. Then another young relative will take her place.

Beatrix is about fifty-five, wears heavy Western make-up in spite of the heat, and dresses traditionally in a Mola blouse, full, short skirt, and dozens of gold bangles on her arms and legs. She goes barefoot on the sandy island. She is easy-going and laughs a lot. Her accent is difficult for me to understand, but she likes to talk about her life, so she repeats until I finally get it.

"Before the time of my great-grandparents, my people came here to escape the Spaniards and the mosquitoes." She doesn't know how many generations lived on the tiny island before her mother was born here. Her mother acquired a second island in order to give one to her sister and one to Beatrix. Ownership and inheritance go to women.

"I love my island. Our children don't like it at all. They think they have good jobs, because they work in offices and have bosses who tell them what to do. Imagine!" She tosses her head disdainfully. Like them, she had to leave the island when she was school age "to learn Spanish and mathematics, but I came back as soon as I could." She explains that Tony is from a neighboring island and never went to school, but it doesn't matter, because he is a good fisherman and knows how to fix everything. By "everything" she means his tackle, boat, the boat's engine, and the generator, "which gives us so much trouble." I ask if he has a sense of humor like hers and she says, "Oh, no, he is serious. But he is a fine lover." Her laugh is a high-pitched, girlish giggle.

I ask about Kula customs, and she tells of her first menstruation. "That is the most important day of all, because it is the day you become a woman. Even your fifteenth birthday party and your wedding are not as important. Your funeral is just as important but you are dead so you can't drink and enjoy it!" She laughs again and so do I.

"When I told my mother I was bleeding, she was as excited as I was. She cut my hair. That is traditional. And then she sent word to my auntie, who came right away. They rubbed this special seed on my face to blacken it, and they put a real gold ring in my nose to show that I was an adult." A small hut was made for her, where she would stay until her menstruation ceased, but that was fun because other girls, who had arrived by boat, sang songs to her and whispered to her through cracks in the bamboo walls all day and most of the night.

When she left the hut she was bathed and dressed in completely new clothing, including her new personal mola, which protects her from evil. She was given many gold bracelets and a new, very special embroidered head scarf that she still wears when she dresses up for parties. There was a feast in her honor with music and dancing. "I was so proud to be a woman!" There are no special duties or taboos, nothing negative about being a woman, "just lots of pride."

She explains the significance of the mola. If I understand correctly, long ago a great woman prophet named Kikadiryai (she wrote out the name for me) drew special geometric designs for molas to protect the wearers against evil spirits. All Kula women choose their own molas from these designs. The molas are sewn onto cheap, store-bought blouses, and when a blouse wears out, the mola is put on a new one. Molas with fish or animal designs are made for the tourist trade only.

Another night she tells me of the burial customs, which is the final celebration of a person's life. The body is wrapped in its own hammock and placed in an above-ground sarcophagus. In the old days the sarcophagus was a room large enough for the person's eating utensils, tools, and, for fishermen, even the man's boat. After the burial there is a very large ceremony, depending on the wealth of the family of the deceased. Sometimes people stay drunk for days on free liquor supplied by the family.

I ask if she ever feels lonely on the island. She says she misses her mother, who is now dead. "I am not lonely. I have great security on this island. I have Tony. And I always have new people like you who want to listen to me."

COSTA RICA

Marian Branch and solo

San Jose: The appeal of Costa Rica is not in its cities. San Jose, the capital, is uninteresting except for its museums. There has been no indigenous culture for more than 300 years. The old churches and even the cathedral are not worth a visit. People wear inexpensive, ordinary clothes, and are busy earning a living. Young adults dye their hair whatever colors it was not meant to be, and wear lip, nose, and navel rings just as in the US.

There are three good museums in San Jose, plus a serpentario. The Gold Museum is being remodeled and will be opened with far better facilities in 2005. At present 200 superb pieces are still on display: necklaces, bracelets, earrings, tiaras, chest pieces, buttons, little frogs, insects, and Mayan gods, all meticulously done in solid gold. The museum is in the center of town. Stroll the pedestrian-only streets to get a feel for the city.

The Jade Museum is my favorite. In addition to its beautiful jade, it has pre-Columbian ceramics: fascinating heads with unique, expressive faces, and large ceramic figures of men and women tattooed in red, white, and black designs. Some wear fierce eagle or jaguar masks. The museum is on the top floor of San Jose's highest building, and the views are fine.

The National Museum traces the archeological and social-cultural history of Central America from pre-historic times through the colonial era. If you are a museum buff, you'll want to spend time here.

The small serpentario has live pythons, water snakes, Costa Rican rattlers, and dozens of others, all coiled or spread out over branches, sleek and slithery and beautifully patterned, with open eyes that don't blink.

Don Carlos hotel, $105 double, a block from the Jade Museum. The Don Carlos is a delight, stuffed with real and bogus pre-Columbian art, old religious tiles, live toucans, fountains, real and ceramic flowers, and in our room two large Colonial paintings of a splendid knight and his lady love.

For a less expensive hotel try La Perla, full of European guests who sit in the patio and discuss in many languages what to see in Costa Rica and elsewhere.

Travel tips: There are many pre-arranged tours, if that is your preference, but they aren't necessary. Costa Rica is an easy country to visit alone. Hotel personnel speak English and will find you excellent local guides. There is good transportation by bus, taxi, mini-bus, and airplane to all major sites. It is the safest country I know. I have never heard of a mugging, and neither citizens nor police carry guns. Medical care is said to be fine. Many people come here for their dentistry and plastic surgery, and there is an ever-growing population of ex-patriots from Europe and North America.

Another tip: Have a meal at restaurants called Soda, which are found everywhere in Costa Rica. They are locally owned and serve traditional, inexpensive food. You'll find them at local markets and road-side stops.

Arenal Volcano Area: Ten years ago when I spent a month in Costa Rica, I wanted to go to the Tilajari Resort near the Arenal volcano, but it was too pricey for my budget. I was practicing the $25 a day theme. Today Tilajari costs $77 a night per room with a fantastic breakfast and is one of the best buys in Costa Rica.

Imagine: Acres of bright green grass, freshly mowed, with literally hundreds of flowering trees and bushes. The swimming pool is large and clean, with comfortable lounge chairs around it. Toucans, canaries, hummingbirds, doves, woodpeckers, tanagers, and others take turns eating papaya from an open bird feeder beside the outdoor dining room. Dozens of iguanas have their private hotel on the branches of a nearby tree. A river drifts slowly below the property and on the shore is a sleepy, very pregnant crocodile fourteen feet long. The river is not for swimming. The banks are perpendicular, so the crocodile cannot visit us, and vice versa.

From Tilajari we take daily excursions with an exceptional guide, Roger, found for us by the hotel. Today Marian, our guide Roger, and I go upriver on an inflated motor boat to visit a local farm. A band of howler monkeys roars from a tree by the water's edge. We see blue heron, egrets, lots of iguanas, and two small crocodiles. At the farm we are served coffee, fried bananas, homemade cheese and cookies. Ticos (Costa Ricans) also come here by boat to purchase cedar furniture hand-made by the family. The ninety-year-old grandfather is in charge of the milk cows, with the help of his eighty-eight-year-old brother. There are no roads to their homestead, so they travel by horseback or by boat.

Roger takes us to visit a zoo for injured (throw-away) animals. There we see the local mammals that we miss in the jungle because they are nocturnal or simply know how to hide. We see tapirs, wild pigs, coatis, small wildcats of various types, plus some luckless big game animals abandoned by a traveling circus. On the road back, high in a tree, there seems to be a discarded, shabby fur coat, the long-haired type that people wore to football games when I was young. Peering through binoculars, we know that this shabby coat belongs to a bright-eyed sloth.

We return to swim in the hotel pool, photograph the crocodile, have a tasty dinner of chicken baked in banana leaves, and visit the iguana tree.

The next day we take an early jungle walk with Roger. We see lots more birds, including toucans, green and red with bright yellow beaks. Flycatchers buzz the toucans to chase them away from their nests. The most fascinating trees are the Chonta palm, that send out spiny stilts which keep the trunk propped even when it decays, and the Giant Suras, with trunks more than twenty feet across, gnarled and buttressed, with roots running above the ground more than fifty feet.

Roger finds the famous, somewhat poisonous red frog with green legs, a tiny, slimy-feeling creature. We see more monkeys and another immobile sloth, whose coat exactly matches the tree because the sloth's coat carries the same fungus as the bark. A rolling sloth would gather no moss, but no one has explained this to a sloth.

I don't believe the sloth is alive until quite languidly it raises its head, looks around, raises one arm just enough for us to note that it is of the two-toed rather than three-toed variety, and then curls up again into a moldy ball of fur. A sloth is only awake six hours a day, partly because the leaves it eats have a narcotic quality. The largest sloth, as big as a large man, weighs less than fifteen pounds. It is all air and fluff.

Roger is a serious, very responsible man. When his four children were still preschoolers, a cousin and the cousin's wife were killed by a truck that lost its brakes, and plowed into their home. Their two babies, asleep in another room, were uninjured, so Roger and his wife kept the children, eventually adopting them. Roger now supports six adolescents on a guide's salary. Maybe everyone ups the tips when they learn about the children. I hope so.

We drive to the Nicaraguan border and go by motor launch up the Rio Frio. (It is well named ... amazingly cold for the tropics!) If I return, I will take the boat in the opposite direction to Blue Fields, Nicaragua. We see: *long-nosed bats plastered against dead tree trunks like inky Rorschach symbols or dead tarantulas; a snakebird; a cormorant swallowing a fish; grebes; blue herons; tiger herons; black vultures; turkey vultures; a swallow-tailed kite; parakeets; the rare brown-hooded parrot; owls; hummingbirds; trogons: ringed and green kingfishers; toucans again; flycatchers; swallows; wrens; scarlet-rumped black tanagers; a lots and lots of Jesus Christ lizards racing over the surface of the water.*

The Jesus Christ lizards remind me of the psychiatric belief that no mental hospital can accommodate more than one patient at a time who thinks he is Jesus Christ. I learn on this trip that no tour group accommodates more than one old lady who needs help. Marian wins the honor hands down, as her vision is impaired and she is older than I am. On past trips I have been the old lady, cared for and babied. "Sit here, Mama." "Mama, be careful." "Mama, give me your arm. Let me help you." Today Marian is escorted to the best seat on the launch, on the side where we will see the wild life. I am told, "Sit over here, where you can take care of her," as I am motioned to the side where the animals aren't. She is escorted by guide, driver, and the young boy who serves as spotter, carefully, carefully over the side of the launch and up the steep hill to the picnic area. I am left to jump off by myself, and find my own way up and down the hill. Though she is a fine and admirable companion, I find myself wondering if I really want her on this trip. The good news is: when I am not being babied, I am able to climb by myself. Hold on to that knowledge, old girl.

Tilajari, $77 with breakfast

We leave Tilajari for the town of **Fortuna**, so named when the Arenal volcano exploded and made the area a Mecca for tourists and a "dream come true" for local merchants. The volcano is a perfect cone, with wisps of smoke rising from the top and from vents on the lava side. We watch red-hot rocks spew out and tumble down the mountain, leaving a trail of steam in their wake. When the clouds roll in, hiding the mountaintop, we leave for the famous Tabacon Resort and Hot Springs. The springs are a huge tourist operation, with pools of varying temperatures and hot waterfalls. We walk along paths between flowering trees and shrubs, and try out all the pools.

Hotels with a view of the lava flow: Arenal Paraiso, Montano de Fuego, Tabacon Resort and Hot Springs.

The next morning we cross Lake Arenal, the country's largest lake, man-made for use as an aqueduct and for sport fishing. It is a beautiful, clear blue, surrounded by mountains. On the other side of the lake a bus takes us on pitted, broken, impossibly winding roads, past the lush fields and rolling hills of the Society of Friends' dairy farms. A toucan flies beside the bus and the Quaker cows moo.

Monte Verde is a green, pristine cloud forest that is one of Costa Rica's major national parks, a must for tourist groups searching for a glimpse of the rare Quetzal birds.

That night we attend a local bull-riding contest at a small carnival. We sit on hard benches and listen forever to the master of ceremonies extol the courage of the cowboys, who are introduced one by one, as are two men on horses covered with silver, two men with red capes, a policeman, and an employee of the Red Cross. In the background we hear the bulls snorting. Finally the first cowboy comes out the gate on a large black bull, the bull bucks once, the cowboy flies through the air and lands on the ground, unconscious. The bull charges the horsemen and the red-caped guys, who try quite ineptly to corner him. Other men leap into the arena with lassos, and in the general excitement it appears that the bull, men, or horses may manage to trample the still-unconscious ex-rider. The bull is finally tied up and tugged back into the pen, the policeman and the Red Cross man carry out the rider, and the music surges. Marian and I leave, with eleven riders still to go. The next day we learn that the rider suffered only a mild concussion, and has recovered completely.

This area is usually damp and foggy because, of course, it is cloud forest. We are lucky. The sun is shining as we walk in a jungle filled with tall, beautiful old trees, ferns, and shimmering green vines. We are searching for the Quetzal, but see only a quite tame coati. Our local guide takes us to several spots and when Marian is tired, he and I continue walking for three more hours, he lugging his huge tripod and telescope, as we search everywhere for the elusive birds. My legs hurt and I can barely keep going, but this is important! Finally, the guide smuggles me into the nesting area, reserved for biologists, and leaves me there. A young woman, who is writing her Ph.D. dissertation on the habits of these birds, tells me two Quetzals were here, but flew away an hour ago.

Discouraged, I leave and go to the hummingbird sanctuary, where a twittering group of British bird lovers are exclaiming over a rare hummingbird whose tail is pointing up. I buy earrings for gifts and get a taxi. I am telling myself I am going to stay in Monte Verde for the rest of the trip if necessary to see these birds when, wonder of wonders, beside the road just outside the park on the lowest branch of a tree, are a male and a female Quetzal, so close to me I can see them well without even using my binoculars.

The male is brilliant red and green with a long, flowing tail, the female stubbier-tailed and mostly green. They really do exist! I am ecstatic. When they fly away, the male's tail floats brilliantly in the air.

That afternoon we visit the frog and toad living museum. Each species is in its own large, individualized, glass-walled environment. The museum guide points them out to us, as many are so well camouflaged that we can't spot them even two feet from us. Brown toads hide under brown logs, and bright green, tiny frogs, cling to bright green leaves. We see our red and green frog, spotted frogs, black and white ones, the precious, almost extinct little frogs that are so transparent that their inner organs show through their skin, and the famous red-eyed tree frog whose eyes, unfortunately, do not open until after dark. There are many other toads and frogs, and the guide is truly dedicated to these tender creatures who are becoming extinct everywhere. They are our "canaries in the coal mines," whose deaths tell of the pollution of our planet and the effects of the depletion of the ozone layer.

Belmont hotel, beautiful, view rooms, $85 without breakfast.

Monday morning we drive back to San Jose around lovely small mountains, past small towns, coffee plantations, fruit trees, and sugar cane. We have an Italian dinner at Campo Le Europe in San Jose, made special by a liter of good red wine. The next day we relax.

Drake's Bay, (Bahia de Drah-kai). We fly in a four-person plane between the mountains, through bright clouds, and over dazzling green fields to a tiny airport. A truck takes us to the bay, which we cross by launch to Drake's Bay Wilderness resort. Sir Francis landed here. How thrilled he must have been to find trees loaded with fruit and nuts,

42

and plenty of fresh water pouring into the sea. Did he decide he had reached heaven? Or was he in such a hurry for naval skirmishes and gold that he barely noticed the richness of this bay?

On arrival we are served coffee and plates of fresh mangos, papayas, and wonderfully sweet white pineapple, all local. As we walk to our cottage, two scarlet Macaws fly by, brilliant against the blue sky. I cannot believe it! I have now seen **toucans**, **quetzals**, and **macaws**, and my bird mission is complete.

We have a friendly cocktail hour, meet two fun guys from Florida, three Costa Rican women in bright clothes and gold spangles, a French couple, and two New Yorkers. We discuss our favorite travel sites. Namibia, especially Etosha National Park, is rated the best in Africa. Du Plooy's resort in Belize is raved about. A guided tour of a coffee plantation here in Costa Rica can be fun. Antarctica is unbelievably beautiful! Don't take a construction elevator in the Los Angeles airport even if you think it is a safe short cut, because the cops will get you! As we chat, we hear the howler monkeys nearby and on the way to dinner Marian and I stop to watch the spider monkeys who are permanent residents of the tree beside the office. This is a rustic resort with good beds and overhead fans, a saltwater swimming pool, and freshwater showers heated by the sun.

We go by launch to **Cano Island** to snorkel: *White-tipped coral, seeming to flare from the dark lava, stingrays, even a manta, puffer fish by the dozen, lots of sergeants, parrotfish, and snappers.* Two flounders, like white dinner plates with both eyes on top, kiss, take turns chasing and catching each other, then lie one atop the other. It appears to me that flounders have nice sex. The water here is about eighty-eight degrees. Do we get to vote on the heaven we desire? If so, chalk this up for me, with a few bright coral for additional color.

> "And in the heaven of all their wish,
> There will be no more land, say fish."
> Rupert Brooke

A little land in heaven would be pleasant. I lie on a hammock, a warm breeze wafts away the super-heat, and I watch a yellow-breasted bird who sits on a bush beside me. The bush has one rose-colored flower with showy petals. Lizards skitter everywhere. On our return trip five, then eight, then twelve spotted dolphin circle our launch. They leap into the air singly and in pairs, putting on a real show. Three baby dolphin play together, splashing each other, while their parents guard them. That night someone finds a baby boa constrictor in a staff bedroom, and immediately a foster home is offered by a young man who works at a neighboring resort. Tourists, be warned.

The next day we motor into the bay to see two islands inhabited by hundreds of ibis, boobies, and frigate birds, swooping, gliding, or just standing a few feet from our boat, looking peacefully down at us. We go up the Sierpe River past crocodiles and many varieties of birds. The two couples with us are passionate bird-watchers, with individual notebooks plus bird books the size of giant dictionaries, filled with descriptions and pictures of every type of bird in Costa Rica, of which there are thousands, it seems. We are swamped with information that I promptly forget. It is fun to hear their muted whoops of joy as they see a bird they have never before encountered, but can't permit themselves to make a noise for fear of scaring it away. We are all having a fine time, when a tropical rain comes out of nowhere, soaking us.

We had been very hot and now the temperature drops to endurable. We go fast down river to find shelter under the tin roof of someone's loading dock, and there make sandwiches for lunch. The rain begins to sweep sideways, as if seeking us out, and both we and our lunches are drenched. The boatman takes off his shirt, wrings it out, finds a dry one under piles of stuff aboard, dries the spark plugs with it, puts it on, and off we go. Briefly we northerners are a bit cool; the boatman shivers wildly. Just as we reach our dock, the rain stops, the sun shines, and again we are quite hot.

One of the men has developed an abscessed tooth, very painful, so all of us give him whatever pain medicine we have, and he takes all of them at once, without relief. He is a tough guy not to die from over-medication. One of the guests suggests holding strong Listerine and/or straight lemon juice in his mouth. I suggest he cuddle up against her, as her perfume ought to anesthetize anyone. Our time in overheated Paradise is over, so we and the tooth sufferer return to San Jose. Marian leaves for California.

Drake's Bay Wilderness Resort supposedly is being turned into a private school. Check it out.

I am in **Escazu** to visit a local family I have known for several years. He was my Spanish teacher in 1992. Since then the oldest daughter has become a professor of education and the mother of an adorable little girl. The oldest son is a gifted woodworker, who specializes in unique frames for photos and art work, and the younger two are still in school.

Escazu is two-tiered: the flat area where the locals live and the hills where the wealthy, mostly Americans, have huge homes with stunning views and large swimming pools. The US ambassador lives in the hills.

During my last visit we in the flats had an exciting strike. The town had allowed so many swimming pools in the hills that there was not enough water to go around. Or perhaps the sewerage system was in jeopardy. Whatever the reason, the town officials' response was to ration the water supply to the locals. Water was turned off in town between 8:00 A.M. and 8:00 P.M. The pools and palaces got all the water they wanted.

There is only one main road from town to the people with "plata" (silver), meaning the rich ones in the hills. The locals barricaded the road with branches, boxes, whatever was handy. I joined in, since I especially detest unflushed toilets. In my honor, the word Internaccional was added to the strikers' banner. It became **Huelga Internaccional de los Sucios,** (International Strike of the Dirty People.) Bus drivers rounded the corner to drive up the hill, saw the banner and barricade, and backed down, laughing and tooting happily their support. The drivers, of course, were also sucios. The rich looked frightened and furious in their cars, as they, too, had to back and wait. The police arrived without guns, since they never carry guns here. I have been through California strikes and peace marches, and this was pleasantly different. The police hugged their friends, the strikers, shook hands with those they didn't know, including me, and phoned the mayor. He arrived and tried to give a speech, which began, "Why didn't someone let me know?"

He was hooted down, as amateur comics improvised loud speeches on the themes of mayoral ignorance and love of not bathing. It was all quite fun, and within the hour the water was turned on and the rubbish cleared away. At that point the mayor made a silent departure.

Who would guess that mostly-mundane Escazu is famous for its witches? They supposedly congregated here even before the Spaniards' time. In the old days, they were famous for their abilities to cure illnesses, but modern-day witches use crystal balls and tarot cards.

45

Most look like hippies but I understand that some are "high class", which means expensive. They are consulted by local politicians, Ronald and Nancy Reagan types, who won't make a move without their advice.

Today I walk up the hill with my friends, past where our barricade had been, and sit on the terrace of the Tara hotel to enjoy a beer and the wonderful view of distant mountains. Starting at the nearby church of San Antonio, there are hiking trails along two shallow, tumbling rivers. It's a place of birds, butterflies, and peacefulness.

Hotel Tara, $75 - $100. Casa Maria, in town, $50, with pick up at San Jose airport.

Manuel Antonio National Park. I leave Escazu by bus to San Jose and then take another bus to Manuel Antonio, a trip of four hours on winding roads through beautiful mountains and small towns, past waterfalls and rock formations to the Pacific Coast, considerably north of Drake's Bay. This is an impulse trip, planned suddenly because I misread my plane ticket to Cancun and thought I had to leave today instead of next week. It is a lovely, lucky mistake.

Travel tips: May you label all your mistakes "lucky ones." The slogan is: Serendipity Forever!

I find a clean, modern hotel, built around a sparkling swimming pool, only 100 meters from the ocean and beside the National Park. The beaches are perfect here, with pure white sand that doesn't become hot, as it consists of coral, finely ground eons ago. I practice body surfing, as the waves are just right for grandmothers. Hermit crabs are everywhere, scurrying about as they carry their shell homes. One crab's home is a bright blue bottle cap that someone must have discarded.

I take a guided walk in the early morning and see six sloths, about forty monkeys, and innumerable birds, including a yellow-headed woodpecker peeking out from his hole in a tree. The next day I sign up for a tour on a river thick with mangrove trees, water birds, and baby crocodiles twelve to thirty inches long, who have been abandoned temporarily while their mothers and fathers mate and then lay eggs in holes away from the river's edge. White faced monkeys jump onto the tin roof of our launch. The guide says they are not begging, because they are well fed from their favorite food, river clams. He thinks they come to the boat out of curiosity. One leans over the edge of the roof and peers deeply into my eyes before darting away. I spend much of the rest of the day chatting with a very knowledgeable local who owns a cafe. As owner, he has plenty of time to read but he says he has few people who like to discuss literature. He reads English and especially likes Mark Twain. We talk Mark Twain and also San Francisco.

Travel tips: I find it is a good plan to alternate trips alone with trips taken with friends. Alone, it easier to meet local people. If I had been with friends or family, Celeste and I probably would not have become such close friends. I would not have spent as much time with the Isla Mujeres people. I might not have gotten to know Beatrix on Coco Blanco. Or the man who enjoys Mark Twain. Still, being with Marian was a real pleasure. We shared lots of laughs and my trip was enriched by our discussions of our experiences.

A SPANISH TEACHER*

Carlos is a handsome, stocky man about fifty-five years old with brown eyes, dark hair, and a mustache. His speech is musical and very clear. He smiles a lot and likes to invent jokes for his students. His classroom, like much of Costa Rica, is shabby by our standards. He has a tiny room, a table with six chairs crowded around it, and a noisy but essential fan near the window. He's enlivened the walls with slogans, advice, and jokes in Spanish, plus an incredible, hand-lettered index of over a hundred items of Spanish grammar. Although he has his college credentials as a teacher of Spanish, he is monolingual. He manages by speaking simply, gesturing, and knowing many ways of saying in Spanish a single thought.

During four weeks in 1992, after Bob Goulding died, he was my Spanish teacher, friend, and confidant. He tells me about his life. He grew up in an impoverished family, with an alcoholic, abusive father, an ineffectual mother, and uncles who were very cruel to him, verbally and physically. In spite of his background, he worked very hard in school and was the first in his extended family to graduate from high school.

At our second-to-last session together, he asks, "What do you do when a person is afraid of heights?"

"Who? You?"

"Yes." He explains that he is comfortable in this office on the second floor, but is very uncomfortable on the fourth floor, where the staff holds their meetings. He is afraid to sit by the window, and never looks out.

"OK, come on, we are going to cure you." I ask him to stand as close to the window on this second floor as he can in comfort. He stands directly in front of the window. I stand beside him. Below us the street is crowded with cars and pedestrians. "Are you OK here?"

"Yes."

"Good." I point down. "Look down. Are you still OK?" When he says he is fine, I ask him to imagine that his mother and father are standing on the sidewalk below us. "Tell them, 'I am not going to jump' and see if that is true."

"Oh, yes, that is true. I would never try to kill myself or hurt myself. I am not going to jump."

"Perfect. Now tell them, 'I am not going to fall.'"

This time he stiffens and looks very tense. "I just remembered something. I think it is the problem." He explains that his mother was always terrified that he might fall. For example, when he wanted to climb trees, she'd scream at him to get down before he fell and injured himself. "She tried to protect me."

I say, "How sad. You are just a little boy and she does not protect you from your father. She does not protect you from your uncles. She does not protect you from important things. You need protection from the dangerous people in your life, from real dangers. And she only protects you from imaginary dangers, like trees or this window."

He is crying. "I was never protected. No one protected me. I needed protection." He thinks about it. "Could I have taken care of myself in trees? I suppose I could have. Of course. I have taken care of myself for years." He is excited. Laughing, he yells to me, "Come on, we're going to the fourth floor!" Usually he walks very sedately to the elevator. This time we run up the stairs.

On the fourth floor, we go to the faculty room, and he stands at the window, looking down. "I am not afraid!"

I tell him that his is the fastest cure in history, and he is very pleased. He says he is going home as soon as my lesson is finished, to tell his wife.

During our last session, we talk about what he has done, and we go back to the fourth floor. He is not afraid.

This session took place in 1992. Ten years later, when I visit the family in Escazu, Carlos tells me he is doing fine, and has no fear of heights. "However, I'm not thinking of doing anything foolish. Don't expect me to climb mountains."

*from A TIME TO SAY GOOD-BYE, by Mary Goulding, 1996

ICELAND

Laurie Barrett, Tara Barrett, Reiko True, Karen Edwards, Bill Kreger: Eldertrek

Reykjavik. At the Reykjavik airport so many officials are stamping passports that there is no wait. The woman who stamps mine asks, "Are you staying a long time?" Her welcoming smile suggests that I may stay as long as I like. I feel a pleasant culture shock.

From the airport to the city we see bare earth, rocks, a bit of lupine, and not a single tree. In the distance larger rocks have formed themselves into snow-covered mountains. Iceland is stark, and starkly different from where I have been for the first half of 2002. I have come from heat, lush growth, and jungles to austerity, from brown skinned people to very white skin and pale hair. Here in June it is **cold** and the wind blows hard.

Everyone I meet speaks English. Cars are new and clean. Adolescents are clean, their hair is combed, and I don't see nose rings. Or lip rings. In this cold, who knows what the navels are like? People in Reykjavik seem sedate. They don't gesture much, and we don't see hugging and kissing, or hear loud voices. But believe me, we are loud! Six of us, five family members plus our friend, Reiko, haven't been together in ages, so we talk excitedly, catching up on family news. The sun is shining late at night, while we, bundled up, explore the city, chatting madly.

In the morning we join seven other tourists and our guide, Erik, and are driven out of the city into the central highlands, a desolate area surrounded by glacial mountains and rivers of a strange, milky white from the glacial run-off. Icebergs drop with a crash from the glacier and float, a brilliant blue, on a glacial lake. The wind continues strong, insistent, and icy. We see a large two-tiered waterfall, then lava beds, hot springs, bubbling mud and water, and cliffs full of birds. Geyser, for which all others in the world are named, no longer spouts. But just 100 yards away, Strokker is a fine substitute. It churns noisily, bubbles, and then with a loud hiss and explosion jets water ninety feet into the air. This world of heat and cold, rock and water, is beautiful.

We visit an oasis which is a residential center for mentally retarded and disabled Icelanders of all ages. They live in attractive, stone-block homes, heated electrically. In their greenhouses the residents grow tomatoes, cucumbers, beets, onions, zucchini, beans, potatoes, and carrots. They also make candles, toys, shampoos, soaps, and various doodads for tourists. They serve delicious lunches to visitors, who include ecological and gardening groups that hold international conferences here. What I find most impressive is the quiet pleasure the residents take in their community.

Thingvellir. Another day of rock and cold, and we reach Thingvellir, where Parliament was held for almost 1,000 years. It's a long, plain, wooden building constructed in 934 during Norse times. Every summer forty-eight chiefs and ninety-six advisors, chosen in their local districts, made the arduous trek to Thingvellir from all parts of Iceland. There were no roads, trails, or even markers to guide them then. They faced extreme cold, terrible storms, and sudden fogs that blotted out everything for days at a time. When all the chiefs and advisors finally arrived, Parliament began. The appointed secretary from the prior year recited from memory all previous laws, as they had no written language during the early years. For two weeks the members of Parliament discussed these laws, local problems in each area, and made new laws as deemed necessary. Then they set out on their long trek home. Until quite recently, parliament continued to meet here; now it meets in the capital. Iceland has the world's oldest, continuously functioning democratic Parliament.

The area surrounding Thingvellir contains dark, fissured lines and deepening chasms that are evidence of the movement of the continental plates. The plates are pulling apart at the speed (dazzling or slow, depending on your outlook) of one meter a year. Though the cracks are old, the knowledge of the existence of continental plates is quite new. It wasn't until 1912 that a German, Alfred Wegener, wrote of this geological fact. He was discounted or ignored by geological societies. Finally, after his death in the 1960's, his facts became a cornerstone of geological knowledge. One of reasons he had been discounted: he was not a geologist. Oh well.

A monument was erected in honor of the old parliament, and the government decided it would be a fitting place for their first national cemetery. An enclosed, raised area, green in summer, was prepared.

The first dead man awarded the honor of burial here was a famous poet. He was also a drunk who was such an excellent con artist that he had even been able to sell the rights to aurora borealis (Northern Lights) to several fools. After some snide remarks about his body being chosen for the first internment, it was decided that the country needed a real hero for the second. They chose a leader who had fought courageously for freedom from Denmark, had been killed in Denmark, and buried there in an unmarked grave. The Icelandic government determined which grave was his, negotiated with Denmark to exhume the body, and the Icelandic Navy brought it back amidst the requisite pomp and ceremony.

A huge national re-burial ceremony took place. Unfortunately, a mistake had been made. Iceland had buried with honor a Danish blacksmith, rather than the patriot. Since then, living candidates for a future home in the national cemetery have publicly written, often with fiery passion, that they do not wish to be buried between a drunk and a Dane. The two bodies remain alone.

A bit of history:

6th century BCE: St Brendan, an Irish priest, came to Iceland, called it a "paradise of birds and flaming mountains," and did not stay.

4th century BCE: a Greek named Pytheas arrived, named Iceland Thule, and also left.

700 CE (over a millennium later): Irish monks set up a monastery, but since there was no begetting and nobody from Ireland was beating down the doors to join them, the order didn't last very long in Iceland.

874: The first Norse settlers arrived.

934: Parliament was established.

1000: Parliament (under great pressure from Norway) adopted Christianity.

1200 to 1220: The great sagas were composed. They are about real men, who supposedly were virtuous, handsome, strong, and very intelligent, but each had one flaw that led to his downfall. One was unlucky in love, one afraid of the dark, etc. The language, Old Norwegian, is unintelligible to Norwegians today, but Icelanders can read it.

1300s: Iceland was devastated by earthquakes.

During all the years under Norwegian rule, conditions were terrible, with rampant disease and starvation. This continued through the 1400s and 1500s, when Iceland was under Danish rule.

1600 - 1602: Denmark monopolized Iceland's foreign trade, and as a result, over 9,000 people died of starvation.

1783: Mt. Laki erupted, devastating the southeast area. One-fifth of the population died. Icelanders began to migrate to Canada and the US.

1855: free trade was restored, but conditions didn't improve.

1855 to 1870: migration accelerated.

1874: Iceland gained domestic rule from Denmark.

Iceland today: Iceland is a well-to-do capitalist country with extensive welfare services. People receive good salaries and are productive. Health care is free to all of its citizens; there is no illiteracy, no regular armed forces, and practically no unemployment. There are only forty inhabitants in the country's federal prison. Part of their wealth comes from the geothermal power the state sells abroad.

Iceland's animals: The horses are small, with short legs and lovely flowing manes. They run everywhere, free of fences, and there is one horse for every two people in Iceland. They are kept as pets, used for herding sheep, rented to tourists, ridden by locals, and eaten. Local markets all carry horse meat. Little lambs in twosomes hop about behind their mothers. They, too, look like pets and, of course, end up eaten. Many people here, especially young adults, choose to be vegetarians, although it is a difficult choice with so few available vegetables.

What else about the people? Erik says, "We are boring. I didn't know how boring, until I went to Spain to live with a family for a summer. They hugged and kissed me, and telephoned all over Spain for their relatives to come to meet me. Nothing like that would happen in Iceland. But we have our good points, too. When I was in Spain, I witnessed a terrible automobile accident. One man was lying in the road, bleeding very badly. The Spaniards were screaming and praying hysterically. I put a tourniquet on the man, which saved his life. We are a resourceful people. In a difficult climate like ours, I think that only efficient people survived. However, I wish I could be emotional as well as efficient."

Iceland is famous in Europe for being the site of wild weekend parties during the summer. There are tales of customers stripping in bars, sex parties, and much drunkenness. However, these are stories about the customers, not the people of Iceland.

We drive across icy, barren plains from Langjokull toward the Hofjokull glaciers, passing geysers and waterfalls, and then stop at a natural outdoor hot pool, but the winds are so cold most of us won't undress outside in order to soak in it. My sister Laurie, who, I swear, swims wherever she can crack the ice, braves the wind, and her daughter Tara joins her. They report that the hot water is magnificent.

At **Hofsos** we see a folk museum dedicated to the saga of the courageous people who bore the hardships of poor land and unending poverty. We see another waterfall and a large lake where there is supposed to be a fantastic collection of ducks. Not a single one shows up. Godafoss is a fine horseshoe-shaped falls, large and powerful, given its name because it was here in the year 1000 that the head of parliament threw his statues of the pagan gods over the falls. For him it was a tragic occasion.

Nearby **Akureyri** is a small city with a sparkling white, painted church that has about one hundred steps leading up to it. Only the fit are fit to pray here. Below are tourist shops, restaurants, and bakeries. Among the souvenirs are plastic replicas of Vikings, labeled "made in China," (like the "made in China" plastic replicas of cable cars and the Golden Gate Bridge in San Francisco.) Just outside of town, in this almost treeless country, is a small forest of birch and conifer. Then the landscape turns bleak again, except for one brilliant yellow farmhouse and its outbuildings. How cheerful they are!

We go to **Husavik,** a pleasant fishing town whose major industry is showing whales to tourists. The sky is almost black with storm, but the bay is calm, as bays so often are, to fool the foolish. Our group sets out happily in a thirty-foot boat. I am also happy, as I wave them godspeed. I see the bones of whales in the local museum, hear a video on whales and whaling, and look for a restaurant. There are none open, but a woman in the back of a tourist shop offers to make me coffee. She tells me how smart I am not to go out to sea today. The waves will be high, she predicts accurately. The group returns, white faced and staggering, except for the few like Laurie and Bill, who love any ship in a storm. Unfortunately, the group saw only one brief flash of a whale's tail. One man was so sick he couldn't lift his head even to see the tail. Erik, as sick as any of the tourists, says this is the day he fears on every tour, because he always becomes seasick, "It is my duty to go with the group." So duty joins efficiency as a positive in the characterization of the people of Iceland.

Another Erik episode: We stop at the largest and most spectacular canyon in Iceland, deep and long and very beautiful. It was formed by tremendous flooding from a glacier. The rain is now heavy sleet, but we trudge along to see the great waterfall. Standing in front of it, erect, his blonde hair sparkling with sleet, Erik sings in full voice the national anthem. The place, the operatic quality of the song, the fervor and beauty of his voice in the sleet and rain are for me Iceland at its most thrilling.

Travel books say that temperatures in June in Iceland are seventy degrees in daytime and sixty degrees at night. We are freezing and it is never night, because this is the Summer Solstice, with dark clouds covering what might be twilight and wind following us everywhere. Our group is wearing newly purchased wool hats, scarves, and mittens; without my thermal underwear and my father's thirty-year-old, very heavy down jacket I would give up and head south on the first plane going to the Equator. Icelanders are walking bareheaded, wearing a single sweater and eating ice-cream bars.

We visit a geothermal power station, where there are seventeen high pressure wells and five low pressure wells in operation. (I take this sort of meaningless-to-me notes.) We get a lecture on the ecological advantages of geothermal power. It is free of undesirable atmospheric emissions and, because the government rather than private industry controls it, people have all the heat and light they want at almost no cost. All schools have heated swimming pools, open to everyone. Children learn to swim soon after they learn to walk.

We see more caves, natural hot tubs, boiling mud, sulfur springs, and a bizarre "village" of lava sculptures made by a combination of ice and lava that spilled out more than 10,000 years ago. Early travelers went days out of their way to avoid this "place of malevolent creatures." We walk among them, fascinated by their grotesque black forms. With fog swirling about the shapes, they do look like malevolent creatures from another world.

We visit a folk museum that once was a very big farm, housing workers and the owners, plus old people without funds, who were boarded there by the not-so-benevolent government of the early 1900s.

After a poverty-stricken life, these old people were stashed in unheated, freezing rooms with miserably inadequate food. The place was run by Lutherans, who forbade alcohol, dancing, card playing, and excessive laughter, should anyone find anything to laugh about. Since 1950, the farm has been a museum, with old tools, saddles, and furniture. Today's old people are well cared for.

It is the day after solstice, and the ground is white with newly fallen snow. I cannot imagine how anyone survives here. My daughter Karen, who lives in Colorado and likes snow, disagrees. She finds everything about Iceland to be wonderful. At the end of each day, she, Tara, Erik, and our driver search out pubs where they can dance with the locals. She says, "I like this climate. What's your problem?" My problem is I like the tropics.

We pass steep mountains and long, beautiful fjords, and visit a typical working farm house with a turf roof and an old kitchen with an open peat fire. A hole in the roof allows the smoke to escape. The new kitchen is modern and warm. A friendly red-haired woman, with an equally friendly red-haired little son, serves us fine pancakes.

We stay at a school (hard beds, rough sheets) in a town called **Djupivogur** on a fjord. After supper we walk along the fjord and see harlequin ducks, lots of skuas, and arctic terns. The next morning we visit the third largest icecap in the world: Vatnajokull. Amazingly, the weather warms enough for us to have a picnic by the ice cap: pickled herring in mustard sauce, beautiful ripe pears, smoked fish (ghastly), and Icelandic pastries. Afterwards we go to a glacier lagoon full of icebergs: white, black, black and white in stripes, and dazzling blue. We cross the huge flood plain, created when a wall of water, from an eruption under the ice cap, crashed across the land in 1996. In three hours, miles of land lay wasted. (Since most of Iceland is what is called wasteland, I am not sure that this devastating sweep of water did much except make a few sheep move to another pasture.) No people lived in the area.

We see puffins! Dozens of these adorable birds! They look a bit like penguins with brilliantly colored beaks or like a toy invented for especially nice children. Baby puffins stay in deep holes in the cliffs, and their parents fly in from the sea, with as many as five fish crammed into their mouths to feed the babies. Adolescent Puffins sit on the rocks, preening and flirting, rather like adolescents of any species.

We see another glorious Falls, Skorgafoss, immense and pure, milky white as it flows over green moss on black lava. At the next falls, the agile in our group are able to walk behind it. As we approach **Reykjavik** at the end of our long, circular trip, we stop at a glass-domed oasis, heated thermally, with palm trees, a tiny waterfall, and many blooming flowers. The Icelanders sit at small tables, eating ice cream in this exotic environment of live, growing plants. At City Hall we re-live our trip, tracing it on a large relief map of Iceland. We tour the city, see the Lutheran Cathedral, the university, and the huge water towers that heat every home, office, shop, and hotel in Iceland. We have a banquet of salmon, plus the slimy cheeks of some large fish.

Our final morning is dedicated to shopping, so I buy a doll from the woman who made it, to add to my daughter Claudia's collection. We spend the afternoon at the Blue Lagoon. This lagoon is the result of a wonderful mistake. Drilling holes for a new geo-thermal plant, the drillers went too deep. Seawater infiltrated, spoiling the project. The drilling was abandoned and the area became a hot lake, loved by neighboring children. The officials realized the possibilities, built dressing rooms, and Voila! The public has this wonderful hot lake all year long! We undress, walk into the shallow water, dab ourselves with clay from the bottom, whose mineral content is supposed to make us beautiful and does make us white, and then like ghosts we bob through the mist. The water is warm in places and very hot where it comes directly from the nether regions. The heat merges, the mist is blown away and returns, and all around us, blonde, clay-covered Icelanders are smiling.

COPENHAGEN to OSLO to AURLAND

Karen Edwards, Claudia Pagano, and Reiko True

Copenhagen. We are booked into the Cab Inn, a new concept in low price hotels. The rooms are like cabins on ships, all plastic, with two bunks, a couch that makes into a single or double bed, and two more bunks tucked away in the walls overhead. The bedding is stacked on shelves for occupants to make up their own beds. The beds are comfortable and the room very clean. The woman behind the front desk seems to speak all western European languages with cool efficiency. This is the first conversation I overhear in English:

A man is complaining that he had booked a non-smoking room and has been given a smoking room.

Desk person: "It's a non-smoking room as long as you don't smoke."

He repeats that he wants a non-smoking room, and she repeats that he has a non-smoking room.

He: "I tell you it's a smoking room. There's even an ashtray in the room."

She: "Put it in the desk drawer. You don't need to smoke just because we give you an ashtray. Lots of people don't."

He walks away, muttering to himself.

I ask her where the closest Laundromat is. She brings out a street map, puts an X for the hotel and another X for the Laundromat, and very efficiently tells us how to get from one to the other. Once there, our problems start. There are no instructions in English. A nice young Scot arrives, and tells us what troubles he had washing his clothes here the first time. "You can't do it without help." he says cheerfully, and goes through the steps with us:

Is this a tip for tourists or a cautionary tale? The reader may decide. To wash clothes in Copenhagen: put clothes in washer, close washer, put coins in slot for soap, put coins in a different slot for activating the washer, push the number of the correct washer to make soap go into your machine instead of another machine. If you need to open the washer (we had a shirt caught in the door), push a special button and hold for thirty seconds exactly, when the door can be opened and then shut again. When washing is done, clothes are sopping wet. Pull them out and put them in a huge tank, put correct coin in correct slot for correct tank number, and clothes will whirl for three minutes. Put them in a dryer, which charges by the minute.

It is so complicated that I make up a quick excuse to leave the others with the knowledgeable Scot. I say I think I have an appointment to see the Queen.

I do what I do in strange towns, get lost, even with the map in my hand. I am walking in precisely the wrong direction, when I see a taxi parked at a curb. The driver explains that he is waiting for his fare, but tries to show me on my map where I went wrong. His fare appears, a local physician who tells me he is going past the Cab Inn and will be glad to take me there. He says, "You look a bit jet-lagged," and adds, "It's easy to get lost in a big city." He is a savior.

The National Art Museum is modern and beautiful, with Van Goghs, Monets, Pisarros, an exquisite early Picasso, and many more. At the entrance is an interesting statue dedicated, I imagine, to birth control: a woman being scrambled over by too many children.

We go to Tivoli Gardens and enjoy the flowers, bright, fun buildings, and happy crowds. We'd expected terrible food, a la Disneyworld, and instead have memorable meals of salmon tartar, lobster-asparagus salad, and "the perfect sole," which we share.

Hotel Cab Inn, (inexpensive, good choice.)

After a tour of the city on a double-deck bus, and a visit to another museum, it's time to take the 5:00 P.M. ferry to Oslo, an all-night trip with dinner and dancing. A Swedish friend warned my daughters to beware of all the single men on the ferry, who tend to be "wolfish", so my daughters happily anticipate this. Unfortunately, the people who show up for the dance are families with children, a few honeymooners, and pensioners. Not one wolfish person anywhere. Oh bore. Instead of dancing, we sit on deck, watching the North Sea traffic, the Swedish coast, and a long, lovely sunset that doesn't end until after 11P.M.

Oslo. We cram in the tourist sites: the countless statues in Frogner Park, the ho-hum folk museum, and then the very fine Viking exhibit. It's impossible to believe that anyone would put to sea in a cold, raging ocean in such flimsy, open boats. The three Viking boats prove that the Vikings were death-defying. No wonder they were the scourge of their time. The only people able to stop them were Genghis Khan and his men. Karen is inspired to buy a book on the Vikings, and from that night on, she reads us to sleep on Viking history. The Kon Tiki museum contains Heyerdahl's famous raft, also a flimsy craft that managed to survive the sea. His amateur movies of the trip are a delight.

The weather is glorious. Norwegians by the hundreds are strolling or rollerblading on the waterfront, and eating in the outdoor cafes. Norway seems the most affluent country we have encountered: new Mercedes, Rolls Royces, and BMWs; houses solid and freshly painted. Everything costs a fortune, especially the food. We stay at the City Hotel, described erroneously in some guide books as being in a dangerous area full of drunks. Perhaps this was true once, but now the streets are clean and yuppified. The only current danger is to our sanity, because the hotel is full of English adolescents in large tour groups, who yell all night, slam doors, and behave as obnoxiously as they know how.

We visit the Munch museum. I had known him only for his famous "Scream," and this museum shows the interesting range of his work. We decide to dine in deluxe style at the Grand Hotel. The dining room is staid, nicely decorated, turn-of-the-last-century, but the food is mediocre, expensive and bland. One front table is permanently reserved for the spirit of Ibsen, who dined there regularly.

City Hotel, (inexpensive.)

On to the fjord country! The train from Oslo to Myrdahl passes pretty, small towns with peaked-roof houses, bright green, perfect lawns, and a wonderful assortment of flowers in spite of the short growing season. Purple lupine, buttercups, and daisies grow beside the tracks, and lambs and goats jump about and chase each other. The train climbs through forests of pine, aspen, and fir until we pass the tree line and reach the altitude of bare, gaunt rocks, and beautiful snow. We see only an occasional home, standing alone, and then descend back to wildflowers and houses, to Myrdahl. We need to change trains to go to Flam, the entrance to the fjords. We independent travelers are told to find cars 1 - 6, which don't exist. All other cars have been commandeered by tour groups, who refuse to let us on. The most militant is the Elderhostel guide. Karen and Reiko spot a guide who looks a bit embarrassed by his role of storm trooper, so push him aside and find us seats. We are off, on the wonderful downhill run to Flam. The train stops once and everyone disembarks for a view of a very full, grand waterfall. At the last minute, I manage to enter the wrong car, occupied by a Japanese tour group who all stand up, bow, and offer me my choice of seats.

In Flam we take a small steamship and sail down the fjord to Aurland. Rocky cliffs rise hundreds of feet, with many waterfalls, some wide and full, others little jagged lines of silver on the rocky walls. Some waterfalls bounce and spray, some travel under the rocks and then gush out again. It is cold today, with a misty rain.

Aurland is an adorable town with brightly painted houses built up a mountainside. Every house has lace curtains in the windows and blooming flowers in pots on the window sills. In the center of the town is a newly plastered and painted white church from the twelfth century that holds forty parishioners. Around it are headstones, many quite old, and lots of flowers. We walk around town, take photos of each other sitting on an iron reindeer, and buy handmade Norwegian sweaters.

The next day we do a round trip, Aurland to Gudwagon at the mouth of the fjord. The mountains are even higher and more splendid than on the way to Aurland, and the fjord narrows until there is barely room for the boat to pass between the cliffs. The guide books say it is the narrowest fjord in Norway. Waterfalls are everywhere. This three-decker steamship is jammed with tour groups getting off at Gudwagon to bus to Bergen. On the way back, we are the only passengers, so drink coffee with the crew, and see the wonderful gorges a second time.

On our return train to Oslo the sun is so bright I can barely look at the snow, even through dark glasses.

KOBLENZ TO BADEN BADEN

Karen Edwards and Claudia Pagano

Koblenz is a beautiful city, rebuilt after the destruction of World War II. We take a short Rhine trip past the famous castles, and then rent a car and head south along the Mosel river. This is wine country. Vines cover every hill, up, down, and sideways, making a huge patchwork of varied greens. We pass lovely little villages, where German tourists are buying great quantities of wine, souvenirs, and hugely beautiful desserts, cakes and ice cream dripping with whipped cream. Oh, to be non-diabetic! Everywhere there are flowers in bloom in every possible color. Europe with my daughters is the best of the best! We have fun laughing at the imps in the fountains, the way people twist their bodies as they shoot photos, or almost anything.

We drive along the river, past villages with gothic churches and dark, timber-framed houses with window boxes filled with flowers, until we reach the fairy-tale palace of Burg Eltz, high on a hill, surrounded by forests and its own private river. The castle is built of yellow-brown stone with dozens of turrets and towers, all crowned with pointed spires. To me it is a perfect site for dwarfs and witches, but in reality it is a private palace built by a wealthy count and countess during medieval times. Although it was an era of perpetual warfare, this castle survived unharmed, because, they say, the count and his heirs used tact and diplomacy rather than armed conflict. Inside are the usual collections of elegant china, heavy jewel-encrusted goblets, tapestries, and old swords and other arms that somewhat belie the story of non-violence. Maybe not. Tact and strength may go together. We see more towns, and watch the barges and tourist boats on this gracefully flowing river. Good wine is everywhere and we imbibe with glee.

Trier is the oldest city in northern Europe, built in the reign of the Roman Emperor Augustus in 15 BCE. Three hundred years later, under Diocletian, it became a Roman imperial residence and western capital of the Roman Empire. If you peek behind the altar of the cathedral, you will see a sumptuous shrine which holds what is supposed to be a cloak used by Christ. We visit the ruins of old Roman baths and a bridge with a black gate like a three-tiered wedding cake. It was originally white, but turned black spontaneously around 1000 CE, the Trierians say. No one can explain this, since the oldest living witness died at least 950 years ago. We photograph the bridge, buildings decorated with stone lions, saints, and little imps, and a colorfully painted fountain. Then we wander among the souvenirs for sale in the hauptmarkt.

Luxemburg. Since childhood, I have had a mental image of a beautiful, fairyland castle surrounded by forests in a land called Luxemburg. I can see it with total clarity, as beautiful as the Emerald City of Oz. For at least sixty years I have been told that Luxemburg really isn't all that great, and yet I still believe in my castle. Even the dumbest places in Europe have castles, right? So I persuade my poor daughters that we must check it out. After a non-interesting drive with lots of traffic, we reach Luxemburg and find there is nowhere to park. There are signs, sprinkled willy-nilly through the center of town, with large I's (Information) and P's (Parking), that lead us nowhere. Finally a parking place opens up. We grab it and look for the castle. It does not exist.

Previously unknown to my daughters or me, (obviously, our combined knowledge of Luxemburg is zilch), the language of this small country is French, which means that nobody admits to understanding anything we try to communicate. A saleswoman actually shrugs when we plead "water," "agua," "wasser," until finally Karen dares go behind the counter and point. We can't find out where there is a toilet, palace, or castle. "I told you we shouldn't have come here!" Karen announces accurately and dramatically. We finally locate a public toilet.

We find a sign that lets us know we are standing in front of the royal palace, a square building that looks like a local bank. On the main street are many banks that look like palaces. Maybe this was done on purpose, to fool invading armies. If an army attacks, the conqueror will immediately attempt to destroy banks, while the royal family remains safe, if the royal family has the presence of mind to remove that one small sign that tells where they live.

We try to leave Luxemburg, but have a terrible time until we discover that we are using a map of Trier rather than Luxemburg. The maps look vaguely alike, if you confuse highways and waterways. Eventually, we escape back to the town of **Schweich**, to recuperate with some fine local Riesling at the Hotel Krone. I still believe that somewhere hidden away is the wonderful castle. Could it be in Liechtenstein?

Hotel Krone, Schweich (about $50. Nice rooms, excellent restaurant.)

All over the world, except in Luxemburg and along the Mosel, there are internet cafes. Beside a palm-roofed cabin in Akumal, in Cuba, even in Irian Jaya years ago, I was able to email home. In hotels in Iceland and Amsterdam, the use of email is free. Internet is as ubiquitous as MacDonald's. For one week in Germany, I have looked in vain. Germans explain that all locals own their own computers and German travelers take their computers with them. No one needs public internet. *%^&*%$*#&** !^!+!#*/*

Baden Baden is a big, beautiful tourist town, with every conceivable bit of art, clothing, and special food that a tourist could want, but still no internet. True, some expensive hotels have internet access, but only for their guests. We decide it doesn't matter, because here we are at the most famous baths in Europe!

We go first to the old spa, in a castle-like building where royalty from all over Europe once "took the waters." Inside (nude bathers only) are: a large, fragrant pool, a hotter pool, a cooler pool, and small pools, all with sumptuous sculptures of nudes and semi-nudes from Greek and Roman times, as well as old paintings from the Middle Ages. The baths are wonderful! We follow the printed instructions, telling us the order in which to soak in each pool, and the maximum time in each. We follow instructions the first time, and then we simply go back and forth in whatever order we choose, and don't bother about maximum times. Before leaving, we wrap in hot sheet-towels, lie on heated wooden couches, and then test the soft lounge chairs. We overuse the famous lotions and drip our way to the hotel.

We spend the next day at the Caracalla Leisure Baths, named for the Roman Emperor Caracalla, who came to Baden Baden to cure his rheumatism. (Except for the hot tubs and steam rooms on the second floor, suits are required.) We jump into a warm, outdoor pool, with a strong current that spins bathers in breath-taking, frightening circles. Next to this pool are two large hot pools and a medium-hot pool with special jets for massaging feet, legs, and upper and lower back. Inside the building is an immense pool with a tall, domed roof and glass walls for viewing mountains, beautiful homes, and hotels that could be palaces. There are snack bars, scented steam rooms, tanning tables, heating lamps, tanning coffins that actually close when you are inside them (perish the thought), and lounging areas.

That night we try to visit the world-famous casino, but we aren't properly dressed, says the guard. Women must wear dresses or "very dressy pant-suits," and men must wear jackets and ties. We plan to dress up the next day, but never get around to it. The lure of the baths is too great.

I take the train to Utrecht to attend a transactional analysis conference. Claudia and Karen drive on to Munich.

BELGIUM AND THE NETHERLANDS

Felipe Garcia, Claudia Pagano, TA conference, and solo

I am in **Utrecht** attending the annual conference of the International Transactional Analysis Association. I wander around the city, enjoying the canals and medieval buildings, but most of my time is spent giving and attending workshops. Claudia visits old churches and takes me to a wonderful temporary exhibit of Russian icons.

Strews Hostel. This is the first time I am recommending a hostel. The major hotels are awful, not clean, expensive, and with personnel who don't offer service. Strews is clean and delightful, as are their guests.

Brugge is a city of views, medieval buildings, canals, quaint houses, churches, lovely squares, plus truly beautiful lace, tapestries, and ceramics. The town square is perfect for people watching, and the best and freshest chocolates imaginable are sold right there at the market place. Even the sugar free chocolates are a glory! We visit the museum Catharijne Convent, which is nice if you like religious art. Claudia climbs the tower. We watch old women make lace by hand, go to the Atlantic to see windmills, and end at a store, Point de Rose, where Claudia buys herself a tapestry and photographs all the ones she doesn't buy. We stay at a wonderful hotel, with a room overlooking a canal. We watch the boats below, and, of course, take a meandering trip on one of them. Our boat is accompanied by ducks and swans. If there is a list of Europe's most perfect small cities, put Brugge at the top.

Bouroensche Cruyce hotel. A wonderful place! Pay a little extra for a room overlooking the canal. The restaurant is also a delight. email: bour.cruyce@ssi.be

Once every ten years in **Haarlem** there is a fantastic flower show. People come from all over the world to see it. Get ready for 2012 and don't let anything keep you away! They stage Spring, Summer, and Fall exhibits, each different, and we are here for summer: hundreds of exhibits, millions of flowers, flower arrangements twenty feet tall, whole fields of indescribably brilliant color, every possible orchid, from the tiniest, almost microscopic buds to the largest, most lavish blooms, and fantastic water lilies! There are acres and acres of beauty all around us. Claudia, Felipe, and I spend a full day here, and wish we had time for a second or third visit. If I lived in Europe, I would certainly go to Haarlem for all three season changes.

Amsterdam is a must-see city. Its name comes from the dam built across the Amster River, to create the town square. In a small, smoke-filled cafe we pore over the long wooden menu of available hash and marijuana, as if we know one from the other. The boy behind the counter does. He is almost lyrical in his description. "This is from the mountains of Pakistan, picked only by moonlight." "This is Afghanistan's glory." He smiles. "And you are Americans? You must appreciate your finest, flown here from Mendocino County." We let him choose for us, and get good, smooth marijuana. Then we walk the cobbled streets to the red light section to see the attractive-looking girls who sell sex.

The next morning I need to buy insulin, which is over-the-counter in every country I have visited, including the United States. Not here. This I do not understand. "I am a diabetic. Here's my card, my old bottle of insulin. What is the trouble?" The pharmacist explains that in the Netherlands I must have a prescription from a physician licensed in this country.

"Can't the doctors make a living any other way than charging tourists for unnecessary exams? I cannot believe that in a country that will sell me hash with no prescription, I cannot buy the insulin I need!" I explain that I have only a little time in this beautiful city, and don't want to waste it in a physician's office. "If I spend the day in a doctor's office, I won't have time for your museums."

Finally, the pharmacist phones a physician friend, tells her my name and says "She's an American older woman and expected to buy insulin here without a prescription. She's a bit upset." The physician okays it over the phone.

Truly, I like Amsterdam, its brooding, sixteenth century stone buildings, its canals, splendid museums, happy crowds, and white-blonde, blue-eyed children. I go to the square to see the Royal Palace, the peace memorial, the cathedral-like church where coronations are held, and then visit the Anne Frank house. It's easy to find, as everyone speaks English and knows exactly how to get to tourist sites. Going through the house is a somber experience. She was a young woman, a child really, who wrote simply about her experiences before she died in a Nazi camp. Many people are crying as they walk through the barren house where Anne Frank and her family had been hidden.

Claudia and I spend the next two days in the splendor of Amsterdam's museums. The Rijksmuseum has the Dutch masters, Vermeer, Steen, Halls, and Rembrandt. If you skip the early church art, you can spend the day without angels, tortured saints, or crucifixions. Instead you'll see the earthy, colorful dancing and carousing of the peasants.

The newly renovated Van Gogh museum is a joy. Every painting is beautifully spaced and lighted. The early Van Goghs are here, including the darkly arresting "Potato Eaters," that tells all one ever needs to know of overwork and poverty. Only a year later, Van Gogh is splashing brilliant color across sunlit fields, flowers, his yellow house in Arles, his cramped, dizzy-making bedroom, and his tortured self-portraits. He once wrote, "My art is a scream of despair." I spend the morning, go outside for a hot dog, and come back. To me the enigma is how a man, so desperately unhappy, could paint brightness so well. I also wonder why people of his day did not recognize his genius and buy his paintings.

Bridge Hotel (inexpensive. Reserve a front room overlooking trees.

In this museum-packed week, I keep aside one day for the Kroller - Muller Museum before going to The Hague to get my visa for the Ukraine. This time I am alone. On the way to the museum by train and then two buses, I meet a young woman from Hiroshima, who tells me that she has only a one-week vacation, and came all this way, halfway around the world and back, to see one painting, Van Gogh's "Starry Night." "When I was in school, I saw a copy of Starry Night and I thought it was the most beautiful painting in the world. Now I will see the original!" We chat about her work in computers, the fact that Japanese receive only one-week vacations, US computer people two weeks, and Europeans four weeks from the same international companies. Big cheat. But she is here, and very happy.

Together we stand in front of Starry Night, so amazing and wonderful. Then we move on to The Cedars, The Olive Trees, and the rest of this beautiful collection. I go back and forth between them. We take a coffee break, and meet an American man her age, who says he recently inherited enough money to live in Europe for one year if he is careful. He, too, loves art. He introduces her to Gris and Bracht and other painters in another part of the gallery, and explains their intellectual beauty.

This museum is in a national park, with bicycle and walking trails through woods embellished with abstract sculptures. I spend an hour outside and then go back to Van Gogh.

Next, **The Hague.** Seventy years ago, when I was memorizing the names of world capitals, I particularly liked this one. The "the" gave it real importance. No one said The Washington or The London. Not even The Paris. I decided The Hague deserved to sound more impressive than other cities, because it was the seat of the League of Nations. In those days, we fervently believed that the League could keep nations peaceful forever.

I am early, so go to a café and share a table with a local businessman, who tells me, "Tourists know Amsterdam, but this city is nicer. It's clean and quiet. You'll like it. It's free of the hordes of scruffy young people who invade Amsterdam for marijuana and hash."

I take a taxi to the Ukrainian consulate offices, in one of the substantial, nineteenth century brick buildings that now house embassies from all over the world. I pick up the proper form, stand in line while filling it out - and am zapped into a "senility state," which comes over me from time to time when I realize that I have made a perhaps irreversible error. The symptoms: humiliation, mental dizziness, inability to think, panic. The problem this time: I forgot that I would need a photo to paste onto the application, and the office is only open two hours each morning to take applications.

I dread encounters with officialdom, anybody's officialdom. When a policeman stares at me, I get sweaty, as if I were again in a US peace or civil rights march, where the police used night sticks and gunned their motorcycles at us, swerving just before running us down. In California, if you want a building permit or a driver's license, it can be hours of frustration. I have grown to hate asking an official for anything, a building permit, a tax rebate, a visa. Like people who are afraid to fly and therefore remember all crashes everywhere in the world, I remember horror stories about the arrogance of those who have the power to give or withhold visas.

Feeling totally defeated, I mumble that I have no photos. "Is there anything I can do?"

The Ukrainian official is young and sweet. "Don't worry. Just leave your papers and your passport here, and I'll clip the photos in when you come back this afternoon to pick up your visa." He tells me where to go to have my photo taken. Silently, I thank fate for such a helpful man, and aloud I over-thank him. He looks surprised and I wonder if he even knows how difficult some officials can be.

A man in line behind me offers to drive me to the photo shop. On the way, he points out the peace palace and tells me how to find an interesting large mural of turn-of-the-century Hague. The photographer, like the Ukrainian official and the driver, is charming and solicitous. He shows me my photo and says, "You look so light-hearted." With three such sweet men, I recover my sanity.

I take a guided tour of the peace palace, then see the mural, a large, round, quaint panorama of dikes, small houses, birds, children, and fishermen that represents The Hague of many years ago. I walk around the Royal Palace, which is not open to the public, and even have time for a much-needed haircut.

I return to the consulate, turn in the photos plus the one hundred dollars in cash (ridiculously expensive) for the visa, and the same official glues the photo onto the application, and returns my passport with a fancy silver seal and YKPAIHA (Ukraine) stamped on it.

BARCELONA

Felipe Garcia, and solo

Felipe and I fly to **Barcelona**, one of my favorite cities. We decide to specialize in Gaudi architectire, which Felipe has not seen. We jump on and off buses, looking, admiring, and by 3:30 PM end up exhausted at our hotel, have lunch, take a nap, and then walk down the Ramba to watch amateur musicians, magicians, tarot card readers, and young people who paint portraits for a couple of dollars. Other young people from everywhere, with impossibly large backpacks, sit on the curbs, also engrossed in the street entertainment.

We go into an internet café with about 200 computers, crammed with the young, typing. It costs only $5 for twenty-four hours of computer use. Are these almost-grown men and women writing their friends, their parents, or searching the web for their next adventure site?

We have dinner about 11:00 PM, and the next day see more weirdly awesome Gaudi: *Casa Vicens, with blue and white tile towers that look like Moorish minarets, and iron security gates like palm fronds; Guell Palace with even more flamboyant ironwork, and deliriously playful sculpture growing from the rooftop; the unfinished park with the famous mosaic lizard fountain, curving pathways, tunnels covered with coarsely finished mud and rock designs, and the wonderful mosaic bench that twists like a brilliantly colored serpent; Casa Mila, with even more fantastic rooftop sculptures and balconies that a modern architect describes as "glistening bunches of seething seaweed."*

The third day we visit his jewel, La Familia Sagrada, the cathedral he took over in 1883 and continued building until his death in 1926. Not nearly finished, it is indescribably vast, beautiful, and surrealistic. The work goes on slowly, as money trickles in for its completion. Perhaps it will never be finished, and that would be fitting, too. I like the idea that Gaudi's dream, if not his life, stretches into infinity. His actual death almost became a mystery. This great architect was wearing his usual work clothes, ragged, torn, and filthy, when he was run over by a tram. Unrecognized, he was taken to a paupers' ward in the local hospital, where he died. People were searching for him everywhere. Just in time, his body was identified, so instead of its being put in an unmarked grave, he received a great man's burial.

We spend three lovely days at **Sitges** on the Mediterranean south of Barcelona in a hotel by the sea. The beach is lovely, and in the early evening we sit on our own private balcony, sipping Cava wine and watching the parade of tourists. Known as a town for gays and lesbians, it is quietly elegant. The two huge swimming pools at the hotel are rarely used, so I have them to myself when I'm not at the beach or people watching.

Felipe leaves for San Antonio, and I take a bus to another beach town, **Tossa**. Marc Chagall called Tossa "Paradise in Blue." A Spanish poet said, "It is the flower of the sea." Sea and sky are brilliant blue, the houses white, the Roman and Medieval ruins buff. Behind the town, the mountains are a brilliant green. The beaches are sand coves sheltered by black lava cliffs in eerie shapes. The sea is calm, dotted with islets. The large beach is alive with beach umbrellas, in plaids, polka dots, flowers, and solid orange.

Two thousand years ago the Romans built themselves a city here, put up a wall to keep invaders out, grew olives, and swam in their huge swimming pool not too far from the beaches. There are hiking trails in the mountains, which I am too old to explore. Besides, when there is a sea anywhere, that is my focus. The water is warm and wonderful.

Unlike Sitges, Tossa is a family town. Mothers and fathers and their little children, covered with sand or all cleaned up, asleep in mother's and father's arms, in strollers, or trailing behind as they try to keep up. Blue-eyed blondes from the Netherlands and Germany, white-skinned British newly sunburned on faces and shoulders, brown-eyed Italian children. I don't see single parent families. Does Tossa send out brochures advertising for family wholesomeness? It's a merry place, but from early morning until late at night the pool and the beach are invaded by little people in their inflated horses, mattresses, and inner tubes. They scream in French, Italian, German, and British English, and are never quiet while in the water. I yearn for the childlessness of Sitges.

The next day I take a plane to Arles.

72

ARLES to CHAMONIX to PARIS

solo

Arles. Chez Irmelin is a lovely outdoor restaurant. I arrive in time for dinner. The weather is ideal, warm, clear, and starlit. I order as a first course a shrimp - tomato salad. The French waiter, who speaks perfect English, brings gizzards, and sets them down with a flourish.

"I ordered shrimp, not gizzards."

"The gizzards are beautiful. You'll love them! Just try them."

"Oh, dear," I say. "My grandmother used to tell me I would love gizzards and tried to make me eat them. That was over seventy years ago, and I didn't eat them then and I am not going to eat them now." I look sweetly into his handsome brown eyes.

He frowns, then suddenly laughs and takes them away. The shrimp are excellent and so is the rest of the meal. A violinist moves from table to table. It's a perfect evening.

A brief history: *First there were the Celtic tribes, then the Greeks, and then Julius Caesar gave this area to his soldiers as a prize for winning the Punic Wars. The Romans built a large forum with statues everywhere, aqueducts to supply water, a huge track for chariot racing, a theater, and a coliseum holding 20,000 people. It was a Golden Age, if you weren't squeamish about the popular sport, gladiators or Christians vs. wild animals brought in from all over Africa. (I don't think civilization has changed much. We have television in place of coliseums so that millions of people from all over the world can watch killings in fact and fiction. The killings in Afghanistan are the current feature.)*

When the pagans began to overrun the area, the coliseum was turned into a fortress with watchtower, church, and homes inside. Most Romans fled. In the twelfth century Arles began to be rebuilt outside the coliseum-fortress. Bones of various saints were brought in to make the city especially holy, and through the years grand churches, cathedrals, and stately homes were constructed. The buildings inside the coliseum were torn down and carted away. The first big bullfight was held in the coliseum in 1830 to celebrate France's conquest of

Algiers. During World War II much of the city was destroyed by bombs, and rebuilt again when the war ended.

In the morning I go first to the new, very modern and impressive archeology museum with its fine displays of Greek and Roman artifacts. Then I set off for the Roman theater. Its stone seats are covered with white plastic chairs, set up for a musical event this weekend. Acoustics are as clear as ever, they say. Next, in the ancient coliseum, I see where the vast crowds sat, and then the stalls where wild animals were kept, with ramps leading into the arena. During the Roman era, the coliseum had a movable roof for protection against the sun or rain, which is fancier than the baseball fields I knew as a child, Wrigley Field and Comiskey Park. There remain only two beautiful white marble pillars that once supported that roof. Scattered in the grass outside are broken pillars and slabs of marble with carved flowers and geometric designs. Up the hill are the ruins of the Roman aqueduct.

Where the old forum used to be, there are now two expensive hotels and the outdoor bistro that Van Gogh painted in Le Cafe de Nuit. His famous yellow house was destroyed during the war. The gardens that he painted remain. Sitting in one of the gardens in the late afternoon I see a Van Gogh-like purple sky. In the morning it has a golden quality. He came to Arles in 1888 and created over 200 works of art, none of which remains in Arles.

I go to a French bullfight, where no one is hurt, including the bulls. They wear little tassels on their horns. The winning bullfighter is the one who collects the most tassels, using a small fork-like object to lift them off. The bulls charge out of their stalls one at a time and do what they are supposed to do, paw the ground and snort menacingly. Ten bullfighters leap around them, running and jumping, more like ballet dancers than toreadors, as they reach for the tassels.

Hotel Le Nouveau Rhone, ($36, nice, run by an accommodating young couple who speak English.)

Les Baux, a short bus trip from Arles, is a wonderful old town built on the top of a high limestone hill for safety during the Middle Ages. Today it is jammed with French tourists, their proper little pedigreed dogs, and their whining, screechy children. Between screeches the children are ingesting spun sugar (cotton candy on a stick), ice cream, and large lollipops, which may be a part of their problem. On the other hand, they may be sick of a vacation that consists of walking up steep, unshaded paths in the heat to see old stone buildings. At their age, I would not have whined, but I would certainly have screeched. The little dogs behave perfectly. They march correctly, heads held high, and when they give even the tiniest yip, they are immediately picked up and carried. Since they weigh only a few ounces, they win the "carry me" battle that the children lose.

There are a few middle-size dogs, too, a labrador, a chow, and a golden retriever, obviously pure bred, who slink along with the "excuse me for living" look of Thurber's dogs. They are no match for the arrogance of the miniatures.

Inside one of the Medieval mansions a lovely, red-haired woman is singing old French ballads in a high, sweet voice and accompanying herself on instruments with wonderful names: crumhorn, rebec, and psaltery. People walk through a deep, jagged cave to see a slide show of over 1000 slides shown on ten walls simultaneously. It's a clever idea, but the show is of modern China. How nice if it had been slides of Provence.

The long uphill march to the castle continues, but there is a reward for children at the end. Enthusiastic young men in medieval dress are teaching medieval games, chess with giant chessmen, lawn bowling, archery, and jousting. Children who want to joust are decked out in small-size armor. When at last the castle proper is reached, there are exquisite views of the countryside below, gray-green olive trees interspersed with grape vines and wonderfully twisted old rocks. I leave Arles the next morning by train.

From Arles to Lyon, fields of bright yellow sunflowers extend to the horizon. The Rhone meanders beside us, turns away and comes back, a lovely river with only a few boats and swimmers. We pass two castles, one in the hills just before Lyon.

The Lyon station is as busy as a major airport, with security police, some police dogs, and railroad officials checking every ticket. I change trains for St. Germaine and find my seat. A very fat, sweating man with a huge backpack is running toward the train with two large strollers collapsed under his arms, just ahead of a disheveled, equally fat, red-faced woman with a huge back pack and their two shrieking children under her arms. The whistle blows, they stagger aboard, and we're off. The scenery becomes hilly and wooded, and then mountains appear with faces like half-dome. I see another castle. The train stops somewhere with a woods and a castle, and behind it a granite-topped mountain that shines like snow. Perhaps the stop is Culoz. I can't find it on my map of Europe. We are in a valley of corn fields, whose stalks are so close together that no one could walk between the rows to harvest them. The corn is stunted compared to the Illinois corn I knew as a child, so I imagine it is silage for cattle.

A little over an hour out of Lyon, we pass a gorgeous lake that also is not on the map. "If I'd known it was coming, I'd have had a swim." Now we are into real mountain country, and the train stops every few minutes to let off vacationers.

At 9:00 P.M. I arrive at **St. Gervais**, starving. There was no restaurant car or even a food vender on either train. I go to the first hotel by the railroad station, dump my suitcase, and look desperately for something to eat. St. Gervais closes down early. I find an outdoor cafe which has just closed and persuade the cook to feed me. He brings out wine and two glasses, plus bread and cheese for me. He speaks English and is delighted to chat. He says he wants to live in America, loves all things American, but supposes it might be easier to find a job in French Canada. When I tell him I'm from San Francisco, he says he adores San Francisco, which he thinks he knows well from what he has seen in movies and TV. Might there be a job for him doing anything in San Francisco? We drink more wine. With a third glass, we both decide that San Francisco is a perfect place for him!

Early the next morning I take the first cable car to the foot of Mont Blanc. Along the way, wild flowers poke out wherever snow has melted, thick enough to make a carpet of blues, pinks, yellows, and bright red. At the end of the cable car line is Mont Blanc, fantastically beautiful, with other mountains dramatically behind it. The trekkers take off, while others sit on rocks, and whip out their cell phones. Their voices are eager and they gesture expansively, as if the listeners can see them. They smile and laugh with pure joy. This is a truly wonderful spot, as I am sure they are reporting.

There are little waterfalls everywhere and many snow-capped peaks in the distance. Gauze-like clouds dance quickly above and below the peaks, disappear, and regroup. A soft white veil moves across Mt. Blanc, becomes opaque, hiding the mountain, then whisks away, and the mountain shines forth brilliantly again. Glacial fields are dazzling, contoured into wonderful giant statues of pure white ice or jagged free-forms streaked in gray and black. I am overwhelmed at the beauty and remain until late afternoon, when the weather suddenly turns cold and the clouds group thickly to hide all views. I race for the cable car, as do trekkers from all over the mountain trails. The rain arrives just after I get aboard, and turns to sleet. I return to St. Gervais and take the late train to Chamonix.

The guide books say that **Chamonix** sits in a valley surrounded by the most spectacular mountain scenery in the French Alps. Today the scenery is invisible. I might as well be in Chicago. I am staying in a cheap hotel run by a group of Australian women who are noisy and friendly (and, big advantage, speak English). There's nothing to do except read and wait. The lifts are closed. From my window I watch strong, active mountain climbers pacing the streets of Chamonix like caged lions, back and forth, not looking at anything. It is actually a pretty little tourist town, with flowers growing in huge pots on the streets and hanging from eaves. But that is little comfort when the lifts stay closed and the mountains remain hidden for three days. Every day I hate Chamonix more.

The food is poor. How do the French survive on breakfasts of white bread, jelly, and coffee? Not even fruit or a piece of cheese. There are no good fresh vegetables and no variety in the salads. Everything is over-priced, and I am sulking. I know that I would consider Chamonix wonderful, if only I could see the mountains. For years I have been planning to take the chairlifts over Mont Blanc to Italy and back. I'd set out to do this twenty years ago from the Italian side, and the lifts were closed by bad weather then, too. Are they ever open? I could wait it out, but what's the use? Rain is predicted for the rest of the week. I leave. I play out in my head a "poor me" drama, which probably would not inspire much sympathy from anyone else, because I am headed for Paris.

Le Trekking, ($60 with bath, cheaper without.)

Paris, Paris, Paris! The world's finest city! I go into my Paris mode: a frenzy of TRYING TO SEE EVERYTHING. Just being here, walking through parks, sitting at outdoor cafes, taking a boat on the Seine, eating fresh fruit and cheese on a bench beside Notre Dame, all of this would be enough to make Paris the finest vacation city in the world. But I have scheduled only four days and the museums are calling me. First, Musee d'Orsay, a major railroad station that was transformed into a magical museum of French art. I saw the old railroad station on my first trip to Paris in 1975 and fell in love with it, as did Monet, who painted the trains there. I returned for d'Orsay's first year as a museum in 1986, I believe, and decided that all old railroad stations should be museums!

Today I start first with artists whose work I don't much like, Ingres, Delacroix, and Corbet, the dreadful paintings such as The Decadent Romans. Why is the great, exciting art banished to the attic? I climb the stairs to visit my old friends: Renoir's Dancing At The Moulin Rouge, Seurat's Le Cirque, Matisse, Toulouse-Latrec, Rousseau's eerie jungles, Van Gogh, Manet, Monet, all the Impressionists. I go back downstairs to walk slowly through the main corridor, twice. It overflows with sculpture. I imagine caressing the marble, imagine hugging it close. I even like the colored marble of the very ordinary sculptured heads. Rodin's The Kiss is here. I go back again to the impressionists, to savor them.

For the rest of the day I walk beside the Seine, past Notre Dame and into St Chapelle church to see the beautiful stained glass and colored tile, then sit at a café and have wine.

Musee de l'Orangerie, with floor-to-ceiling Monet water lilies, is closed for remodeling so instead I visit the Musee Marmottan the next morning. I am there when it opens, to see the Monets before the crowds arrive. I adore his glorious trains with the steam from the engines blending miraculously into the fog and the yellow engine lights piercing the white and gray. I look at all the Monets with affection, even devotion. Then I take the time to admire this elegantly restored mansion.

Two museums in one day is pushing it, but I decide to spend the afternoon at the Musee du Moyen. Who is this Moyen anyway? Seems to be someone who composed beautiful music, made tapestries and stained glass, was obviously a pious Catholic and yet seemed dotty over pretty ladies and unicorns. I decide she must have been a fantastic woman of her period, perhaps a collector rather than artist. She seems famous enough to have an entire age named after her, like the Napoleonic Era. Well, guess what? Moyen means Medieval in French. My fantasies go kaboom.

The museum is beautiful and not crowded. The building is a

brilliant stage for its contents, founded in 1843 by joining together the mighty ruins of Rome's thermal baths with the Medieval mansion that had once been the residence of the order of the Cluny Abbotts in Paris. There are rich tapestries, some featuring unicorns; Roman tiles; the sculpture gallery of Roman kings; the fabulous Golden Rose of Basel in the jewelry section (made in 1330); wood carvings; stained glass; enamel work; Gallo-Roman baths from 200 AD.

For supper I have good, inexpensive spaghetti at a restaurant a block from the hotel Louisiane. I have a window table, perfect for watching the scene in the street below. Afterwards I join a group from Japan who are sitting in the philosophers' corner of a nearby cafe. A few of them speak English, none speak French, and we tell each other what we most enjoy in this superb city.

The last day is for the Louvre. Although I come early, tourists are already jamming the route to Mona Lisa and Winged Victory. Ropes are up and the guards are on duty. I choose to avoid the crowds, so go to Napoleon's opulent apartments, and then decide to spend my time in the Egyptian rooms. In the past I left them for last, when already tired, so barely glanced at them. This time I walk in refreshed. Almost no one else except the guards is here. Egyptian coffins are mummy-shaped, with faces, wigs, arms, and hands carved and painted on them. The ancient Egyptians believed that the more coffins a mummy had, the greater its chances of getting eternal life, so coffins were made like Russian dolls to fit inside each other. Beside a mummy's coffins is the coffin for the vital organs, which supposedly will be united with the body at Egyptian resurrection. There are coffins for mummified pet cats, fish, even crocodiles, all of whom will accompany the mummy to the next world. Each set of coffins has a stone or marble sarcophagus elaborately carved with images of gods and symbols that tell who the mummy was during his or her lifetime.

Then there are the statues of the gods. I particularly enjoy Bes, a bearded, ugly gnome whose tongue sticks out to frighten away both demons and poisonous snakes. Wealthy Egyptians had a stone Bes beside their beds to keep the sleepers safe. There are statues of the falcon god Horus, who for 3,000 years protected Egyptian kings. During all those centuries, Egypt maintained its culture and political system, its language, art, science, and religion. It won and lost wars, erected monuments, mined gold, and made beautiful jewelry which it traded with its southern neighbors for feathers and ebony. It had its oppressors and its multitude of oppressed. Then in the 5th century of our era, Egypt became christianized, made Greek the official language, and lost its own language and culture. I find the end of any culture sad. The last known written hieroglyphics are here, a prayer to the goddess Isis.

I learn all of this in one lovely half-day. Afterwards I sneak around the crowds, smile winningly at tired guards, and am able to see Psyche and Cupid, one of my favorite sculptures. I hurry through back rooms, again smiling at guards, and in a very short time I am standing beside Mona Lisa, having avoided all the lines. I admire her for a few minutes, and then wave her good-bye. She really is a fine woman.

Travel tips: If you are seeing Paris for the first time: take a sight-seeing bus for an overview of the city. Look in any Paris handbook for a minor museum that interests you and go very early in the morning before tour groups arrive, to buy the museum and castle pass for three days or a week. A pass lets you avoid the long lines in front of all major museums, including Versailles and the Louvre. In the metro buy a metro pass for the same reason. Walk a lot. Eat lunch from sidewalk venders, because it is fast. Leave a museum when your eyes start to glaze. If luggage weight is not a problem, buy the museum art books and look through them in the evenings.

Stop for a glass of wine at an outside cafe and enjoy the street life. If you care about food, have your fine dining experiences in the evening, after the museums are closed. Passes don't get you up the Eiffel Tower. No matter what time of day you choose, you will be in line one to three hours, so if you insist on getting to the top, it is best to be there an hour before it opens, and bring your guide book to read while you wait. Plan exactly what you are going to do each day.

My daughter Claudia carried the Louvre floor map and crossed out each room as she left it. Every day a different set of rooms is closed to the public, so you must have three days to see them all. Claudia did not miss a single exhibit, but she is a fanatic. Go to Versailles on Sunday, when the fountains are turned on. The rooms are decadently extravagant and the Sunday fountains are superb. Enjoy the acoustics at the concerts at St. Julien le Pauvre church, built in the twelfth century. Have a plate of mixed shellfish at the restaurant near the old Opera House. Ride the giant Ferris wheel at Tuleries garden for great views of the city. See the Rodin museum.

The Chantilly castle out in the country is fairy-tale-beautiful with its moat, statues, and paintings. Its village is great for strolling, as is the nearby village of Senlis. Leave time for Monet's Giverney. Paris is so rich, I could write on and on, describing must-see wonders

Hotel Louisiana, Left Bank, cheap. Sarte and DeBeauvoir lived here. Splurge with a night or two at Hotel Brighton, close to the Louvre, in a room overlooking Tuileries gardens.

UKRAINE

solo

Lots of places are on my "must see" list; lots more on the list of "maybe, some day." The Ukraine was on neither list, until I received an email invitation from a woman named Nadyezhda Ivanova, asking me to do a workshop in Kiev. I would need to pay my own airfare, and they would put me up in a new apartment and prepare for me delicious vegetarian meals. "We want you and we can't afford to pay you. Psychiatrists earn $45 a month here and have to grow their own food so as not to starve." At my age it is nice to be wanted and it is nice to be able to give of my talents. I send an email, "I'm coming. But why is everybody so poor? Capitalism and democracy aren't working?" "It's a long story," she writes back. "But we are thankful to be an independent nation for the first time in our history."

Kiev. Nadyezhda and her driver are waiting for me at the airport. I'm amazed to discover that she is American, since her name is so impossibly (for me) Ukrainian. She's a very attractive woman in her early sixties, who dresses with style and walks with the grace of an actress. Her driver is a cousin, who speaks no English, so smiles and nods. Nadyezhda bought him an old car in return for his chauffeuring her as needed. He uses the car for his business of buying and selling used clothes and other articles. He drives us across town to the workshop condominium, in an old red-brick building which was built in Soviet times as a dormitory for students. The area and the building remind me of Chicago housing of my childhood.

We walk up four flights of dirty stairs, while I wonder what I have gotten myself into. Nadyezhda opens the condo door. It is beautiful inside! She purchased this old apartment, tore out everything, enlarged the windows, added skylights, and faced the walls with natural light wood and the original brick. On one side of the very large group room is a long table used for meals, and on the three other sides are stacks of bright futons, which participants sit on by day and sleep on at night. Educators and psychotherapists come from all over the Ukraine to attend her workshops, for tiny fees that include room and board. She and I have private bedrooms behind the group room. The kitchen is large, immaculate, and well equipped.

After I stash my suitcase, she takes me sight-seeing in old Kiev. We visit Orthodox churches to see their fine icons, and listen to a strikingly beautiful mass sung by a male choir, then walk past solid, eighteenth century brick buildings to the Dneiper river, where we have a fish dinner as we watch the river traffic. The two of us chatter and laugh as if we are old friends. Nadyezhda is an amazing woman, who was born in New York of Ukrainian parents, worked in New York, and now lives permanently in the Ukraine. A lifetime member of the Society of Friends, she feels as I do about the US for countering violence with violence. We are appalled by the war against Afghanistan.

From her earliest years, her father told her that someday the Ukraine would be free, and they would return to their homeland. He also told her that she would be a leader in a free Ukraine. Her parents died before this freedom occurred, and here she is. She speaks Ukrainian, Russian, and English, and she does have a mission here. Years ago, she went to a transactional analyst, who she believes saved her life. Her mission is to bring transactional analysis to every psychotherapist and educator in the Ukraine.

She has accomplished an amazing amount toward this end. There are TA therapy and training groups in most Ukrainian cities. Educators are teaching TA in the schools. Business leaders are exploring the possibility of TA leaders training their staffs. Nadyezhda receives no money for any of this, and does none of the training. She promotes TA, has arranged for a basic text to be published in Ukrainian (my standard textbook and others are already available in Russian, which all Ukrainians can read), and she brings foreign teachers like myself to give workshops. Already several Ukrainians are certified as advanced TA practitioners in the European Transactional Analysis Association.

The next day I decide to sight-see on my own. Nadyezhda is appalled. She says, rightly as it turns out, that I won't find anyone on the trains who speaks English and, besides, I won't be able to decipher place names. The Ukrainian alphabet does seem upside down, backwards, or perhaps from outer space.

"Not to worry," I tell her, as I copy carefully all the names of train stops I will need, plus her directions for finding them. I'm especially careful about the return trip: Down two steep escalators, walk past first metro stop, turn right, then right again, get on train (I draw-write the name) and go five stops. Go up escalator and turn right. Find the stop named (again I draw-write the name) and take train there to the end of the line. Cross the street to a funny little bus with lengthwise seats like sofas, and go to the end of route. Turn left and walk to the only brick building among the dozens of concrete buildings. Knowing that one misstep can prove fatal, I also have the address of the apartment.

The weather is spring-like. I sit at an outdoor cafe and do my usual peeking to see what others are eating. Most of it looks meat-laden and heavy, so I settle for a toasted cheese sandwich and Coke Light. I watch students, business men and women, and women carrying shopping bags. Everyone looks very serious. There is no easy-going chatter, touching, laughter, or even loud arguments. The people remind me somewhat of small-town Germans going about their business. They wear inexpensive, bulky clothing, and a lot of them are fat. Nearby are exclusive clothing stores and a series of new, modern shops dedicated to Dior, Helena Rubenstein and other extravagant odors. These are obviously stores for wealthy Ukrainians and tourists, and today they are empty. I go inside one of the perfume shops to chat with the beautiful young saleswoman, who speaks perfect English. I ask if she likes her job, and she explains that she is hoping to find a husband among the male clients. I wish her the best of luck.

I visit the Taras Shevchenko museum. Shevchenko (1814 - 1861), a genius who was born a serf and orphaned at age eleven, painted more than 2,500 works of art and wrote poetry and essays that elevated the Ukrainian "peasant language" into a language of great depth and beauty. His work fills this entire museum. He organized and laid the groundwork for a united, independent Ukraine, so is considered the father of Ukrainian independence as well as one of its finest writers and artists.

Because it is the end of August and still vacation time, the only people in the museum are old ladies, guarding and guiding. They ask my language, I say "English," and they bring out their English-speaking companion. Though she keeps apologizing for her pronunciation, I understand her easily. She shows me Shevchenko's self portraits and I agree that he painted beautifully in the style of the

1850s and that he was a most good-looking man. Then she finds me samples of his poems translated into English and I appreciate them, too. I like his landscapes and still life, as well as pen and ink sketches for books. He wrote prodigiously, but she has no copies of his books in English. I am delighted with the museum and the woman who guides me.

Brief history of the Ukraine:

Scythians swooped in on horseback and captured the area. Next came the Ostrogoths from northern Poland, Huns, Slavs, Khazars from Turkey and Iran, the descendents of Ghenghis Khan, Turks, Poles, Islams, Lithuanians, and bands of Cossacks, the peasant warriors under the Tsars.

1840s The quest for Ukrainian nationalism began under Shevchenko. Brief attempts at independence were quashed by Russia.

1932 - 35: Six million Ukrainians starved to death when Russian troops confiscated the harvests, killing everyone who tried to hold back food. (This number sounds horrendously large, but I am told it is accurate.)

1941 - 43: Nazis slaughtered the entire Jewish population. (Anti-Semitic Ukrainians also killed the Jews and turned over Jewish neighbors to the Nazis.) Non-Jewish Ukrainians were also killed in great numbers.

1944 – 1991: At the end of World War II, the Soviets arrested and imprisoned in Siberia all Ukrainians suspected of being nationalists. Ukraine continued to be a part of the USSR.

August 24, 1991: The Ukraine became an independent nation after 2,700 years of subjugation.

I have learned a great deal in one day and it's time to find my way to the apartment. I get out my careful directions and carefully set out, but something goes wrong. I get off the final train and the area looks as unfamiliar as most areas always look, whether or not I am lost. The nice little buses with the sofas inside are there, but when I show them the address I am seeking, the drivers all waggle their hands in fervent "No way" gestures. They cannot discuss this with me, they cannot tell me what to do, so they drive away. I go up to people, forlornly holding out the address, and they back away.

Then a hero arrives on the scene. He grabs my arm, pushes me into a taxi, and jumps in beside me. We head for what seems to be the other side of Kiev. I keep showing him the address and he keeps shaking his head affirmatively. Forty minutes later we pull up to the only brick apartment building in a sea of concrete buildings.

He comes with me to the fourth floor, to scold whoever lives there for allowing a poor old American lady to be on the streets unaccompanied. Nadyezdha and the cook vigorously deny their guilt. They couldn't stop me. All of this is translated to me by Nadyezhda.

After much discussion and translating back and forth, wine is brought out, and he agrees to have supper with us. All ends well. I find out later that the trains occasionally skip a stop. When that is going to happen, it is written somewhere on a board, in Ukrainian of course. How was I to know?

The workshop begins the next morning and is excellent. The participants are well grounded, ask interesting questions, and are eager to be therapy clients. Over dinner the first night I ask what is going on that the country is so poor. All agree that the government is corrupt. The leaders have teamed up with corporate America to keep wages low and profits high. They tell horror stories of greed and the collapse of local factories since privatization. People with influence are allowed to acquire old factories, sell the machinery for scrap metal, and abandon them. They stand derelict in all the cities. The people at the dinner table insist that these factories should have continued as nonprofits to help the people. Other factories are sold to foreign conglomerates that pay the workers almost nothing and ship the products to overseas markets. These factories are thriving, but do nothing for the local economy.

Salaries for physicians and other health workers in state-owned clinics are abysmally low. Teachers' salaries are also low, and often payment is deferred. I wonder aloud why people with the intelligence and diligence to become doctors and teachers do not use their intelligence to organize for decent salaries. (This is a question I have through the years asked teachers and social workers in the United States and elsewhere.) As in the US, the people at the dinner table talk about their moral obligation to their patients and students. One woman says I have a point. The other day she was treating a patient who noticed that the ceiling was rotten and crumbling above them. He said, "Where is your self respect? As long at the government can make you work under these conditions, you don't deserve better." She asks the

86

dinner group, "How have we lost self respect?" Someone says, "Bit by bit over thousands of years." Self-respect becomes the theme of the workshop.

The participants explore their childhood decisions that get in the way of self-respect: "I am only worthwhile if I can make father happy and that isn't possible," "I am only worthwhile if I don't bother anyone," "I am not important except when I take care of my mother and baby brother," "I'm not important no matter what I do." Like members of the helping professions all over the world, they treat their patients and students better than they treat themselves. Now they are excited, as they return in fantasy to their individual childhood scenes to make redecisions about themselves. We have a lively, productive, and loving week.

The workshop ends on August 24, National Independence Day. Nadyezhda and I watch the fireworks from a participant's apartment, and then go to downtown Kiev to be part of the celebration in Independence Square. Music blares from loudspeakers, as families and friends stroll together, eating ice cream and smiling.

The next day we are driven to **Pereyaslav,** where Nadyezhda lives in a small rented apartment while her own home is being built. We visit the home of a local physician, Dzuhuzha Tetyana Vassylivna, and her physician husband. She says she got so much out of the workshop that she wants to give me something. She offers me much-needed laser treatment for my legs, and a daily massage. I accept joyfully. It has been seven months since my laserpuncture treatment in Cuba; I am again having difficulty walking, and my night-time cramps have returned.

Their house is tiny, with a small living room, their bedroom, their son's bedroom, and now they are slowly building a second floor for their married son and his family. It is a pleasant but sparse house, with photos of family on the walls but no decorative touches. Their furniture is old. They are both charming, intelligent people who barely earn enough to survive. He is crippled, and a physician in the local hospital. She, too, works there, and also keeps up a vegetable garden, cooks and cleans, and now is making time for my treatments. (Before I go I send her money for the treatment.)

Nadyezhda has arranged for us to eat at another home, because, like me, she hates cooking. That home is decorated with small ceramic animals, and has the old-fashioned, somewhat claustrophobic feel that goes with mismatched floral designs on wallpaper, carpets, easy chairs, and the sofa. The cook is a happy woman who cooks well.

Homes in the Ukraine are large and appear prosperous, with bricks in attractive patterns and heavy, stained doors and shutters. However, it is best not to look inside. People construct the outer walls and roof first, and move in. It may be years before they can afford running water. They may never achieve indoor kitchens. Some of the loveliest houses have outhouses for bathrooms. There are no gas lines to some villages, so there is no affordable way to heat a home during the freezing winters except by a wood stove.

Pereyaslav is a museum town. We visit the only museum in the world dedicated totally to minstrel singers. On display are lutes, lyres, and kobzas (a seven-stringed, Ukrainian instrument,) sheet music, and photographs of famous minstrels. The museum director, who looks like a minstrel in his pink shirt and long flowing white hair and beard, shows us each instrument and demonstrates its sounds. Minstrels were often homeless, blind musicians who roamed the country-side, playing and singing for board and room. They were considered seers by some, who believed their songs foretold the future. Their folk songs kept alive the Ukrainian national spirit, and this made them traitors in the eyes of the Soviets and their lackeys. One year all Ukrainian minstrels were invited to a huge folk festival. Forty came, and were promptly murdered. (Maybe those who stayed away were the ones with ability to foresee the future, so hid out.) In the Ukraine today, pro-nationalism minstrel songs are very popular.

Another museum is the one-room college of a teacher who died in the 1700s. It contains his original desk and the rows of benches for the students who studied philosophy under him. The teacher lived in a very poor bedroom behind the classroom. Some of the teacher's and students' clothes hang on pegs in the back of that room.

We visit the Folk Architecture Museum, a series of old farmhouses, windmills, a church, a tavern and brewery, and a school, brought here from many parts of the Ukraine. The houses have floors of tamped mud, as shiny as brown ceramic, covered with fresh grass, and changed daily, which keeps the houses fragrant and the floors clean. (I think it was this sort of peasant directive that was responsible for my mother putting newspapers over all her freshly scrubbed linoleum, which I also did, following her custom, when I was first married.)

The old brewery has a huge beer barrel and many wooden beer mugs on a long table. The church, for display purposes, is covered with rushniks, long, linen scarves, embroidered with red flowers on white linen, or red and black on natural linen. They are worn as scarves, put on tables, and draped around icons. Women begin making them early in life for themselves and their future families. A soldier takes one with him to war, babies are wrapped in them, and in death they form the funeral shroud.

Another fascinating small museum is the Museum of Clothing. Under their dresses women used to wear one-piece blouse-skirts, with full, colorfully embroidered sleeves and lace around the bottom of the skirt. They wore these to bed and in the morning simply added a layer or two of embroidered skirts, plus vests and jackets. It made dressing and undressing easy, but after a while the women must have smelled awful. There is also a section displaying examples of old embroidery styles on modern dresses and shirts.

On the walls are modern paintings made with bottle caps, gold candy-wrappers, sea shells, broken glass, and oil paints, all in brilliant colors. One is an exciting maelstrom of flying birds, another a sky filled with bursting stars around a banal woman with flowers in her hair. Because I say that I like the art, I am taken to the home of the artist, a seventy-two-year-old, lifelong spinster, outspokenly anti-sex and anti-male. She will not sell her art, which she keeps in hopes of a major exhibition somewhere. Meanwhile, her studio bursts with fascinating works, stacked against all the walls. She asks if I know anyone with a New York gallery where her works could be displayed. I am truly sorry I don't.

On my final Saturday, we sail on a catamaran across the part of the Dneiper river which was turned into a lake by a dam the Soviets built in the 1960s. Everyone here still complains about the dam: it flooded out ten villages, doesn't create extra electricity for this area, and destroys the river fish that everyone needs for food. In town and again while we sail, the discussion of this dam is as emotional and dramatic as if the flooding occurred last week. I think the lake is beautiful, but keep quiet about my opinion.

The catamaran is the work of a man who spent all his free time for seven years building it, and for the next fifteen years he lovingly kept it in excellent shape and added decorative touches. His family used to take three-week vacations sailing to the Crimea and exploring all along the Dneiper. "Now," he says, "with our terrible economy my wife and I work day and night and can't even afford to buy gas, so we don't go anywhere." (Under communism and the hated Soviets everyone had full employment and long, paid vacations.) Because Nadyezhda bought the food and gas, his whole family, wife, two daughters, their husbands, and two grandchildren, joins us, thrilled to be on the water. It is a glorious day, sunny and bright.

We anchor on a lovely sand beach to swim and picnic. There is lots of food, plus homemade wine and vodka. By sunset, when we start back, the captain is red-faced and uninhibited. He sings loudly in a beautiful bass voice, stopping only to announce with tragic passion the names of each "drowned village" as we pass over it.

Sunday is my last day in Pereyaslav, and we visit the market. Once a week Ukrainians cram into buses to travel to Turkey, where they stock up on cheap merchandise, and then sell it in the Sunday market. To Nadyezhda this is a symptom of the collapse of the economy in the Ukraine. People are also selling cabbages and beets from their gardens, and pigs and chickens.

We leave for the airport. I will miss Nadyezhda, an extraordinary women and fun companion. I plan to return.

A VILLAGE NAMED LENIN

The Ukraine near Pereyaslav has dozens of small villages strung along the main road. Every village has a World War II memorial in the center, a City Hall of brick, and sometimes another large brick building, now divided inside into small stalls where individuals sell soap, candy, used clothing, and various home-made sausages. Between the houses are fields of sunflowers, silage corn, and other grains. There are tiny herds of cattle, each watched by a caretaker. Geese and ducks run everywhere. All homes in every village have individual vegetable gardens in front.

The tiniest hamlets no longer exist, except for one. In the late 1920s the government in Moscow decided to consolidate Ukrainian hamlets to keep tighter control over them. Those with less than fifty houses were destroyed. Soviet troops marched in, counted the houses, and if there were too few, gave the people an hour to evacuate, and then smashed everything. The people were forced to move wherever they could. (The US has a history of village-smashing, too. Remember Vietnam?)

In one hamlet of twenty-five houses, a town councilman had a brilliant idea. He told the others and got their approval. They renamed the hamlet and put up the sign: LENIN.

When the Russian troops arrived, they stared, confused, not knowing what to do. How could they destroy a hamlet named after Lenin? They whispered among themselves, and then asked, "Why is this village named Lenin?

"To honor the great founder of the Soviet Union."

The soldiers marched on. The village still exists, thanks to the cleverness of one of its citizens.

SWITZERLAND: A WEATHER REPORT

solo

Lucerne, rain. I wander about, see the old buildings, and leave.

Interlaken, rain. I like the bright green hills, the lake, the red-roofed houses, the window boxes filled with flowers. I leave.

Brigerbad, icy rain. I go to a spa. Body temperature pools, some with jets and some for lap swimming, and a very hot pool in a grotto. Fine restaurant on the property. What's a little rain, when I can enjoy a spa? I'll answer that. "What's a little rain?" is a Polly Anna response, unworthy of me. I can make yowling, screeching, bitching into a fine art. I came for mountains, not hot soaks. Unfortunately, I am a stranger in a sedate land, so my screams are silent even as I swim fast in the lap pool. Blah, Bad, double blaaaaaah. And then I run around in nature's cold shower, shaking my fist, before I am ready once again to enter the grotto.

Saas Fee, fog and rain. I walk a bit in this touristy town, read, and the next morning wake up to miraculous sunshine. I jump out of bed, hurry to the cable car, and take the world's highest funicular to Mittelallalen, 3,500 meters above the valley. I get there in time! All is sunshine and snow-covered mountains. There is a 360-degree view from the restaurant on top, with the names of each mountain carefully etched into the wood signs along the lookout rails. Bless the Swiss for their compulsive labeling. I circle the area, reading names. There are thirteen mountains over 13,000 feet tall, including the Jungfrau and even, farther away, the Matterhorn. I see the Dom, and countless glaciers glittering with new snow. It is breath-taking beauty. I gasp and choke up just from the wonder of it.

Skiers with jackets from everywhere, even Bratislava, are strapping on skis and zigzagging down the mountain. To celebrate the sun, even though it is still morning, I have a cup of coffee with schnapps. Later in the day, when the clouds have gathered, I walk through pine forests and wild flowers below the mountains.

Hotel Bergheimat (bathtubs for soaking tired feet after a long hike. About $75)

The next morning the mountains are hidden again so I set out for two spa towns, **Leukerbad** and **Burgerbad**, past bright green grass, darker green pines, large homes and hotels stained dark brown, with window boxes and flowers under every window, and smaller homes with rocks on the roofs to keep the shingles from flying away in the wind. In Leukerbad I try first a nicely warmed pool with many jets at various levels. I am enjoying the jets against my lower back when suddenly there is a clap of music and a bright red sign flashes ominously. I wonder where the danger lies, and am trying to jump out when I see that other bathers have moved one jet ahead and are motioning me sternly to do the same. A minute later, another burst of music plus the red sign, and we forward march to the next jet.

In about fifteen boring minutes we have finished the line, and may get out and start over or go on to another pool. I go to a hot pool with lovely recliners, and sink happily into one. Jets bubble all about me. Then the bubbling abruptly ceases and all must leave these recliners to allow others (there are no others) to have a turn. I find this regimentation not quite relaxing. But the pool for lane swimming is lovely, and I do know to keep in a medium-slow lane. Your lane depends strictly upon how fast you swim.

I am the only person swimming the crawl. Others, heads held well above water, breast stroke. In the 1930s I was embarrassed that my mother swam this way. It was so desperately old-fashioned. When I offered to teach her how to swim right, she reminded me that she had to wear her glasses in the water or she couldn't see a thing. So I let it go, though sometimes I wished my friends weren't there to watch her pokey, German breast stroke. Now I am surrounded by those who still swim as she did, with and without glasses. Even the young don't use the crawl or butterfly.

The next day it is still raining. I try Burgerbad, with four outdoor pools, twelve indoor ones, and fine sun rooms. I go to the very hot pool, 110 degrees, and then relax on one of the lovely lounges in a sun room. The mountains become wonderfully visible! I spend the day swimming, relaxing in the various pools, and basking in the sunshine as I view the mountains. I am a spa addict.

Grindelwald. Sun again. I spend over-budget for a room with my own deck overlooking the Eiger and other mountains. Two floors below is a beer garden in case I get thirsty. The mountains have huge, sheer cliffs with snow on the peaks, the sun is setting, and I am on my deck, having a supper of bananas, cashews, and beer. In Grindelwald the street signs tell the number of minutes it takes to walk to ski lifts and to nearby towns. Double the time if you are my age, and then double it again if the hike is uphill. I go to Grund, take the tram to Mannlichen, the cable car to Wenger, and return. There are not enough superlatives to describe the beauty of the Alps when the sun is shining! They are glorious. I sit on the grass in Mannlichen, enraptured.

The next day is cloudy, so I take a fine ten-minute walk in the glacier George, with shear, vertical walls, at some places only a meter apart. The river races noisily below. It begins to rain hard and is so cold I have to buy a second sweater. I need my father's old jacket, which I left in Iceland. My raincoat is tearing, my clothes are getting shabbier by the washing, but after my Switzerland workshop I will be back in California to change wardrobes. I stay in Grindelwald one more day, hoping. The rain stops, but the fog remains thick.

Hotel Spinne is fine. Rent a room overlooking mountains.

I take the train back to **Interlaken**, and halfway there the fog blows away and the mountains dance into view. I see the Jungfrau in all its beauty. I take the funicular to Harder Kulm with both lakes gorgeous below, pastel blue with the darker Aare between. (After all these years, I now have seen this famous crossword puzzle river.) Yesterday's rain gave the mountains a covering of new snow. I watch them into the night under a full moon. The next day I am off to Zurich to do a workshop. When I pass Lucerne, the weather is crummy.

Hotel Metropole is OK

Zurich. I work hard, and afterwards spend time with an old friend. The next morning I fly to California.

JAPAN

Reiko True, Inger Acking, and solo. Reiko designed much of this trip.

Tokyo's International airport is a shock after a horrid, all night flight. It is so very bright and busy, so full of hurrying people. No one saunters in Japan. Reiko's brother meets us to hand deliver our train and bus tickets, and bows us on our way.

Shirakawago is a World Heritage site of old homes and inns that have been built in the same style since prehistory. The owner of the inn where we will stay meets us at the bus station and drives us to the local look-out point to see how the town is laid out. He is a cheerful, enthusiastic man, who wants Reiko to translate accurately everything he says. "Do they understand?" "Did you explain that I am a newcomer here, because my family has lived in our inn only four generations?" "Did you tell them that the biggest house, right below us, has had the same family in it for at least eight generations?" From above we see the entire town, spread out in a wooded valley ringed by tall mountains. The sun is shining, the maple leaves are beginning to crimson, and a creek dances over rocks beside us.

After we admire the view, he drives us to the inn. It is made of dark, rough wood four stories high, with a sharply pointed roof covered with thatch three feet deep. It was built without a single nail. The lovely old wood expands and contracts with age and the seasons, and doesn't split. Our room, like all bedrooms in Japanese inns, has tatami mats and cushions. We sit on the cushions in front of a low table, and one of the owner's daughters serves us tea and rice cookies. At night the bedding will be laid on the mats, and then rolled up again before breakfast. There are modern touches: electric lights, modern plumbing in the bathroom, and even a heated toilet seat. After tea, we are taken on a tour of the rest of the house. The top floor was used for raising silk worms. The family keeps a few to show the process to visitors. Nearby are spinning wheels and looms.

The town was isolated from the rest of Japan until recently, when the first road was finally built. Large, extended families lived together and were self-sufficient. They raised silk worms, spun their silk, made their own clothing, raised their animals, cultivated and gathered food. About every seventy years each roof has to be redone, and this is planned a year ahead. Sufficient thatch has to be gathered, straw ropes made, and 500 people assembled to do the entire job in one day. Barring emergencies such as fire, usually one roof is done every summer in the village.

For supper we are served rare mountain vegetables, collected by the family, including several species of tasty, delicate mushrooms and a vegetable that looks exactly like a cooked, middle-size worm, though Reiko swears it is not. After supper, we luxuriate in the outdoor hot bath under a sky crammed with stars. The mountains are black-dark around us.

Without Reiko, Inger and I wouldn't be here. The owners of these old inns choose to rent to people who speak Japanese, so that communication is possible. It is Reiko's task to make sure we wear the correct slippers in the main rooms, into the bathroom, and to the outdoor bath, and to explain the rules for washing before soaking in a communal bath.

Takayama. We are here for the famous Fall Harvest Festival. The streets are swarming with tourists, almost all Japanese. Eleven huge floats are being wheeled through the streets, guided by men in medieval costumes. The floats are bright red and gold with high, peaked roofs, and are festooned with dragons, phoenix birds, tigers, and swaying lighted lanterns. The street lights are turned off, and the evening is magical! Between floats musicians play and dancers in dragon costumes run after children and pretend to grab them in their mouths. The children run, screaming with fear. Being put in a dragon's mouth is supposed to bring a child good luck, though it is obvious the little ones disagree. The streets are narrow, and the floats sway back and forth, almost tipping as they are pushed and pulled around street corners. The crowd gasps and then applauds loudly each time a corner is turned without disaster.

Takayama is famous for its wonderful old architecture, sake tasting rooms, antique and modern ceramics, and its many museums, most of them old homes of wealthy merchants, now open to the public. We visit several. Then we taxi to the Hida Folk Village, a collection of farm houses brought from many parts of Japan to this lovely, wooded area around a small, quiet lake.

I plan to return to Takayama when there are no festivals, to walk the streets, explore the museums, and sip sake.

City Park Hotel, on a hill slightly above the town, has western beds. The owners' son is a chef, who blends French and Japanese food exquisitely.

Kyoto. Unlike every other traveler I have met, I don't enjoy Kyoto. The crowds are oppressive and the city noisy and dirty. Once we are back on the train, I scarcely remember which shrines and temples we visited.

Travel *Tips: If you want to enjoy Kyoto, find a quiet inn somewhere on the outskirts and spend at least a week calmly experiencing the temples and gardens.*

Shinhotaka. We stop here at another fine inn with wonderful outdoor baths, and ride the double-deck gondola to the top of a 7,000 foot mountain to see the view. The leaves have turned and we see whole mountainsides of vivid red, yellow, and orange, interspersed with dark pines and pale green birch.

Shin Zanso Inn, (very pleasant and not expensive.)

Hiroshima. I remember my despair in 1945, in the midst of national jubilation that the war was ending. Why didn't we bomb an uninhabited island instead, and give the Japanese government time to assess the destruction? We could have bombed several outlying islands if necessary. What was the hurry to murder so many thousands of people? I was sickened by the reports of the atomic bomb. Since then, the US has focused on more and more weapons of destruction, and has become the most dangerous country the world has ever known.

For years, when teaching in Japan, Bob and I avoided Hiroshima. Now I am here with Reiko, who lived in Japan during World War II, and Inger, a Swedish citizen born after the war. In the Memorial Park we stand in front of the peace pond, the simple, modern sculpture, and the eternal flame. Across the river is the burned-out shell of a building left standing as a symbol of the destruction. We go inside the museum, dedicated to the banning of all nuclear weapons. There are photos of burned men, women, and children, as well as a collection of their destroyed possessions, including a poignant, half-melted, twisted tricycle. Garlands of paper cranes adorn the children's pavilion, made by school children from all over Japan. Still the US refuses to support the banning of nuclear weapons.

Reiko leaves us here, to fulfill her professional commitments in

Japan and then return to California. We'll miss her help and, even more, her laughter. The three of us have had a fine time together. Inger and I go on to **Miyajima,** the island with the much-photographed, bright red-orange Torii gate which seems almost to be floating on the inland sea. Behind it is the five-tiered red-orange pagoda, also much photographed, and a large, long temple. Deer wander everywhere, plump and surprisingly aggressive. Don't try to eat a sandwich in their presence. They will nudge you hard until you hand it over. Inger and I have fun playing with them and she runs with them while I watch, but we don't feed them.

We stay at a guest house, totally non-descript but with Western beds. If I could choose, I would combine the best of both worlds: inns with outdoor hot baths and beds with soft mattresses. Inger and I walk through a pretty park to the cable car that takes us to the top of Mt. Misen, for glorious views of the inland sea.

Travel tips: When you don't know the language of a country, keep with you a card on which is written things you must let people know, such as "I am a diabetic and do not eat sugar." Or, "I am a vegetarian."

Japanese trains arrive on time, so you can gauge when to get on and off by what time it is. To be doubly sure, show your ticket to one of the train men on the platform. Inside, most trains have electric signs at the front of each car, with the name of the next city in English.

Buses, taxis, and launches are more complicated. Have someone write your destination and hotel on a card in Japanese before you start out. People want to help you find your way.

Note that in Asian countries people often laugh because they are embarrassed or don't understand you. They are not laughing at you.

The next morning, Inger leaves for Osaka and home. To prolong our time together for a few more minutes, I ride with her on the ferry to Hiroshima. A mistake. After we hug good-bye, I have no idea where to catch my ferry. "Speak English?" gets me nowhere, so I find a uniformed official of the ferry line and point to Matsuyama on my map. He escorts me back onto the boat, and together we return to Miyajiwa. As we ride, he tells me with gestures and a few English words that he has once been to Las Vegas and that it was a "very good" trip. He leads me to the correct pier, next to the one to Hiroshima, helps me buy my tickets, and introduces me to the captain. I thank him and bow good-bye. After a short ferry ride to Ujima, the captain escorts me to the ferry to Matsuyama. This ferry is plush, with reclining seats, head sets, and a drink menu. (I order "Coke Light," which the bartender understands.) The one-hour trip on the Inland Sea is gorgeous. The sea is bright, and full of tiny and medium-sized islands covered with bright green pines and ringed by golden sand. Some islands are bare at the base but crested with pines, like a head with stand-up, green hair.

Matsuyama. I have with me the name and address of my hotel, written in Japanese by Reiko before she left. I show this to a bus driver, who actually gets off the bus to help me on. At the end of the line, Dogo Onsen station, he escorts me to a policeman, who walks me two blocks through a maze of shops, mostly selling sweets for Japanese tourists, to my hotel. Without Reiko and Inger, everyone offers assistance! I suppose they feel sorry for an old lady traveling alone.

Across the street from the hotel is the famous Dogo Hot Springs spa, sometimes called Bath of the Gods. At this very spot 3,000 years ago, says the legend, a crane put his injured leg into hot water gushing from a crevice in the rocks, and his leg was cured. The people who witnessed this miracle built a pool to collect the water, and people have been bathing here ever since. The first spa building was erected over 1,000 years ago. The current one was built in 1894.

Like all bathers, I walk to the bath-house in a kimono furnished by the hotel. It doesn't easily encompass my belly so "just in case" I wear underpants. It is also quite a bit too short for me. Japanese women suppress their giggles. Well, at least I do know to wear it crossed to the left. Crossed to the right is only for corpses in caskets. (I wore it the wrong way at the Shinhotaka inn, and Reiko was scolded for allowing me to make that mistake.) The spa is a very tall, three-story building, classic Japanese style with a slate roof that looks like pewter, and old-fashioned windows of white, oiled paper. White iron cranes line the iron fence surrounding it.

For only $2.80 one can luxuriate in the men's or the women's public baths. For an additional fee one can go to the second-floor lounging area to be served tea and cookies after soaking. There are also private baths for couples or families, and scheduled tours of the Royal Baths on the third floor. I pay the fee, rent a very small towel for fifty cents, and go to the women's dressing room.

After disrobing, I hold the towel against my chest, as others do, in such a way as to almost cover nipples and crotch. The pool area is decorated with a female Buddha and many cranes. About twenty women are preparing to bathe and six are soaking in the large, marble pool. I am the only Caucasian in the room, and everyone smiles at me and gives a tiny bow of welcome.

I sit on a small stool, fill a small aluminum basin with hot tap water, wet and soap my small towel, and use it to wash very slowly. Then I throw the water from the basin over myself, and start again. Japanese women spend much time washing, doing their cuticles, using pumice on their heels, and washing their hair. I work at slowing myself down but am finished, while those who came in with me have barely started on the second foot. I learned in childhood to bathe quickly. With one bathroom for seven people, someone was always knocking on the door, yelling, "Hurry up!" I soap and wash again. And again. Finally, I can wait no longer. I rinse and wring out my towel, hang it, walk to the edge of the pool, and sink inch by inch into the almost-scalding water. Pure bliss!

Several of the women in the pool are at least as old as I am, and some are quite bent. They are helped in and out by woman young enough to be their grand-daughters. I move from water to ledge and back several times, and when I am finally ready to leave, my muscles are so relaxed that climbing out is difficult. Two young women help me without my asking. I dry with the small wet towel, as the others do, and sit in my robe on a lounge chair in a calm, quiet room. It's a glorious way to spend an afternoon.

The Royal family no longer comes to the spa, but tourists line up to look at the Royal suite. The walls are decorated with gold paint and royal symbols. In their room for lounging and taking tea, the emperor's throne is a simple overstuffed chair, exactly like the one that was my grandfather's favorite. Others in the family have only stools or mats. The emperor's bathroom is stone and austere, with no decorations. His toilet is a black lacquered, squat type. The entire suite is very plain compared to the ostentatious baths in European palaces and in the Hearst castle.

The next day I go to Matsuyama Castle on a mountain above the city. A chair lift lets you solo over green and red trees to the top. The castle is massive, many-winged, with thick timber and stone walls. Inside are displays of armor and quite awe-inspiring (which means "scary") protective face masks.

Dogo Springs Hotel, across the street from Dogo Hot Springs. (About $150.) The other hotels in the immediate area are much more expensive.

Okayama. It rains hard all day, so I stay inside the hotel and read. That evening I find a very tiny tapa restaurant, with tossed salads and spaghetti with garlic and seafood, a lovely change. The cook and waiters are all in their twenties, and laugh with each other as they serve the diners. I sit on a high stool beside the open kitchen and watch the cook as he creates several dishes at once. A waiter, who speaks a bit of English, tells me they are all from the same family. Their restaurant is new and they are obviously proud of it.

The next day I visit the restored Black Castle, with fancy gold trim and "one of the three loveliest gardens in Japan," according to my guidebook. We would call it a park rather than a garden. With each turn of a path, there is a new view of small pagodas, beautifully pruned trees, and colorful, twisted rocks beside reflecting pools. Although I am not a tea drinker, I try the ceremonial tea, served in the beautiful tea house. There is a special exhibit of chrysanthemums and bonsai.

In the morning, I take a fifteen minute train ride to **Kurashiki**, past bright yellow rice fields and clusters of yellow wildflowers growing along the tracks. Yellow and yellow under a pewter sky, interspersed with the dark wood of old farm houses.

I am here to see the Ohara museum of art. The museum was assembled by a rich man, Magosaburo Ohara on the suggestion of his friend, the famous modern Japanese painter Torajiro Kojima. The museum has an impressive collection of his art, plus representative old European masterpieces and paintings by Picasso, Matisse, Chagall, and others. Kojima chose well. Each painting is beautifully displayed, nothing is crowded, and the museum in its entirety suggests the truth of the saying "less is more." Between the rooms are corridors with floor to ceiling windows looking out on a canal banked with red Japanese maples and bright green willow trees.

A parade is forming outside, so I go to watch it. The procession is led by costumed dancers and drummers in red and blue jackets and white face masks. In one float a female drummer is pulled by costumed women, who are shouting slogans and laughing. Boy Scouts march in uniform. Young girls in dark blue shorts wave red fans. An Afro-American man, his Japanese wife, and their two handsome children lead an international group of inter-racial families. A women's group wears kimonos. A group of children carry lanterns. There are many onlookers, including several Japanese tour groups and quite a few aged tourists in wheel chairs. Afterwards, one of the English-speaking participants tells me that this is the annual autumn festival and that the participants are all locals. The organizers pass out prizes, large boxes of fruit, to each participant group. It begins to rain hard, and the people scatter. I go back to my hotel in Okayama and the tapa restaurant.

Nara. It's misty, almost raining, as I walk up the path toward Kasuga Taisha, the largest shrine in Nara, past hundreds of concrete lanterns softly green with moss. Gnarled trees are spotted with the same green. Deer are everywhere, because they are holy, but these are much more sweet-tempered than in Miyajima. The temple is the same red and green as the maples and pines in the background.

This is an historic city, the capital of Japan, 710 - 794 CE, and the seat of Buddhist art. The stone Buddhas here are of a mature, realistic style with an accurate portrayal of the human body. The bronze statues have an appealing individuality. The city is bursting with temples, shrines, pagodas, museums, and ponds.

With a map in hand, I take a self-guided tour. I walk along the main street, Sanjodori, and pass three pagodas, including a five-story pagoda,
splendidly red-trimmed. Then I veer to the right a block, then to the left, and there is the Kofukuji temple complex with life-sized statues of Buddha, the eight imaginary guardians of Buddha, lacquered figures of his major disciples, the exotic heavenly generals, and the fierce gate guardians. Each is unique and beautifully crafted. Guarding the edges of the slate-roofed buildings are dragons, horned beasties, and other little monsters.

I keep walking to the National Museum, quite interesting, and later follow the ever expanding lines of primary school students to the Todaiji Temple, the world's largest all-wood, nail-free building, but barely large enough to hold its massive image of Buddha.

The mist has turned to a cold drizzle. It's a day that demands noodle soup. I walk into a restaurant where several men are sitting at a counter, slurping noodles. I smile and point to a bowl, and am served a delicious stew-soup that seems to contain practically every imaginable food. I practice slurping noodles twenty-four inches long. I stay three more days, returning for second and third visits to the museum and temples. I love Nara.

Osaka. There are castles, one in the city and one a few minutes by train, a bird sanctuary, and lots of opportunities to shop, but I choose to spend my one free day at the aquarium. My choice turns out to be a good one. The world of the Pacific Rim is partitioned into specific areas, each three floors high. California has its salt water fish, harbor seals and otters, and a redwood tree. Central America has its wonderful reefs with brilliant fish, monkeys and a surprisingly alert sloth who is preening and playing as he looks at himself in a full length mirror. It's the first time I've seen a sloth play anything but dead. There is a huge tank for rays and sharks. Smaller tanks hold collections of jelly fish, white, green, maroon and brown, parachutes in a blue sea.

As I am leaving, a young man asks if I am a tourist. He tells me, "I think you will want to see a ceramics exhibit," and leads me down the street to a small exhibit of ash-glazed jars from the eleventh century BCE to the twelfth century CE. They are exquisite, and exquisitely displayed. I am reminded again that good things happen to old ladies who travel alone.

I go to a puppet show, Bunraku, of love, war, and samurai. The puppets are five feet tall. Each puppet has three puppeteers wearing black robes and hoods to make themselves almost invisible against the black curtains. One puppeteer manipulates the head and right arm; another, the left arm and body; the third, the legs and feet. Five men chant the story line, while a sixth plays a lute-like instrument. Because there is no English translation, the plot is impossible to follow. This is definitely what I call "should" entertainment. One SHOULD attend classic puppet shows. My mother's reasons why I should attend boring things, like symphonies and my piano teacher's recitals, were "It's good for your immortal soul." She did not explain further. Within minutes, even though the ticket was expensive and my immortal soul may be in jeopardy, I am looking for an unobtrusive way to escape.

I take the bullet train to Tokyo, and watch villages, towns, and cities hurtle past.

A JAPANESE PROFESSIONAL WOMAN

The Empress Michiko of Japan told this children's story, the earliest she remembers from her childhood. "One day a snail became aware that the shell on his back was stuffed with sorrow and he went off to see his friend, saying he could no longer go on living and pouring out his tale of woe. But his snail friend said, 'You are not alone in that. The shell on my back, too, is filled full of sorrows.' The little snail went to another friend and then another friend and told them the same tale of woe, but from every friend the same reply came back. So the snail at last came to realize that everyone had his burden of sorrows to bear. He stopped bemoaning his lot."

From a keynote speech sent by video to the 26th Congress of the International Board on Books for Young People, New Delhi, 1998, by the Empress Michiko of Japan. The speech was later published in book form in Japanese and English.

"I was born in 1935, so was six years old when the War started. When I was in the 4th grade my two young sisters and I were evacuated from Tokyo to a small town at the foot of Mt. Fujiyama to live with paternal great-uncles we did not really know, while our parents remained in Tokyo. I was responsible for my sisters because I was oldest. I thought it was my duty to make sure they did nothing to offend or inconvenience my uncles, who probably didn't really want three little girls in their home. I went to a country school, where the children hated the "city kids." Once, when they found out I was afraid of snakes, they put a snake in my pen case. The teacher also disliked me because I knew more than the other children, and in my young arrogance I corrected several of her mistakes.

"One night the sky was bright red from the fire-bombing of a nearby city, and for years afterwards I hated sunsets. Our home in Tokyo was burned to the ground, so when we children returned our home was gone.

"After the war I went to a very fine private school, and then was one of the first females accepted into a national university. I majored in psychology and had an internship at a prison for juveniles. I was horrified that many children, ready to return to their families, were not accepted by the families. In essence, they were permanently rejected because of the shame they had brought on their families. I decided to

104

become a social worker instead of a psychologist, in order to help families understand their children and reconcile with them.

"I received a scholarship to do graduate work in the United States. My father had been ill when I left and died while I was abroad. I couldn't go home to say good-bye or even attend his funeral, because US immigration rules might have prohibited me from returning. Both my parents wanted me to finish my schooling. Before he died, my father reported to the family his contented dream: My daughter is in an airplane and she tells me, "Don't worry about me, Father. I can take care of myself." Neither of my parents pressured me to marry, which is unusual in Japanese families.

"After I received my Master's degree in Social Work, I worked for a time in the United States, at the notoriously difficult Cook County hospital in Chicago, and later returned to Japan to work in various hospitals and clinics. I co-led workshops for national businesses. Fifteen years ago I was appointed professor of medical psychology. I teach psychology, medical psychology, and family and patient psychology to undergraduate and graduate students, and I work in the university psychotherapy clinic. I have always spent my summer vacations in the United States, where I attended post-graduate workshops, visited my friends, and taped interviews for my radio work.

"I had an exciting collection of extra-curricular jobs. For years I wrote an advice column for Japanese newspapers. You might say I was the Dear Abby of Tokyo. I did radio shows in which I consulted with people who called in their problems.

"In the United States I interviewed people who would be interesting to Japanese audiences. One was Andy Warhol, who was delightful to me. I also interviewed the author Studs Terkel; the head of the Air Force Academy; the head of the Chicago Crime Commission; policemen who could tell me about Chicago gangs; well-known American psychiatrists; musicians; and people with unusual jobs. I played these interviews with my translations on Japanese radio, and published them as articles in magazines and newspapers.

"I was a disk jockey for American music, mostly Jazz and Blues. I chose the songs, translated the words, and spoke the translations as background. I discussed the songs and singers, and read poetry that fit the songs. Sometimes I did "theme" programs: jealousy, American women's names in songs, Valentine's Day love songs, and songs that told stories of poor or unhappy lives. Mine was an exciting life, which in my day would have been impossible for a married woman.

"Three years ago I had to give up all my traveling and my extra jobs. My mother, who had been a very capable, intelligent woman, became ill with Alzheimer's disease and could not be left alone. I now teach by day, while a care-taker is with her, and then hurry back to be with her every evening and, of course, weekends. What else can I do? I want to continue to visit my good friends in the United States and I miss the professional conferences. I would like to regain my freedom. However, my mother does not want to live in a nursing home and I honor her wishes. When I first suggested that she go into a hospital or nursing home, she said, "I have been a good person all my life. I don't deserve to be put in jail." I think it is my duty to allow her to live in her own home.

"Friends urge me to put her in a nursing home. They say that I am old-fashioned and ridiculously self-sacrificing, even that this unfortunate change in my life style is 'the outcome of a symbiotic relationship.' This, of course, is absurd. I have led a very independent life.

"If her illness becomes so severe that she needs to be in a hospital or nursing home, I will make other arrangements for her. Until then, we will live here and enjoy our time together. She still looks after herself, paints Japanese Sumie, and goes to Sumie classes once a week. I retire from the University in one year. I will stay at home with her and finish the book I am writing. The publisher is pushing me to do it as quickly as possible."

CHINA

solo and tour

Beijing is 3,000 years old and has been the capital of China for 700 years. The streets are clogged with traffic and smog hangs heavy overhead.

I stay at an inn, Halo Yuan (Good Garden), a stately if aging residence in the Chinese classic style, built during the Qing dynasty. Its last private occupant was one of Mao's generals.

My small suite is magnificently ostentatious and totally uncomfortable. The ornately carved king-sized bed is as hard as the floor, but fortunately there is also a carved wooden couch with a modern futon, which I manage to drag onto the big bed. That helps some. A wardrobe, equally ornate, is behind the bed and can only be reached by walking over the top of the bed. There are several huge, absolutely straight, gorgeously carved chairs, made for giants who at all times sit erect. Adjoining the bedroom is a huge ante-room whose only purpose seems to be to display a shrine to Buddha and a thermos bottle of boiling water for tea. The mammoth bathroom has the tiniest possible shower and a toilet almost as small-sized, crammed together at one edge of the room. The rest of the room has wall paintings and empty space. In past eras it perhaps had a beautiful commode and giant, hand-filled bathtub. I giggle and feel quite merry in this place of luxurious discomfort.

I need a duplicate pair of reading glasses, so in the morning set out on a quest for the right store. Like a gift from heaven, I find a sign with a huge drawing of eye glasses. Inside, I use sign language to explain that I need duplicates, as sales people crowd around and one of them figures out my prescription from the pair I am wearing. I pick out bright blue frames. Total cost: $24. They'll be ready tomorrow. At that price, I should have ordered several, considering how quickly I can lose them. I have only a few days alone here before hooking up with a tour group, so choose primarily the sights that are not listed on the tour. Plus, I will spend an extra day at the Forbidden City, where I won't want to be rushed.

I hail a taxi and take off for the Temple of Heaven, a World Heritage site considered a masterpiece of Ming and Qing architecture. Long ago, emperors made animal sacrifices here at winter and summer solstice. It is a splendid place of bell towers, ornate temples with decorated green walls and bright blue tiled roofs, clipped lawns, ceramic dragons, fascinating rocks, and gnarled trees. The bark of one 500-year-old cypress looks as if dragons are climbing the trunk, and is venerated appropriately as "the dragon tree." The temple grounds are crowded with Chinese tour groups, happily picnicking, taking photos, and praying in the temples. Each group has its own distinctive orange or red vests over black, poorly tailored Western business suits. Gone are the blue Mao jackets and baggy pants. Only a few Caucasians are strolling through the grounds, and I hear no English.

The temple interiors are lavish, with bright scrolls and colorful scenes in painted plaster and wood. Beside the Emperor's throne is a secret door leading outside the complex. To escape enemies? Not at all. In 1779 the aged emperor had a problem with his aged bladder, so he ordered an exit for a quick pee. He decreed that no future emperor could use this exit until he was at least seventy years old. It turned out that none of his descendants lived long enough to use his special door.

Tips for female travelers: If you see a monk nearby, help him not touch you. If he accidentally brushes against you or your clothing, he will have to spend hours or days in penance.

From here I go to Jingshan Park to see the twenty-four small aquariums containing rare goldfish of various colors. Most have long, diaphanous tails and large, bulging eyes, some framed in black as if they are wearing diving goggles. The park, made from rock excavated when the Forbidden City was built, consists of exotic small hills and ridges. At one end is an amusement park with bumper cars and other rides for children.

On the way back to the inn I study both a map and a "guided walk" in my travel book, and get hopelessly lost. What good are directions such as "turn north" or "east" when the sky is hazy with smog and the sun seems to be directly overhead? There are no street names similar to those on the map, and streets seem to veer in weird directions. Besides, Getting Lost is my inexorable fate at home and abroad.

When I was eighteen and alone in Mexico City, I learned to ask "Where is Mina Street?" so clearly that people thought I was Spanish-speaking. They would answer in fast Spanish, and I would walk away clueless, ask again, and again receive an incomprehensible answer. After a time I had explored most of the city while lost.

Travel *Tips: **ALWAYS** carry a hotel card in the language of the country and have your destinations written on a blank card each day by the hotel clerk. Also, if you are lost, any international hotel can give you directions in English, or send you back to your hotel by cab.*

I swallow my pride, hail a cab, and point to Tian'amen Square on the map. It is in exactly the opposite direction. Who knows what hidden marvels I might have discovered if I were young enough to walk all day? Today is an ordinary weekday and, even so, the square is alive with Chinese tour groups. There are so many Chinese in the square that I wonder if they are preparing for a massive funeral or demonstration, but someone explains that it is always this crowded.

Men and women are selling postcards, flags, photos of Chairman Mao, and lots of gorgeous kites that are flying overhead: butterflies, dragons, rainbows, and various birds. I want very much to buy a long-tailed dragon, but don't. Everyone is trying to press close enough to view the flag lowering ceremony at 5:00 P.M. I can't actually see the action, because hundreds of Chinese tourists have squeezed in ahead, but I get a glimpse of soldiers leaving the Forbidden City as they march stiffly toward the flag pole. The flag is lowered. I go back to my inn and ask where they would recommend I eat dinner. They point me in the direction of an excellent restaurant.

Travel Tips: If there is no menu in English, walk around the restaurant to see what others are eating. When you find something you might like, bring the waiter over and point.

I hire a taxi to the Pearl Market, on the third floor of an immense warehouse. There are dozens of individual stalls. I go to a stall recommended by an Austrian businessman I met at the hotel last evening. An earnest young saleswoman gives me a lecture on pearl-buying, explaining the importance of color, luster, and sizing. She and her aunt rent this space, and she is proud of the quality of the pearls. She also has a bit of jade, and tells me about it, too. The pearls are incredibly inexpensive, so I buy Christmas presents for all the females in my family. Probably none of them wants pearls; that is a problem I have with overseas bargains.

More *Tips: I have to keep reminding myself not to buy just because*

*items are so much less expensive than at home. If I succumb, I promise
myself I won't be upset if no one likes my gifts. Children prefer the
plastic junk I can pick up at the airport on my way home. I've learned
from them never ever to get them fancy, embroidered clothing, or any
other clothing that differs in any way from what their friends are
wearing.*

Next morning I visit the Tibetan Buddhist temples, freshly restored
and re-painted. Monks are in residence here, guarding the temples,
praying, and sweeping the grounds. Signs in English explain China's
version of Tibetan Buddhism. One Buddha, eighty-five feet tall, is
carved from a single sandalwood tree. The prayer wheels around the
temples are kept whirling and, as I pass, I too give them a whirl. Inside
the temples are brilliant thangkas (painted cloth scrolls detailing
Buddha's life) and mandalas for meditation, plus a multitude of statues
of past, present, and future aspects of Buddha. I see Paradise in
bronze, a world of love and plenty, which I think should be the goal in
this world and is unavailable to most people everywhere.

The next day I wander in the Gugon Bowugua, called The
Forbidden City by the English-speaking world. Twenty-four emperors
and two dynasties have ruled from this Forbidden City, until the last
was overthrown in 1911. Everyone who has seen the movie THE
LAST EMPEROR knows its vastness. There is so much of everything:
temples, moats, ponds, small parks, theaters, apartments for
concubines, apartments for the royal family, for hangers-on, business
areas, temples for royal examinations. The rooms go on and on. Many
have been turned into museums filled with jewels, clocks, costumes,
swords, paintings, and many statues.

The actual living areas are quite bare, containing only a throne for
the emperor and mats for everyone else, because the decorative pieces
are in the museum areas. Only the concubines' apartments contain
their lounges and some decoration. A three-story pagoda, open in front
like a child's doll house, has multiple stages on three floors. A single
stage might be used for music recitals or small dramas, but in epic
theater all of the stages are used simultaneously for casts of hundreds,
including racing horses, Samurai and their soldiers, or huge Chinese
operas and dancing troupes. The Royal Family sat in special tiers in a
lavishly decorated building facing the stages. I spend the entire day at
the Forbidden City, seeing everything.

When I return to the inn I meet Larry, a friend of the manager, who is marking time until the date he leaves for graduate school in Australia. He offers to go with me tomorrow to visit the Eastern Qing tombs. (See the next chapter: A Chinese Dilemma.)

After my day at the tombs with Larry, my freedom ends. I join a tour group of fifty aging Americans. In the morning I march with them behind the gallant flag of the tour leader, just as the Chinese are doing in their groups. Instead of red or yellow caps or vests, we are given black sweat shirts, all size XL, with the name of the Chinese tour company emblazoned on the front. Obviously, someone believes all Americans are giants. Most of the group refuses to wear them, but it doesn't matter. We are the only white-haired people in a sea of black hair, and many of us are quite tall, so we are highly visible.

At night we have a lecture from a local professor on Mao and the Revolution. It's a canned speech, carefully memorized. "Eighty percent of what Chairman Mao did for the country was wonderful. Twenty percent was not good." How is this figured? Millions died of starvation because his agricultural policies failed and because of his crazy obsession with steel production instead of food production. Millions were tortured and killed during the Cultural Revolution. How do you assign percentages to starvation, torture, and slaughter?

The next day we go through the Forbidden City very quickly, omitting most of the rooms. I am pleased I spent a day here before this tour. I buy a cappuccino at Starbucks and sit contentedly in the royal gardens beside a lovely pool. Though I am disgusted that Starbucks is allowed inside the Forbidden City, this is my first good cup of coffee in Beijing, so I forgive the sacrilege.

After our tour of the Forbidden City, we are taken to the Qing summer palace, quiet and calm, with beautiful trees, a large lake with boats that look like dragons, lovely pagodas, an outstanding temple high on the hill, and about 500 meters of covered walks with over 1,000 old paintings on the ceilings: Chinese style jousting, daily life of peasants, court life, plus lots of birds and flowers. The dowager empress, the one whose tomb I visited with Larry, was mean, avaricious, and a traitor who built herself a decorative concrete boat here at the Palace with money given her to improve the Chinese navy. But this summer palace is lovely. I wish the group had time to walk more slowly among the paintings, and enjoy the beauty of the high hills and lake.

We drive to **Badaling** and from a distance see the **Great Wall of China**, stretching mile after mile, up and down the hills and across plateaus, solid and enduring and, like all fortifications, eventually useless. It remains a wonder of this world, and but it is only a rumor that it can be seen from outer space. When I was very young, I saw photographs of the Great Wall in the National Geographic in my grandfather's dental office and planned that some day I would be right here. I am grateful to myself for making that plan come true. The wall is truly fantastic. I stand on it and see a huge expanse of curving wall that is only a very small part of the whole.

We fly to **Xi'an** and visit the leaning Tower of Buddha and the Wild Goose Pagoda. Long ago, a monk named Xuan Zang went to India to study Buddhism and was gone seventeen years. On the way back, when his group was very hungry, he prayed for meat. A wild goose fell dead at his feet. Because he believed it to be a sign from Buddha, he refused to let it be eaten, and instead buried it properly. He is hungry, prays to Buddha, and Buddha sends a goose he shouldn't eat? The holy man refuses a much-needed gift from his own god? And such a story glorified? Religious stories are sometimes silly.

From last night's lecture by a local guide: *China has the world's longest **recorded** history. Old bones were found by peasants tilling their fields. Since they were shiny and had strange markings, the peasants believed they were dragon bones, and sold them to be ground up as a cure for impotency. In 1899 scientists began to take an interest in these bones, which proved to contain ancient writing from the eleventh century BCE. They were so elaborately done that for some time Western scientists considered them a hoax. They are "divination" bones. The bones were heated until they cracked, the cracks were interpreted, and then the interpretations were written on each bone, along with the events of the time. In effect, these are the state archives and religious beliefs of that period.*

The Terracotta Warriors: Six thousand full-size warriors stand in a huge, covered cave bigger than several football fields, infantrymen, cavalry, archers, officers, and each statue has individualized, unique facial features, expressions, and clothing. The figures were once brightly colored, but time has eroded the colors, and exposure to air shattered many. They stand in pale terracotta, magnificently restored by present-day workers. The scene is awesome, incredible, a high point of any trip. I walk round and round this huge arena, trying to see every warrior.

There are also horses with reins of gold and silver, and a bronze sword that is still sharp enough to cut bamboo.

No one knows how many more statues are still buried nearby in Qin's vast mausoleum, which has yet to be opened. Two thousand years ago, over 700,000 men spent seventeen years on this gigantic project, and at the same time another million men were building the Great Wall. These two projects so weakened the economy that collapse became inevitable.

On the way to the airport, we visit the archeological remains of a 6,000 year old, matriarchal village, **Bampo,** to see the clay huts and houses, polished stone tools, and painted pottery.

After the wonders of the past week, the city of **Kunming** is a disappointment, being just an ordinary Chinese city. Besides, I wake up to an aching neck. The group goes off without me on a long bus trip to see a stone forest.

I decide to buy a neck brace, which has helped my neck in the past. The hotel clerk explains my need to a taxi driver, who makes everything easy. He drives to a medical supply store, which does not carry neck braces but tells him where I can find one. Totally solicitous, he wants me to lean on him, although there is nothing at all wrong with my legs at the moment. He guides me up and down stairs of a giant department store, until we find the counter where neck braces are sold. The store has four salespersons for each twelve-foot counter, and there are dozens of counters. I am the only customer on that floor. When they see me, there is a crescendo of female chirping, before a clerk emerges who understands a bit of English. Only one type of brace is sold: a three-tiered inner tube, fake fur on top, with what seems to be a rubber tennis-ball hanging down to the chest, to inflate and deflate the contraption. I complain, "This is not what I want."

"Oh," she says, smiling.

"Do people wear this outside the house?"

"Oh, no. They stay inside and no one sees them."

I laugh, the four saleswomen at the counter laugh, then saleswomen from surrounding counters join the merriment. We are having a fine time.

"What other ones do you have?"

This time the laughter is even more widespread. No one can conceive of a different one. "No other. Very pretty." After all, this has lovely fake fur around the collar. She puts it on me and brings a small mirror.

I don't really want something prettier; I want something less conspicuous, but I don't know how to explain that concept. I buy. The rubber neck-tire seems to help. At least it gives me something to do, expanding and contracting the gadget instead of focusing on how much my neck hurts. And in this cold weather, it keeps the soreness warm. I walk around Green Lake, a famous park beside our hotel, where old men usually bring their caged birds to sing with other birds, magicians perform, old and young practice tai chi, play mah jong, sing, and play their lutes. So the tour guide told me. Alas, due to the cold weather, I walk alone in a deserted park, and then take my neck to bed.

The others return with tales of a hard bus trip over bumpy roads on the way to the twisted rocks that are not worth going so far to see. I know I would have liked it, as it sounds similar to the Iceland stone forest, which was eerie and wonderful. But my neck would have hated the trip.

Dali, home of the Bai people, is an old town, nestled in a valley beside a long, lovely lake and surrounded by mountains. This is a small city that has for centuries escaped destruction. With its hodgepodge of streets, alleys, and old wooden buildings, it's a perfect place for wandering alone, peering into strange shops and sitting at outdoor tables, drinking tea and watching the people walk by. Bai men wear embroidered vests and Bai women have embroidered skirts and vests, plus caps that are brightly colored and shaped like crowns with ermine on the top. (The ermine matches the fake fur on my neck brace, so I feel quite stylish here.) Young women add white tassels to their ermine. Here many Chinese are still wearing padded trousers and Chairman Mao jackets. Backpackers, many of them Asian, are dressed like backpackers everywhere, in jeans. Dali's most important early tourist was Marco Polo, who arrived in the fourteenth century, certainly not in jeans. His was a luxurious retinue that fit right in with the classy court of Kubla Khan.

We drive along the lake, whose colors change from cobalt to azure to misty sapphire, sometimes with the speed of a cloud across the sun.

Behind it, green mountains reflect in the water, and behind these is the magnificent snow-capped Cangshan mountain range. The wind blows, the water becomes briefly white capped and dark, then in a few minutes it flattens and lightens, and mirrors the mountains again. Camellias and azaleas are blooming everywhere and the weather is mild. What a relief to leave the cold weather behind us in the North. This evening a full moon scatters trails of shimmering silver on the now-black water.

The Bais, who arrived here in the seventh century BCE, are rice farmers who own the land by the lakeside and in nearby river valleys. Their houses are pure white and in this season the doorways are framed with bright yellow, drying corn. After marriage, a Bai man moves into the home of his wife's family. To honor guests, Bais offer three teas, one bitter, one spiced, and one sweet, representing three common aspects of life. They tie-dye cloth blue, with white flowers created by the intricate knots they tie in the cloth. They also make fantastic stone pictures by polishing a slab of stone to highlight the "grain," which then looks like luminous mountains, lakes, and valleys. I would love to own one, but they are too heavy to lift, so getting one home would present problems, even if I had a home.

Today we visit a rich man's garden, not a Bai. It is filled with orchids and carefully pruned trees, like giant bonsai. His front gate and outer screen are intricately carved, and stone statues stand among the trees. His sitting room is splendid, with rosewood furniture, silk pillows and beautifully carved scrolls of birds, flowers, and Chinese landscapes. With all this loveliness, there is no indoor plumbing! And the only method of heating is live coals in an urn in the center of the main rooms. I'd sell some scrolls and buy a toilet and an indoor kitchen. And heaters.

The Saturday market is packed and boisterous, with shrill, earsplitting shouts from buyers and sellers. Along with the usual fruit, vegetables, and meat, they sell live kittens and puppies (for meat?), and mice (I don't want to know what for), plus tourist goods. I buy several strands of hand-painted ceramic beads for one dollar a strand. The beads have painted birds' heads, children's faces, and even a Santa head.

High above the lake are three pagodas around a large reflecting pool. I struggle many steps higher to see a temple with a big bronze bell and a lovely bronze statue of the plump female Buddha. As is common throughout China, rock formations are show-pieces in the garden. They are as beautiful and intricate as fine carving.

On to the **Yangtze**, the world's third longest river. (First is the Nile, then the Amazon, they tell us. In Peru the people include the tributaries and say the Amazon is longest.) We arrive at the town of **Chonquin** after dark and board our ship, the Victoria, US-managed, with nice staterooms and plenty of deck space. We start off down river before breakfast, with much blowing of horns. Over 100 Chinese are squatting silently on the riverbank near us, probably waiting for their boat. The water is a deep brown, the fog intermittent and sometimes thick enough to envelop us completely. The river is almost empty of cruise ship traffic, though dozens of ships stand unused on the shore, some shabby and some deluxe, like ours. The tour season is over and already the authorities have closed off river traffic near the dam, eliminating our final day's boat trip to Wutan. The dam is complete and the flooding will begin next month.

We pass a town of almost vertical streets, where men are transporting huge loads of goods by means of carrying-poles balanced on their shoulders. Among the awful jobs in this world, theirs must rank near the top. The town is bleak, with dozens of cement apartment houses that haven't the slightest adornment. The smog is deep yellow.

River traffic: a long, flat boat filled with sand; several small, shallow boats rowed with very long, thin oars; junks, sails drooping in the non-wind; a small, old freighter pushed by a tugboat; and boats in which families are cooking and eating together. All buoys are shaped like miniature gray rowboats with tiny red plastic sails. They bob cheerfully in place.

I go inside briefly to hear a lecture on the dam. Everyone, including this bright young female speaker, knows that world authorities have overwhelmingly condemned it. Though China has moved many national treasures from the area to be flooded, archeologists mourn the loss of those that cannot be moved and the loss of whole sites which have never even been explored. International engineers lambaste the design, talk about the inevitable build-up of silt, and say the damn will cause more problems than it can possibly cure. Environmentalists talk of the impact on animal and plant species, some of which may become extinct. Political commentators say that the dam

116

is being built because of the arrogance of the current rulers, who don't want to appear subservient to the rest of the world.

The young Chinese speaker, while acknowledging some of the concerns, insists that the electricity generated will vastly improve the lives of the Chinese people. She speaks of the jobs created by building and then maintaining the dam, and assures us that the Yangtze will be equally beautiful after the flooding.

I go back on deck. On both sides are steep rocks, then flat areas where people are cultivating what will be their last crop of winter wheat. As in other parts of China, we see the bare hills where whole forests were demolished because of Chairman Mao's bizarre decision to use all potential lumber to fuel the smelters in order to have a higher steel production than the US. With the death of Mao, sanity returned and trees are now being replanted everywhere except here, where the dam will make the water rise above the bare hills. Is the dam today's insanity or will it truly help the people?

We pass derelict apartments, five and six stories high, abandoned stores and shacks, and an abandoned, once glorious mansion on a small peninsula jutting into the river. For long stretches, there are no people on the land. All along the river huge signs painted into the rock indicate the dates at which flooding will reach the various heights. It will be about two years before the flooding is completed.

Our first stop is **Fengdu** to see "The City of Ghosts," built long ago, during the Han dynasty. Two officials, bored with the Imperial Court, came to the mountain above Fengdu, to practice Tao teachings and make vivid scenes of their version of Hell. In the first, a newly dead spirit goes before the bureaucracy of the dead. Those decreed pure are rewarded; however, that doesn't much interest these two ancient Taoists. They concentrate their enthusiasm on the tortures of hell, with scenes of demons and torture chambers, and signs reading: "Great Torturing Pass," "Tower of Last Glance At Home," "No Way Out" bridge, "River of Blood." Much of this gruesome stuff was destroyed during the Cultural Revolution, and now has been rebuilt for tourists. Even a chair lift has been added.

The town of **Fend** is being taken apart and rebuilt on higher land. Hundreds of people are dismantling walls, cleaning the bricks by hand, and stacking them onto trucks. Truckers move the bricks to the new Fend, where other workers use the bricks to build new homes and stores. Lung-burning smog hangs over both sites. Guides tell us that old people hate this change, because they want to stay near their ancestors' burial grounds and be buried beside them. The young are happy to have the construction work, and the new houses will be considerably better than the old. One week from today the water will begin to rise. Over 3,000,000 people along the Yangtze have already been evacuated to new homes and 300,000 more await homes.

We are taken up the **Daning**, a clear, beautiful river that joins the Yangtze, on motorized sampans guided by men using long poles with steel spears to dig into the sand. The walls on each side of the river stand 3,500 feet high, and in places are very narrow. High above us are square holes in the rock for narrow platforms that supported a wooden walkway dating back at least to 3,000 BCE, built to transport salt from the mines. It was destroyed by the Imperial Ming army in the seventeenth century. Also in the gorge are hanging coffins suspended from caves by the Bas people 3,500 years ago. There used to be hundreds of coffins suspended a thousand feet above the river. The caves are inaccessible today, and no one knows how the Bas reached them to hang their dead. Or why, come to think of it.

About this area, Bai Juiji of the T'ang Dynasty wrote:
> "Summits tower high
> above the restless water
> between cliffs blanketed with greenery
> the space between sometimes wide enough
> only to insert a reed."

We see wild monkeys, waiting patiently along the river's edge for handouts. They will move themselves to higher ground and, no doubt, be fed by tourists on the higher river.

We leave the Victoria at the last stop, and are bussed to the dam and then on to **Wutan**. On the way, we just have time to race through the **Hubei** Provincial Museum to hear a glorious Chinese symphony: Sixty-four elaborate bronze bells of various sizes, all with intricate designs, are played with long, hammer-like objects and poles. The concert ends with Beethoven's Ode to Joy. We are rushed back onto the bus and driven through terrible slums to the airport.

Shanghai is a modern city of interesting skyscrapers and beautiful parks. Our tour guide sings praises to capitalism and seems to believe that all Shanghai Chinese will soon be as rich as US tourists:

"Shanghai has the most skyscrapers in the world," "the most parks," "the most new businesses," and therefore "Shanghai will become the world's greatest city."

The new museum is wonderful. I happily spend a full day there, avoiding our guides. This is my idiosyncrasy, and no fault of the guides. I feel trapped, just as I did in grade school and high school when our classes were taken to the Field Museum, Art Institute, the museum of the Chicago Fire, Science and Industry, the County Jail, and Hull House. Except for the jail, I had visited all of them many times on my own, read all the signs and studied them carefully, and prbably could have given the lectures as well as the tour guides. Now I know how lucky I was as a child! I was allowed to go to Chicago alone, a one-hour train trip, from the time I was about nine years old. I spent days in museums or walking the streets, discovering new worlds. Fortunately, I had parents who never believed anything bad could happen to me (who would want to kidnap me?), and nothing bad ever did. I got lost then, too, but people pointed me on my way. I still avoid guides, and enjoy headphones because with headphones I am in charge.

In this modern Shanghai museum, there are explanations in English beside each exhibit, so guides truly aren't needed. The rooms are filled with clothing from all ages and ethnic minorities: costumes, masks, and fantastic court robes embroidered in pure gold. There are stone sculptures, funereal figures, pottery, many different portrayals of Buddha, jade from Neolithic to modern times in all its lovely colors and carvings, and in one room are paintings forty feet long, done by four masters of the seventh century. There are samples of the world's earliest writing, tiny, clear characters on old bones and turtle shells, and samples of writing on the first real paper. Inscriptions on bronze bells date from the sixteenth century BCE. One room is dedicated to the step by step process of making porcelain, and adjoining it is an exhibition of precious porcelain through the ages.

Before breakfast the city parks are filled with men and women doing Tai Chi, exercising with fans and swords, and dancing, while old men air their birds and chat with each other. I go alone, avoiding our "gang of fifty," to find people who want to practice English with me. One man my age shows me how his parakeet dances in time to his finger movements. A university student hopes to visit her relatives in

Vancouver and wonders if she will be able to see the aurora borealis.

I really like Shanghai and hope to return. When I do, I will stay at Longhua, a Buddhist hotel that serves superb vegetarian food. I am sick of the monotonous Chinese diet with the same eight platters of food for every lunch and dinner. Perhaps I would become just as tired of the vegetarian menu, but there are also pizza parlors and European restaurants in Shanghai. I yearn for the freedom of solitary traveling.

Guilin and **River Li**. Guilin seems an attractive city, but we have no time to explore it. Immediately after breakfast, our bus sets off to the river. Boats are docked to the right, left, ahead, and behind us. The officers on all the ships wear bright blue uniforms with lots of gold buttons and stars, and look as if they are about to burst into a lively chorus from the HMS Pinafore. They help us clamber from boat to boat, until we reach our own. When all are aboard, the whistle toots and, with much poling, the ship is eased into its place in line. Then we steam ahead single file, dozens of boats and hundreds of passengers, but the boats are spaced so that we seldom see each other.

The river meanders, a glowing ribbon, between the rounded, beautiful green and gray limestone hills that are famous from 3,000 years of Chinese paintings. The sun is bright, without the characteristic mist, and the reflections of the hills are clear and sharp. Along the way, children are playing in the water and men are using cormorants to do their fishing. There are bamboo groves, waterfalls, and bright green ponds. This river is so much more exciting than the Yangtze! I want to return to see it in all its moods.

I sit on the floor of the top deck, my legs dangling between the rails, and I imagine I hear Cuban Celeste singing, "Gracias a la vida, que me ha dado tanto." (Thanks to life, that has given me so much).

Travel tips: *There's a small resort along this river, Crown Cave Resort, which I would check out. In Guilin, look for the best guide of our trip, Wei Marie, who escaped against her family's wishes from their rice farm beyond all roads, to educate herself. She is full of stories, and knows the area well.*

Be wary of mass tours. The itinerary may be wonderful, but mass dining, mass marching from place to place, and mass line-ups to use the too-few toilets are definite disadvantages. If you are looking for a tour of China, I suggest choosing a group with no more than fifteen participants. Fifty is a nightmare!

A CHINESE DILEMMA

I meet Larry at the Halo Yuan Inn in Beijing. He has a bachelor's degree in business, has worked two years for an international computer company, and recently won a scholarship to do post-graduate work in Melbourne, Australia. He'll leave for Australia in a month, and is now on vacation. In order to practice his English, which he speaks very well, he offers to go with me to the **Eastern Qing tombs**, 125 kilometers from Beijing. He's twenty-six, small, lithe, and eager. He looks like a high school student, but at my age almost everyone seems younger than they are. The inn manager vouches for him.

"I don't know what to do about my girlfriend." We are in the taxi on the way to the tombs. Larry gazes at me intently, his cheeks glowing with embarrassment. "Yesterday you told me you are a psychotherapist, so I hope you will guide me. Please pretend I'm your patient."

"Oh, dear." So this is today's hidden agenda. I'd be irritated if he were American, but because he is Chinese I'm intrigued, as I'm curious about relationships in modern China. "What's the problem with your girlfriend?"

"There is no problem with her. The problem is, I ought to marry her because she is my fiancée." As we drive past small villages and lovely hills, Larry continues to explain. "I'm a modern Chinese man. I consider myself a free-thinker. For instance, I am not a member of the Communist party, even though my parents are party leaders. But I'm not really free. That's where the problem is. You could call it a Chinese dilemma." He explains that he must eventually settle in Beijing, marry someone who will help him care for his parents when they are old, and have the maximum-minimum one child.

He is leaving Beijing to study and learn, of course, but mostly he is leaving to avoid marrying his fiancée. He predicts that if he marries this woman, whom he chose years ago, he will have a disastrously unhappy marriage. "At her age, she must marry or no one will want her. I don't know what to do." He asks again for my advice.

"I am not the kind of psychotherapist who gives advice." I offer to keep listening, to help him figure out what is the best solution for him, his fiancée, and his parents. "In my culture we may over-rate the importance of the individual. In your culture, you may over-rate the importance of family."

"We don't think about the individual at all." He tells me about his parents, who obviously love him very much. They approve of his studies, his scholarship, and his wife-to-be. "Because I am an only child, I will always be responsible for them. We are very fortunate in China to have the one-child rule. We have to keep our population down. China used to be swamped with children whose parents couldn't support them. The one-child rule is what permits my country to be successful today. It also increases my personal problem. I have no brothers and sisters to give my parents grandchildren. It is all up to me."

Larry believes in capitalism but not democracy. "Our country must control dissidents to keep our economy flourishing." He believes that under capitalism people succeed according to their willingness to work hard in school and later in a profession. "I think I get A-plus in both." He says this in a straight-forward, non-bragging way.

Obviously, he is as naive and prejudiced as any of the privileged of the world, but with the combination of his ability plus family connections he will always be able to pretend to himself that his willingness to work hard accounts for his successes. It's the "born on third base and think you made a home run" attitude. We argue a bit, congenially, and I am amused that I am the one who sounds like a communist. He is an example of the new capitalist optimism in China.

Perhaps I'm irritated by his self-centeredness, because I say, "Some people report that an only child in China is spoiled by parents and grandparents."

"Oh, we are!" He is a member of the first generation of one-child families. "People say that all of us are spoiled. My parents gave me everything I wanted. All I had to do was ask. But that's only one side of it. I have to be as perfect as possible, because I am my parents' only hope for the future. You understand how that makes my problem greater? If I don't marry my fiancée, she and my parents will suffer."

"If you were the absolutely perfect only son, what would you do?"

"Marry her right now, and not leave China until she is pregnant. My parents would have the grandchild they want and also a daughter-in-law to care of them in their old age. But for me, this would be a disaster."

"In your culture would she rather be married, no matter how unhappily, than risk not being married?"

"Yes, but neither of us would be happy."

I tell him that in my experience, people work hard to make their negative predictions come true. Therefore, I believe him when he says he will be unhappy.

He looks straight at me. "I think I know what you mean. Thank you for saying that, even though I don't like what you said."

We reach the tombs. I seem to be the only Caucasian here, though there are many Chinese tourists. Larry switches gears, to become a most efficient tour guide. He tells me the history of the area. He shows me who among the locals are Mongolians, descendants of Genghis Khan. They serve as tour guides and caretakers, although the Qings were their historic enemies. The finest tomb complex is that of the emperor Quianlong, who ruled for fifty-nine years during the 1700s. The chambers leading to the tomb are of polished white marble covered with carved sutras and images of Buddha. In the tomb area are the coffins of the emperor, empress, and two favorite concubines.

In another tomb complex is the body of the traitor Empress Cixi (1835 - 1911), who sold China out to Western Imperialists. She was a notorious man-hater, whose funeral carvings place the Phoenix (for women) above the Dragon (symbol of the power of Emperors.) She had tons of jewels surrounding her coffin, which were stolen during the Maoist revolution by those who fled to Taiwan. Were they as avaricious as she?

We watch a small festival re-enacting the journey of the second emperor to pay homage to his dead father, Qianglong: lots of music, bowing, and marching up and down the courtyard.

We sit on the terrace overlooking the graves and drink good Chinese beer. Larry speaks quietly. "Love is a complicated part of life. I do better with computers. I don't know much about love."

I ask about his fiancée. "What's she like?"

He says she is pretty and wants to please him. "But she is not interesting. She quit school after we became engaged. She just did nothing, until my parents got her a job in a bank." He sighs. "I cannot marry her, but I lack the courage to say this to anyone. Whenever I think of telling my parents or my fiancée anything about my feelings, I am filled with shame. Probably I will just go to Australia and not say anything."

"You have been, you tell me, a very dynamic person. You actively chose your profession, you got yourself a job, then competed for and won a scholarship. Only when it concerns your choice of a life partner do you collapse and become passive."

"Yes. About marriage, I feel like a balloon that's lost its air."

"That's not your style. I imagine that you'd be less ashamed if you made a decision and announced it."

On the way back to Beijing we pass three serious accidents, a head-on collision, a rear-ender, and a car that missed a curve and flipped. Like all taxis in Beijing, ours has no seat belts, and I am nervous. We reach Beijing after dark. When we arrive at Halo Yuan Inn, Larry and I do not bow. We hug each other. He says, "You are very wise. Perhaps I will start by telling my parents about our conversation. It will take great courage."

Travel tips: For me, an advantage of traveling alone is meeting local people. Another advantage is making spur of the moment plans with them.

NEW ZEALAND

Bill and Bette Kreger, Laurie Barrett

Auckland. This is a family vacation and a respite from writing, except for a note here and there. On the first day sister Bette, brother-in-law Bill, and I go to a zoo to see a kiwi, which looks enough like an extra-round hen to be quite uninteresting. Auckland has some fine roses.

The museum has an interesting collection of Maori artifacts and the Maoris give a dance presentation with much bulging and rolling of eyes, sticking out of tongues, and stamping in time to loud drums. All of this, in the old days, was to scare the enemy. I wish that were today's technique, with a few spears if absolutely necessary.

Hotel Rydges, (full of tour groups, but good location near the Sky Tower, within walking distance of the water and the Auckland explorer bus that runs all over town with fourteen tourist stops).

We take the ferry to **Davenport**, a nice little town on a nearby island, majoring in tourist goods, antiques, and delicious lunches.

Our sister Laurie arrives all the way from the Virgin Islands, exhausted. Never mind that tiredness stuff, we pick her up at the airport and drive north. First stop, an ocean motel at **Waipu**. We see the sea, eat pizza, chat with the restaurant people, and spend the night.

Waipu Cove Cottages (Ocean view: $120 US for a cottage for four)

On to **Whangarei** and Clapham's Clock Museum, pretty small stuff after the clocks in the Forbidden City. The best part is the woman in charge, who flits about, rapidly rewinding and re-setting clocks so that we can hear each one strike the hour. She, like the clocks, is wound up. Nearby is a pleasant park with a waterfall, Parahaki Scenic Reserve.

After lunch on a wharf, we head north again, but make a stupid choice. We take a back road instead of the highway, because it looks interesting on our map, as it winds to the sea. The highways here are back-road enough, two-lane affairs that suddenly with no warning become one-and-one-half lanes to accommodate a rocky spot, a view, or perhaps merely the sadism of a highway engineer. In addition, there is this "wrong side of the road" problem, since no one in our car has expertise in left-hand driving. The back road begins with one and a half lanes, but this is a land of many little streams and rivers, and all the bridges are one-lane only.

There are no markers to designate who has right of way. A tie goes to the undertaker. I am in near-total terror, although there is almost no traffic and the road is obviously safer than any in California.

The road twists up, down, and around lovely hillsides, mostly getting nowhere. Bette, recuperating from surgery on her still-aching right arm, decides she must drive to avoid nausea; she opts for pain rather than vomit and we agree to her choice. For newly reunited, usually jolly sisters, we are quite glum. At the end of this long day we finally reach **Russell**, a quaint town that would have made a pleasant stop for a few days.

However, we are planning All Of New Zealand In Three Weeks, so quickly scan the big trees, lazy waterfront, and white clapboard houses. We sleep in a fair motel, and are off at daybreak to **Paihia** (short ride on a small car ferry), then to Waitangi national reserve, honoring the spot where a treaty was signed between Maori and Caucasian New Zealanders. In this greenly beautiful park is a huge carved and painted war canoe that used to seat 150 warriors, a carved treaty house, and a video that explains the history. We eat a tasty lunch in an outdoor restaurant in the park, overlooking a small creek and many birds. A waiter serves us, then hand-feeds a small eel that lives in the creek.

South again. Just by luck we see a small sign, "Kawiti glow worm cave," outside of **Waimio**. It is a must! The cave, long, black-dark, dazzles with thousands of blue-white glowing lights of the tiny worms. Lucy in the sky with diamonds! Our Maori guide, a middle-aged woman, is a member of the family who has owned this cave for twelve generations. "The first Maori was Roku from the tribe Ngattu, who ran away from her husband. She took her little daughter with her, and they hid right here in this cave. She collected shellfish, raised kumaras (a potato-like vegetable), and made fires deep in the cave to keep themselves warm." The next three generations, starting with the daughter and a couple of cousins who joined them, hid from the British, fought them, and had their children. Their descendents kept the rights to this cave plus 150 acres where the family raises sheep. "Through the years we have chanted the names and deeds of all our ancestors, starting with Roku. That's how I know all about them."

Nowadays, family members go to college and become professionals, thanks to the family income from the glow worm cave and the sheep farm. "No matter where they live, they come back for our holidays. We sing and dance and have work parties to shear the sheep and fix the cave." The cave is beautifully kept, with new-looking, strong wooden rails and floors. There are also wooden paths over the cave through the trees. (Later, when we go to the more famous glow worm caves, we know how lucky we were to have found this out-of-the-way gem. The other caves are jammed with tourists, and the speeches are canned.)

In **Kawakawa** for the first time in all my wanderings, I stop to gawk at public toilets. They were designed by an Austrian architect, Friedenreich Hundertwesser, a fine, lofty name. The bathrooms have ceramics, shells, beads, driftwood, and glass shards in fascinating combinations in the walls, columns, ceiling, and even in the fixtures. The building is topped with a grass roof.

Laurie drives us almost to Auckland, and stops at the Red Beach, a resort town. We are too late. All rooms from here through Auckland are occupied by spectators of the American Cup yacht races. We are forced to drive back to **Waiwera** and get rooms in a dingy motel. It is exactly where I wanted to stop an hour before, because the town has a local hot springs. Laurie and I go there immediately. There are warm pools, a wonderfully hot pool for adults only, and one huge, crowded pool where the locals sit neck-deep, watching on a giant screen the most bloody possible series of wrecks of cars, boats, trains, and planes, shoot-em-ups and bomb-em-downs. That leaves the lovely hot pool quiet and almost empty for those of us who do not enjoy carnage.

The next day is a total dud, rain, wet sheep, nothing, nothing for hours. Laurie is the driver. (I gave up my license in the year 2000, joyfully.) How I long for a big safe bus or train! Finally we reach **Rotorua**.

On Lake Rotorua we visit a Maori Anglican church famous for its Jesus in Maori dress, etched onto a large glass window in such a way as to make Him seem to be walking on the lake just beyond the church. The interior of the church is decorated with bright red, painted carvings of Maori figures with mother-of-pearl eyes. Nearby, the meeting house is similarly decorated.

Lake Rotorua has coves and inlets edged by trees of many shades of green. In the background are the dark shapes of mountains. We go to **Whakarewarewa**. (Wh is sounded sometimes like F and sometimes like V. For the rest of the letters, we are on our own.) This is a thermal village, with trails winding past steaming pools, boiling mud, and many souvenir shops. Lunch, just a wee cut below edible, includes corn on the cob cooked in one of the boiling pools. From various look-out points we see acres of steam, geysers, and rivers of hot water. The Maoris put on a dance, complete with tongues sticking out, rolling eyes, and stamping, almost exactly like the one we watched at the Auckland museum. The women dancers twirl balls on strings and keep the drumbeat by bouncing the balls against their hands and bodies.

We drive to the famous blue and green lakes, somewhat grayed on this cloudy day, and visit a partially excavated village, **Te Wairoa**. June 10, 1886, Mt. Tarawera erupted. Fireballs exploded from three vents, and in five hours over 1500 square kilometers were covered in lava, ash, and mud; 153 people were buried under the flow. Excavation began only recently, and so far a few huts ("whares" with the F sound again) have been uncovered, plus broken tools belonging to the village ironsmith. There are more tools, glasses, plates, and some pots in another whare. A very lush valley has grown from the ashes.

Wamangu, twenty miles south of Rotarua, is an eerie hell of steaming cauldrons and multicolored mineral terraces. We walk down about a mile, and then a bus picks us up for the return trip. We overnight in **Taupo**.

The very best of the thermal areas is Orake Korako, with its yellow sulfur pits, blue-green ponds, red algae, silica terraces, geysers, and a natural cave with jade-green water.

Next we visit a geothermal power plant, and see a lot of water go through a narrow gap at Huka Falls. A couple of miles down the road is the Aratialia Dam, whose control gates are opened three times daily to spill large quantities of water over the rapids. Watching the water gush out, our gang gets concerned about a mother duck and her two chicks. They look as if they are going to be separated forever. They aren't.

Travel tips: *Note that grocery and liquor stores in New Zealand are closed Saturday afternoons and Sundays.*

We take a long trip to **Tongariro** National Park, a dud. Maybe it's OK for skiing in the winter, but there is nothing to see now. In China I learned a fine word, Mamahuhu, which means lousy, and I use it here secretly. After another day of rain, we finally reach Wellington and fly to **Queenstown**.

The next three days are a glory! We spend a day on the mountain behind Queenstown, overlooking Queenstown and gorgeous Te Anua lake. We take a bus trip to Milford Sound, with fantastic scenery from beginning to end. We go by bus and boat to Doubtful Sound. The boat trip across Lake Manapaui, with snow caps reflecting on the bright, calm water, is as beautiful as any place in the world that I have ever seen. After these three perfect, wonderful days of sunshine and spectacular beauty, I leave to fly to Florida to be a speaker at the Erickson Brief Therapy Conference, while Bette, Bill, and Laurie continue the trip.

I spend Christmas holidays in California with my family, where I sing (alone in the shower, as I cannot carry a tune) a paraphrase of the Danny Kaye song:

> Everywhere I wander
> Everywhere I roam
> When I'm in the arms of my family again
> My heart has found its home.

But after a couple of weeks, I choose to escape. I hate the news in our newspapers, the bias on TV. To keep my mind off the present, I am reading about post-World War I, an informative book by Margaret MacMillan, PARIS 1919: "Faith in their own exceptionalism has sometimes led to a certain obtuseness on the part of Americans, a tendency to preach at other nations rather than listen to them, a tendency as well to assume that American motives are pure where those of others are not." That is a polite assessment of the US eighty-five years ago, and describes basic flaws in our national character today. Back then, our politicians were not as single-mindedly and ruthlessly focused on overpowering the entire world. I hate that every year seems to find us worse.

Beyond all this, I am a rambler at heart:

> My hat hang on the same nail too long
> My ears can't stand to hear the same old song,
> Cause I caught this ramblin fever

After a year of travel, I know that I like homelessness. It will soon be 2003. I am setting off again.

CUBA AGAIN

And that's why I have to go back
to many places in the future,
there to find myself
******
and then whistle with joy.
Pablo Neruda, End of the World (Wind)

"I promise that I will be with you, if you so wish, for as long as I feel I can be useful; if it is not decided by nature before, not a minute less and not a second more. Now I understand that it was not my destiny to rest at the end of my life."
Fidel Castro, Granma international newspaper, March 16, 2003

solo

La Habana. I'm back. The downtown is one huge reconstruction zone. With money from Canada and European countries, a great many old buildings are being rebuilt all at once. Havana air, which last year seemed fresh and clean, is now heavy with construction dust. I notice a downtown elementary school that last year looked as if it would collapse if anyone leaned against it. Now it is like new, and painted a brilliant blue and white. I mention to a passerby how wonderful it looks. She tells me that every elementary school in Cuba has been totally repaired and repainted in less than one year. This was a national project, carried out by the people who volunteered their free time for the rebuilding. When the project was completed, each school received a new computer. "Who knows what next year will bring?" she says happily.

I am living at the medical center, sharing a lovely home with five young Spanish dentists who are here to learn methods of tooth implantation that are not yet taught in Spain. Later I will move into Celeste's apartment. I am back with professor Hecheverria and his laserpuncture. When I told him that my legs had been in fine shape for almost six months after the last sessions, he said, "You should have come back as soon as you needed me. Don't stay away so long next time!" I understand him more easily, now that he has gotten the hang of adding a few consonants to his lovely vowels, for my sake. We even have a discussion about whether an old guy should change his ways and buy his wife chocolates for Valentine's Day. I think the old guy should. He grins. (I know for a fact that he does bring her presents!)

I invite a military psychiatrist, who is helping to arrange my workshops, to go to dinner with me tonight. It feels a bit strange, doing the inviting and paying. My age shows. I don't think my daughters would be at all embarrassed to do the same. Like all physicians, he has a minuscule salary. He phones to say that his car has broken down. "My mechanic is arriving any moment. Will you wait for me?" Of course I will. In Cuba people who fix cars are available at all hours, like emergency-room doctors. He arrives a bit after eight and we go to the paladar owned by his friend and mentor, a retired psychiatrist. The fish is fresh and very good, and our conversation in English is easy. He tells me about his life during the Revolution.

I am teaching three weeks this year, at different medical centers. I teach, as always, with a minimum of lecturing and a maximum of demonstrating, with participants as clients.

I help a woman decide what she is willing to do about her senile mother, who can no longer be left at home alone. This universal problem is always difficult, because none of the options are pleasant. In Cuba, where family ties are very strong and lack of housing is a national crisis, the problem is especially painful.

A participant with marital problems decides to give up trying unsuccessfully to change her husband, and figures out how she will change herself to let herself find enjoyment. Another universal problem.

A woman wants to stop being afraid of frogs. It seems a good idea; this beautiful rehabilitation center is surrounded by farm land and appears to be overrun with frogs. I guide the woman to fantasize a frog in an imaginary locked cage on the other side of the room, to dress it in a silly costume, and to give it a name. She fantasies conversing with the frog, first tensely and then humorously. She allows herself to imagine the cage closer to her. While she is desensitizing herself, a little white frog, very alive, watches impassively from the other side of the window. After she has finished, she sees the live frog and touches the glass where it is clinging. She is very excited by her lack of fear. On the last day of the workshop, she touches a live frog, and she says she is going to practice this version of desensitization with her phobic clients.

A therapist decides that her problem is the combination of long hours at the hospital and the pressure of taking care of her parents, husband, and children when she finally gets home. (In Cuba it is common for three generations to live together.) She realizes that she was programmed in childhood to be overworked and overwhelmed, like her mother, and makes plans to change her work schedule to give herself a chance for time alone. I hope she will. In a country where almost everyone overworks and homes are crowded, this is a difficult goal.

The workshop is a success. We stop a bit early on the last day, so all of us can attend the Valentine's Day party for staff. The party committee has arranged the staff into "couples." Everyone lines up, names of couples are read aloud, and, amid much giggling, each "couple" goes arm in arm to sit together at the decorated tables. (Two real husbands "happen" to drop by, hug their wives' escorts, passionately kiss their wives for all to see, and leave.) My partner is the physician who helped set up the workshop. A fried chicken dinner is served, with rum and beer at each place. Silly love letters, written anonymously, are read to various men and women, as everyone laughs loudly and applauds.

I spend Saturday with the chief social worker from the hospital, the workshop translator, and her three-year-old daughter. At my request we visit the literacy museum commemorating the thousands of youth, age twelve to twenty, who in 1960 formed the Literacy Brigade to eliminate illiteracy in Cuba. They reduced illiteracy from over forty per cent to less than one per cent in one year. It was dangerous work in some mountain areas, because counter-revolutionary guerrillas were nearby. Sixteen boys were shot or hanged by counter-revolutionaries.

I am impressed with the book of instructions they received. On the first page is emphasized: make the lessons pleasant and exciting, praise each student every day, acknowledge what each student does well. The chief social worker proudly takes us to the file room to show us her husband's file with his photo at age sixteen. She was only ten, too young to join. Cubans who were part of this literacy brigade still consider it a high point in their lives.

We go to a convention center to see a miniature replica of the city.

The tiny buildings are in different colors, depending on the period in which they were built: colonial, 20th century before the revolution, or after the revolution. The two women point out their own homes on the model. The three-year-old is especially excited. "That little block is my house!"

The next day my friend Rivas and I stroll through the old city, La Habana Vieja. He points out Studebakers from the 1950s and old Fords. I have never cared to learn which car is which, and have no idea what cars my family owned, except that I know my grandfather the dentist always drove a Cadillac. There are relatively few cars in Cuba, even fewer than last year. Cars must be bought with US dollars, an impossible expense now that the days of cheap Soviet cars have ended.

We wander through Bellas Artes, enjoying the air-conditioning. Rivas has studied art, so is a fine companion. He explains modern Cuban art, and shows me examples of the work of one of his teachers. We also see paintings by Mariano, Celeste's ex-husband. Next we walk the waterfront. Because it is Sunday, the area is quiet, without the din of rebuilding. It's a nice time to admire the renovations. At the newly renovated hotel, Las Frailes, we happen upon a small group that includes the chief of restoration for all of La Habana, as well as Fidel Castro's personal secretary. The next weekend Castro attends an opening ceremony here to welcome a new order of nuns to Cuba, and to receive a personal gift from the pope.

I am reading a biography of Jose Marti, Cuban hero and martyr. In 1893, while living in the US, he wrote, "The exclusive, vehement and restless love of material wealth has miscarried here, and gives the people an air of colossi and children; it does not appear to me to be a good foundation for a people." I think about this. Consumerism is part of the US success story and seems to be addictive. I read somewhere that we are the only country in the world where people are spending more than they earn. How does that work?

In Cuba consumerism cannot become an addiction, because people do not have enough money to buy unnecessary things. The life style is similar to what I remember from Depression years, when clothes were handed down, and people used the same old furniture and cars year after year. I wonder what will happen in Cuba, now that some people have dollars, either from relatives in Florida or from the new private enterprise. I am told there is a surgeon who moonlights as a waiter in an international hotel in order to receive tips in dollars.

Maria La Gorda. I finish my workshops, and decide to take a week to vacation at this hotel and beach. The name (Fat Maria) is in honor of a long dead prostitute who was dearly loved by the sailors who landed on this deserted northern strip. I take the bus to Pinar Del Rio (three hours), then a cab (two hours).

The tourists are divers from Canada and Europe. Three German men in their sixties, all with trimmed white beards, big stomachs, and bright red, yellow, and blue diving outfits, look wonderfully like oversized dwarfs in a German fairy tale. One speaks English. We talk of an impending war against Iraq. We are both pessimists. He is proud that the German people were the first to oppose Bush and thereby ignite world-wide opposition.

I snorkel from the shore the first afternoon and then decide to try diving. "Try" means I don't know if I can clear my ears, because I had so much trouble clearing my ears two years ago in Bali. I discuss it with the dive master, who suggests I do afternoon dives, which are never over thirty-five feet, and says he will stay beside me during the dive. I dive and, amazingly, have no trouble at all. My ears are fine! The water is clear, the fish and coral beautiful. For the first time in my life I see a whole wall of black coral. I swim every morning and dive every afternoon.

Travel tip to older tourists: We too often assumed that any health problem is part of a natural deterioration and therefore incurable. Diving is an example. Last night at dinner a young woman was complaining that she can't clear her ears. She said, "I must have some damned sinus infection," and began taking antihistamines, hoping to unplug her ears before she has to leave. Two years ago I said about my plugged ears, "I'll never be able to dive again. I am too old to dive." And here I am, diving, and my old ears are fine.

I make friends with a delightful young diver from England, whom the dive master is obviously flirting with. They are cute together, she so very English pale and he so beautifully dark. She asks me, "Do you think it would be appalling if I had sex with him?" I tell her I can think of a bunch of appalling things she could do, and sex with Roberto certainly is not one of them. Seemingly, they had a wonderful week together. When I left, he came to the taxi, grasped both of my hands, looked into my eyes, and said, "Mil gracias, senora." (A thousand thanks.)

I return to La Habana and move in with Celeste. Celeste and I spend an evening at the Casa de la Trove, a place where Cubans go to dance. The musicians and singers seem to be whoever wants to perform, and they are good! For anyone who likes son, Cuban folk music, and salsa, this is a treat. Nobody dances better than the Cubans. At 10:00 P.M. the bands and their followers move on to another place, but we go back to our apartments.

I see a couple of dreadful movies, then two beautiful ballets. One, honoring an anniversary of Nureyev's death, shows film clips of him dancing and then the same dances by local dancers. The evening concludes with a heartbreaking and stunning performance of an original ballet entitled SIDA (AIDS).

My time here is winding down. The war news is more ominous. Everyone in Cuba is distressed. I decide to spend my last week in Trinidad. At the bus stop there, at least twelve people are holding colored photos of their homes, soliciting guests. I pick a home that offers me a private balcony on the second floor, overlooking an interesting street. I go for a short walk, and come back to find Cocu, the landlord, on my balcony. He explains it is his favorite place in the house. "So why not?" I ask myself. With that shrugging statement, I realize that I am becoming Cubanized. Boundaries are not that important here. I no longer fuss when Celeste spends half her time in my part of the duplex, and barges in enthusiastically without knocking. I used to try to get her to knock first. She "forgets."

Trinidad turns out to be a shabby sort of city even though my guide book compares it to Guanajuato, Mexico. Goodness! My recollection of Guanajuato is very steep hills, whereas these are quite modest, and spring-like weather instead of so hot you could fall down dead in thirty feet. I don't remember Guanajuato shabby, though I haven't been there in many years. There are several uninteresting museums here, old houses filled with Spanish antiques and firearms.

Cocu's family consists of four dumpy old ladies, one blind, one diabetic and unable to walk, and two who shuffle about, half-heartedly cleaning but mostly watching Novelas (soap operas). They are all sisters who once had their own husbands and families. Cocu is the only surviving husband; I don't know which of the sisters is his wife.

He is lean, gallant, lively, brings me beer, makes breakfast, usurps my bedroom balcony, and invites me to go to a dance with him this Sunday afternoon. The women are in full agreement with his invitation, as none of them dance. I don't either, I say, but he answers, "Not to worry. This is a traditional Cuban dance party, and you must see it."

For the occasion, he wears a loud guayabera (shirt) and a natty panama hat. We walk down the street to a shaded courtyard, where about seventy-five people, couples and singles, sit in folding chairs along the walls, waiting for the music to begin. There is no one here under fifty, and many are about my age. The band is warming up. Cocu finds me a seat and introduces me as "My friend, an American," as people lean over to kiss my cheek. He asks loudly, "Where are the drinks?" Others are asking the same question. A large, plump woman moves to the center of the courtyard, claps for attention, and announces that no alcohol is to be served at this dance. "Who made that stupid rule?" asks Cocu. The man sitting at my left, already well lit, says portentously, "There cannot be a dance without alcohol." Cocu shrugs, disappears, and returns with a large tumbler of amber rum. All drink from the tumbler, including members of the orchestra. Other men vanish, to return with more tumblers. They may not be serving rum, but no one goes without.

The music starts with a fine, fast samba. Cocu flicks his wrist toward a woman, who stands up and moves toward him. All of the men choose partners with the same wrist movement. Cocu is very good and so is his partner. Men ask me to dance and I decline. I thoroughly enjoy watching.

I treat myself to dinner at the Trinidad Colonial, an elegant old mansion. Fine shrimp al diablo. An accomplished middle-aged black violinist alternates with a young white man who plays classical guitar. Then they play together. In Spanish, the young man asks where I am from. "California." He switches to English, "Brave of you to come here." He is speaking about the US blockade, not the war. He came from Canada on vacation several years ago and "Never got around to leaving. I like Cuba." He gives me a thumbs up, and starts to play again.

The next day I go to the **Playa Ancon**, twelve kilometers from Trinidad. The snorkeling trip to a reef is a worthless waste of a day, but I spend two more days swimming in the waves and lounging about lazily. The hotel serves buffets with the best food I have had in Cuba. My balcony overlooks the sea and a tree with white blossoms that flutter like butterflies.

I return to La Habana and see Dr. Hecheverria for a final session. My legs are fine. No cramps, no pain, no "restless feet," little numbness. I tell him I'm afraid to admit that I am fine, for fear of being overheard by the Evil Eye. He smiles, but does not think the Evil Eye is my problem. "Don't stay away so long this year. Come back sooner." When I return from his office, I learn from Celeste that the US has started the war against Iraq. She is watching the bombings on TV, and the war protestors all over the world, including San Francisco. I try to recognize friends, but the San Francisco clips last only an instant. Bush has told the Iraqis "We are coming to help you. Do not destroy your oil wells." He told Americans, "They will welcome us with roses!"

I go back to my apartment and refuse to watch more, even when Celeste yells that there are new scenes of San Francisco protesters. I feel dead, soul-wounded, the way I imagine a woman would feel on learning that she is married to a serial killer. All day Celeste rants and watches the war, while I cry.

A Canadian friend, who has lived here with her American husband for more than twenty-five years, gives me a farewell lobster dinner. Two years ago, her husband suffered a very damaging stroke and is still scarcely able to communicate. Before his accident he was head of the US news bureau in Cuba. He would certainly oppose this war. She keeps the TV off, because at this point in his life he doesn't need to know what the US is doing.

The next night Celeste also cooks lobster, and invites Rivas to join us. We keep from talking about the war by talking instead about past lovers, grown children, and grandchildren.

I am leaving Cuba two weeks early, to get yellow fever vaccine before I go to the Amazon. I tell Celeste I will see her February 6, 2004.

Hotels and private homes cannot be booked from the US. Come to Cuba and find your own.

A CUBAN PSYCHIATRIST

We are studying dream work, and he volunteers a dream he has dreamt several times: "I am on the top deck of a huge cruise ship. The ship is totally white. It's new and very beautiful. It has more decks than any real ocean liner, maybe twenty or more. I am very high, on the tip of the bow. The boat is cruising along the coast of Europe. First I am seeing towns in Spain. Then we are cruising along France, I think. I see a village where all the roofs are of gleaming tile. It is very beautiful, and even though I am so high above the cities, I can see everything perfectly. I don't always know exactly where we are; somewhere along the coast of Europe, perhaps Denmark or Sweden, perhaps England. It is a wonderful dream."

As a child, he lived in a one-room apartment on the sixth floor of a building in the slums of Havana. Up to twelve people shared the small room, including his parents and himself. All slept together on the floor. There was only one outdoor toilet for the entire building. On the first floor was a terrible bar for sailors and marines. The music played loudly most of night, and prostitutes were always outside on the street and in the bar, soliciting. He used to see them being sexually abused and beaten by their pimps and by drunken US Marines.

His mother had TB, and from early childhood he would need to get her to the hospital when she was coughing hard and bleeding. His father was a longshoreman, who was paid less than a living wage. When he was twelve, his mother had an especially serious attack, and afterwards he told his father they had to move to a better place, where his mother could rest. They needed an apartment of their own. His father said it was impossible, but he kept arguing. When his father said he didn't know where there were any apartments, he went apartment hunting, found a two-room apartment that he knew would be quiet and away from the dust and prostitutes, took his father to see it, and they moved there. To pay the rent for this apartment, his father had to take a second job, as night watchman. His mother got better but not well.

Both of his parents wanted him to succeed in school, and he did. He says he had a very happy childhood, playing with small cars and airplanes he made from scraps, and wandering the water-front. They were a family who loved each other.

At sixteen, he volunteered to be secretary to one of the anti-Batista leaders. The former secretary had been tortured and murdered by the Batistas. When the revolution ended, he learned that his own name was on the death list of the Batista forces. For him, the revolution succeeded just in time. He signed up for the Literacy Brigade, and taught reading and writing to children who lived in the mountains, far from any school. Later, in medical school, he arranged for his mother to receive surgery that cured her tuberculosis.

Today he is an officer in the Cuban Army and a psychiatrist; his days are over-full. He sees patients, consults, lectures, teaches psychiatry, attends staff meetings and writes reports, all day and half the night. When he should be off duty, he is often called back. Yesterday, his beeper sounded just as a party was starting. "Sorry, I have to go to the hospital. There's an eighty-six-year-old woman who wants to kill herself because she believes she caused her nephew's heart attack. She's very agitated, and I need to help her calm down." This particular night, he will have to bicycle to his home when he finishes working, because his car has broken down again.

I wonder if he notices three things: 1. He works about the same hours his father worked. 2. As in his childhood, he is unendingly "on call" for adults who need him. 3. He is not as good to himself as he is to others.

He lives like most professionals in Cuba, on little money. His salary is $35 a month. He is sixty-one, divorced, has a government-issued twenty-year-old car and the gas to drive it, a bedroom in a government-owned home with eight other physicians, and government-issued meals. He can, when he takes the time, treat himself to world-class ballet, opera, symphonies, baseball, and movies for about ten cents a ticket. Ice-cream in the city park costs four cents.

Clothes are very cheap, and this year people are dressing conservatively. Latex in wild colors is no long fashionable. I think the reason is that everyone now has access to television, so they dress like people in other countries. Doctors, such as this psychiatrist, have always dressed conservatively and often wear their military uniforms.

He is on national and international psychiatric committees, hosts conferences inside, Cuba, and occasionally is sent to a conference outside Cuba. He is very positive about Castro and communism. He told me his father was even more proud of his being an officer in the Army of the Revolution than he was of his being a psychiatrist.

His life is rich. He is a happy man who is respected and loved by a great many people.

And sometimes he dreams of a white ship.

PERU

Les Kadis, Ruth McClendon, and solo

I go to Peru two weeks early, a result of luck, poor planning, and poorer memory. Six months ago I signed up for an Amazon cruise with friends, but kept procrastinating about getting a vaccination against yellow fever. I could have gotten it in San Francisco in January, but forgot about it in my excitement to get back to Mexico and Cuba. Last week my physician friend Dr. Rivas and I spent one of his precious free days driving from hospital to hospital in Cuba, looking for yellow-fever vaccine, but there was none to spare. Cuba's meager supply is being saved for medical personnel leaving on two-year assignments to areas of Africa and South America, and for Cuban fishermen who may encounter mosquitoes along the Central American coast.

I have to be vaccinated at least fourteen days prior to any encounter with the dread mosquitoes. My plane ticket, Cancun to Lima, gets me to Lima the day before the Amazon trip, and is written in stone. It will cost almost $800 to change it, says the airline. Air Cubano changes my Havana to Cancun ticket without charge, so I leave Cuba two weeks early to search in Cancun.

At every hospital and clinic I am told, "The vaccine is not available here, but go to…" I am assured I will find it at the next hospital, the clinic for foreigners, the "other clinic" two blocks away, the one across town. It seems that Mexicans are congenitally unable to give bad news. They tell me everything except the truth, that my quest is hopeless. There is no yellow fever vaccine in all of Cancun and probably hasn't been for the fifty-some years that Cancun has existed, simply because there has never been yellow fever in Cancun

I feel hopeless. I imagine writing a book entitled: I Am Too Old For This! I *am* too old for this. It is incredibly hot, I am discouraged and panicky, and there is nobody to help me decide what to do. Cancel the Amazon tour and go back to California to sit in front of a TV, which is what old ladies should do? I hate TV, and my friends are meeting me in Lima. Stay with friends at Isla Mujeres (near Cancun), and then fly to Lima the day before the Amazon trip and risk dying of yellow fever in a far-off jungle? Rivas has already told me that death by yellow fever isn't nice.

In desperation I drag my suitcase back to the airport and, eyes tearing up, tell my problem to a very lovely woman behind the airline counter. My only hope is an immediate flight to Lima, where the vaccine is available. She does something magical on her computer, writes me a boarding pass for this afternoon's flight, and charges only an additional $8.75. Not the $800 she is supposed to charge. "You can always go stand-by without paying extra for changes," she says. Of course! How could I have forgotten one of the best deals in flying! I overnight in Mexico City, arrive in Lima the next day, and get the vaccination at the Children's Clinic there. Now I have two extra weeks serendipity. I will spend the time seeing more of Peru. I am no longer saying, "I Am Too Old For This."

Travel *Tips: If you want to leave an area early, ask the day before if the plane has empty seats. Then go to the airport on the day of the flight and fly stand-by without an extra charge. (I have just been told that many airlines charge extra for stand-by tickets. Nothing about airlines can be guaranteed.)*

I scan a Peruvian travel book, and decide to go to the Collca Canyon to see condors, and next to Nazca to see the near-miraculous line drawings in the desert. (I went to Cuzco and Machu Picchu twenty years ago with my sister Bette.)

I fly to **Arequipa,** a town whose buildings are made of soft, pearl-like blocks of volcanic rock. It reminds me of Oaxaca, Mexico, with its plaza in the center, the cathedral on one side, and on the other sides colonial buildings now converted into stores and restaurants. I walk through the plaza and up two flights of stairs to have lunch on a balcony overlooking the plaza. As I am eating, an anti-US demonstration appears below, winding around the plaza, closing traffic in all directions. The demonstrators have built an effigy of Bush sitting on a warhead, with swastikas on his shirt and an Uncle Sam top hat. Their signs read, "Down with Imperialism" and "Stop the Killing." Other demonstrators, self-identified young socialists, carry huge photos of Che Guevara as well as anti-war and anti-imperialism signs. When I finish lunch, I walk among them. They tell me they are demonstrating daily, and that today's group is small. "Weekends we have big crowds."

A block down the street from the plaza is the Museum of Textiles, with weavings and clothing from pre-Incan and Incan times, plus copies of meticulously drawn sketches of Indian life, by a seventeenth century chronicler. An enthusiastic young woman takes the small entrance fee and then serves as guide. I am the only visitor. She shows me samples of the various wools, and explains that vicuna was reserved for decorating the garments of the elite and was worn only for special ceremonies. Alpaca was also used for the elite, while llama wool, cotton, and even grasses woven into llama wool, were for ordinary people. Indian men wore long, very wide pullovers and scratchy woolen loincloths. Women wore the same type of pullover, plus woven skirts and no underpants. Also on display are baskets, bags, and mats made from sedges, rushes, and grasses. I remember the old rhyme, "Sedges have edges and rushes have none, and grasses like asses have holes." I do not attempt to translate this to the guide.

There isn't much else to see in Arequipa, so I visit Santa Catalina convent, founded in 1579, and still an active, cloistered convent of about thirty buildings, spread out over several acres, volcanic white, pearl-like, or painted in bright blue, red, rust, or orange. Mixed together are new and old buildings, and ruins. This is earthquake country. Whenever a building collapsed, it was left as rubble, and a new one was built beside the rubble. The over-all effect, in spite of the ruins, is both picturesque and jolly, and not at all what I expect in a monastery. Only the current cloister is off limits. The rest is a sprawling museum of old statues, over 400 religious paintings, beds, dressers, spinning wheels, ancient ovens, cooking utensils from the sixteenth century, even an ancient shallow pool in which the sisters bathed together.

A sign near the off-limits section where the current sisters live, explains that their mission is love, and their prayers of love are for all the worlds' people.

La Casa De Mi Abuela (the home of my grandmother), ($20 a night, with gardens and very small swimming pool.)

I found this hotel by asking at the airport. As soon as I reached the hotel and knew I liked it, I asked the woman at the front desk to recommend a travel agent. She told me to use the one next door but "be sure to ask for Cecilia. The young girls don't know anything."

Cecilia and I discussed all the options in the area; I bought a tour to Collca and a ticket on a special first-class bus to Nazca. She recommended that I buy it immediately to get the front seat. Then she phoned Nazca to get me a seat on a plane to fly over the Nazca lines. I was set.

Travel Tips: don't shy away from a trip that is planned "on the spot." It is easy and often inexpensive. To book this trip from the United States would cost much more, and the booking agent would not know the area.

The tour to Collca leaves at 5:30 A.M., so that we can see the mountaintops at their bright, early morning best. Indians consider these mountains to be gods who watch over them and bring them what they need. Our guide, Geraldo, says that they revere the actual mountains, not spirits within the mountains. They talk directly to the mountains and hear the mountains' replies. As they converse, they pile small stones vertically into cairns and towers. A tower may be only three stones high or may be an elaborate structure of more than one hundred stones stacked carefully together. These stones, piled by Indians over many years, now cover several acres of land and look like strange, miniature cities.

They also carved rocks to resemble the terraces they built on the mountains, and drilled holes in the rocks for offerings of food and animal blood. Indians still use these same rocks when they pray. The oldest known inhabitants of this land, the Paracans, elongated babies' skulls by binding and exerting pressure on their heads while the bones were still soft, to make their tribe look more like the mountains they worshipped. The mountains are truly magnificent. No wonder they are considered gods.

We pass many Incas on the road, carrying their potato harvest in huge bulky sacks on their backs or on loaded burros. Others are walking with their herds of goats, sheep, or cows. There are only a few cars and trucks. Between the river canyon and the mountaintops are the famous terraces, cut by hand through the ages. The highest on the mountains were built by the Paracans and other ancient tribes, next high by the Incas. The early terraces were abandoned in the 1600s, when over half the Indian population was killed or died of diseases after being forced into slavery by the Spaniards to build their cities and work their mines. All terraces were so well constructed that they are still intact. The newer terraces are on our level and below us, close to the river. Today there is much activity, harvesting the potato crop.

We ride higher into the mountains to the barren land of the vicuna, alpaca, and llama, those lovely, delicate-appearing animals who walk so daintily over the rocky mountainsides. The vicunas are a protected species whose area has been designated a national park. They are delightful, brown and white, smaller than llamas, and sufficiently tame to come within a few feet of us. They can be sheared only three times in a lifetime. Inca specialists are hired to corral them, shear them quickly, mark their ears with the date of the shearing, and release them. A sweater made of vicuna would cost about $1,500, Geraldo says. Vicunas, alpacas, and llamas live about eighteen years.

Alpacas and llamas come in a variety of colors, from black to gray and from dark brown to beige to white. The easiest way to tell them apart is to look at their tails. An alpaca tail grows tight against the animal's butt, whereas llama tails curve away from their bodies in an open semicircle. This is the sort of information I record studiously, like the difference between frogs and toads, and rarely remember. Alpacas may be killed for meat before they reach two years of age; after that, they are useful only for their wool, which is harvested yearly. Llamas are beasts of burden, their wool, also, is harvested yearly, and they are never eaten. Llama and alpaca herds are privately owned. In the daytime they are watched over by quite young boys and their dogs. At sunset they are herded into a grassy corral where they feast and sleep.

One herder, an adorable, very small eight-year-old, comes up to our van to ask if our group wants to exchange pens or fruit for photographs of himself and his llamas. He especially likes bananas, he says. He collects several and puts them aside, perhaps to share with his family.

The road climbs to 15,000 feet. I feel a bit dizzy and short of breath, so when we stop at a cafeteria at the top of the grade, instead of the offered coca tea, which in the past I have found to be totally non-helpful, I buy and chew coca leaves Indian style; that is, wrapped around a piece of hard ash. I did this with my sister Bette when climbing around Machu Picchu twenty years ago. To absorb the coca efficiently, saliva needs alkali, too. Baking soda, ash, or limestone will serve this purpose. In a few minutes I feel better. (Supposedly, coca leaves, which are non-addictive, combined with the ash from a local plant, allow the red corpuscles to carry more oxygen.) Andes Indians

146

chew coca constantly. It is very rich in vitamins and minerals, which they need and cannot get from other foods in their diet. The Indians will suffer and may die if we are successful in destroying their coca plants, something both the US and Latin American countries seemingly ignore.

As we continue up the mountains, we sight Andean geese, Buzzer eagles, little Andean flickers, and the wonderful pink Andean flamingos that live on a small, high river and pond, where for some strange reason there are enough very tiny shrimp to sustain them and give their feathers the wonderful pink color that all shrimp-eating flamingos attain. It is strange to see these usually tropical birds living in the cold, clear heights of the Andes. How lucky for them that people in the Andes don't consider the shrimp a food for humans.

We descend slowly to a region of terraces that look like an artist's giant palette, rising from the Collca river to above our road: brilliant yellow barley, reddish-brown quinoa cereal, green corn stalks, lavender potato flowers, even squares of commercial flowers in all colors.

Geraldo tells us that the potato is a New World vegetable, which the Spaniards brought back to Spain as plants. They knew nothing about cooking potatoes, being conquerors rather than housewives, so didn't get the word out that the flower is poisonous. People became ill, so the Spanish government banned the importation of potatoes. One hundred years later, somebody said, "Well, duh. Eat the potato, stupid. Not the flower."

We arrive at **Chivay** and go immediately to the spa, a large outdoor pool surrounded on three sides by sheer, rock mountains, higher, snow-capped mountains behind them, and the fast flowing, white-water Collca river below. It is wildly beautiful! As I soak in the hot water, the sun sets, a soft rain begins, and all around me I see the darkening mountains through a lovely mist.

We start out again at 5:30 A.M. to reach the lookout at the **Collca** canyon just as the condors are leaving their nests. Bob Goulding said that every trip became in my mind "the trip of a lifetime." It isn't the trips. It is the moments - the double click, five star, shining, unforgettable moments:

Twelve condors soar, barely over our heads. They glide and dip, their wings white on top and black on the underside. They glide below us, a dazzling white, and above us, jet black against the clear blue sky, with eight to ten foot wingspans. Their bodies and heads are black, with white like a flyer's scarf around their necks. They are magnificent, breathtaking, and so close we see clearly their fierce talons and bright, peering eyes. They seem to fly, like horses run, for the sheer joy of it. Condors, like vultures, eat carrion, and find the dead by seeing the gases of putrefaction that are invisible to us.

Chivay is a small Indian town where I decide to spend another night, so say good-bye to the others. I'll return the next day by public bus. I walk around the market, admiring the women. They are splendid, in stiff white underskirts and full, colored cotton overskirts with wide embroidered stripes in every color imaginable. Some wear a third skirt of a different color, open in front and brightly embroidered. Their blouses, vests, and wide belts are also embroidered, with birds, flowers, and geometric designs. The women are as round and highly decorated as Christmas tree ornaments. Perched on top of their black, plaited hair is either an embroidered hat, cowboy style; a traditional black fedora; or a hat I have never seen before, round, snug against the hair, soft-brimmed, and alive with bright embroidery of flowers and birds. I love their clothes, and wish San Franciscan women would let themselves be dressed so colorfully, instead of believing that chic equals black. Wouldn't it be exciting if everyone strode down Market Street in full color and roundness!

The women's teenage daughters already have voluptuous figures, wear very tight jeans and sweaters, and lounge about, looking modern. Very soon, voluptuousness will turn to obesity, and they'll look like their mothers.

I watch a man embroider a skirt, using a treadle machine with a detachable electric motor. The multicolored designs appear as if by magic on the bright red skirt. He takes off the motor, re-threads the machine with heavy gold and silver threads, and embroiders on top of the other embroidery, this time using only the treadle. He explains that the motor can't handle the heavier threads. In only a few minutes the skirt is finished.

Early in the morning, I go to the spa again. This time it is full of local Indians, most of them sitting in the indoor pool. They live among the magnificent mountains all their lives, so I suppose the indoor pool seems more luxurious. As locals, they pay only a few cents for this wonderful beginning to Sunday. The air is crisp and totally clear, and the mountains, their snow-decked gods, are worthy of adoration.

I go to the plaza beside the church. Mass has ended, so whole families are now sitting in the park. It has stone benches, a stone fountain, grass, many bisecting paths, and is surrounded by flowers, trees, and the mountains. Church bells are still ringing; tower bells, louder and not musical, boom out the hour and quarter hour, and Peruvian popular music blares continuously from amplifiers on each corner. A bird repeats sharp, long whistles. Some of the children wear white Communion dresses, and sit properly. Others chase each other or play a game like checkers, using bottle tops. A small group of German backpackers are lying on the grass. An Incan man takes off his sandals to wash his feet in the fountain. The brightly embroidered women pass out candies to their children and indulge themselves.

Five young boys, probably about nine years old, approach me shyly. Usually children begin by asking my name and age, and then gasp as they learn that I am the oldest person they have ever met. Today the question is, "Where are you from?" "California. Los Estados Unidos." They all look solemn. "Do you know about the war?" When I tell them I do know and I hate the war, they rush to agree. "There were dead children." "One has no head." "We saw a dead mother." TV has reached even this seemingly isolated village.

A woman, Indian but dressed in Western clothes, is sitting nearby. She says she is a local teacher, and volunteers that this is the children's first experience of war, as the Sendero Luminoso (Maoist group) were not in this area. International TV is quite new here. I tell her I haven't seen TV recently. She describes scenes of mutilated corpses, and U.S. military bragging about winning. "We are a Catholic country. Like the Pope, we are against what you are doing," I tell her that most people in the United States are also against this war. Does she know that the Peruvian president has come out in favor of the war? She hates the new president, and hopes he'll be thrown out of office. She doesn't like Fujimura either, "but he did more for the people." She says, "Your president Bush has our president in a stranglehold." She puts her hands around her own neck, demonstrating what she is saying. I heard these same words and saw the same gesture in Cancun and Arequipa.

Changing the subject, she asks if I would like to go with her this Sunday afternoon to watch horse, burro, bicycle, and foot races. It sounds fun, but I have to return to Arequipa, because I've already bought a ticket on tonight's bus to Nazca. I leave the park, and return to Arequipa by public bus.

Hotel Rumillaqta, quite new, about $60. I am told there is a fine inn just fifteen minutes away in a town called Copiague, on nobody's map.

That evening I board the 10:00 P.M. special to Nazca, a first class, double-decker. I have seat number 1A, above the driver. I put my suitcase on top of the footrest, pull out my favorite travel luxury, a down pillow, and make a bed. It is more comfortable than a business class plane seat. I take a sleeping pill, and wake up eight hours later in Nazca.

The famous Nazca lines, geometric figures and abstract animals up to 1,000 feet long, are scratched into the arid crust of the desert with mathematical precision. They were made more than 2,000 years ago. How and why are still mysteries. Those who have studied them have various theories: it is a gigantic zodiac; imaginative representations of the major constellations; a calendar for knowing times for planting; deities to be worshipped. A few people still espouse the discredited and demeaning belief that ancient Indians could not have had the ability to draw such straight and beautiful lines, so extraterritorial folks must have swooped to earth and drawn them.

It is early morning and the heat is already unendurable. I have never been in worse heat except for a couple of days in Hanoi once. To get my reserved seat on a four-person plane that flies over the drawings, I have to push and shove, shout that I have reservations, damn it, and then wait almost an hour in line. I am too excited to believe my mantra, "I Am Too Old For This", but do imagine myself writing another still-to-be-started book, "If I Were In Charge!" At the very least, places like this would be *organized*. People would sit in air-conditioned comfort when they have to wait. All of this is insignificant. If I were in charge, there would be no war.

It is a triumph that I am flying at all. In the past I was too phobic to ride in a plane without a back-up pilot. What if the only pilot has a heart attack? My turn finally comes, and I climb into the seat where the second pilot belongs. The hell with phobias. This is important. We take off and I begin to see the lines, eerie, beautiful, mesmerizing. A monkey with a tail like a Fourth of July pinwheel. A bird, created in wonderful parallel lines of wings, tail, and splayed feet; another bird with a pelican's beak. A tarantula. An elongated lizard. All these gigantic geoglyphs, as they are called, are bisected by non-parallel lines that bring the whole together. It is intensely modern art, kilometers long. We see each part of the whole, as we circle back and forth, but the whole is too vast to see in its entirety even from the air. I am awed. Afterwards, I feel reverence toward whoever conceived the grand design, and had it made so well that it is still like new here in this desert.

When the plane lands, I am still euphoric. That explains my craziness: I agree to take a tour of graves and conduits, in spite of the heat.

Graves: the ancient graves were dug about ten feet into the ground and lined with stones. The bodies, stretched out or bound into a tight fetal ball, were wrapped in fine textiles and buried with whatever the people thought would be useful in the next life: pots, pans, jars of seeds, plus the gold and silver ornaments and jewelry that are now in museums. People were buried with killed and wrapped pet dogs, who supposedly guided them to the first level of the universe, where the sun and moon and principal spirits live. (The second level is the earth and the third is under the earth where monsters live.) Because of the dryness of the desert, even soft tissue mummified naturally, including scalps with long elaborate hairdos. Enough bodies are left unwrapped in open graves to interest tourists.

Aqueducts and conduits: Paracan Indians made elaborate underground conduits to bring subterranean water to their fields. This is a remarkable and admirable engineering feat, on a par with the Roman system of aqueducts, and equally boring except perhaps to engineers. In this heat even an engineer might have to feign enthusiasm.

I ride a first-class bus another four hours toward Lima, this time headed for three days of self-indulgence at the hotel Las Dunas in **Ica**. It is built on a large oasis at the foot of a high sand dune, with big swimming pool, second pool with water slide, tennis, golf, disco, skis for riding down the dune, lots of birds, elegant flowers, a green lawn kept trimmed by wandering alpacas, and a collection of pre-Inca pottery that would put most museums to shame. The food is first-class.

I walk around the grounds, pet the alpacas, watch the sand skiers, swim, and read, and on the second day I run out of books. A manager takes me into her office to find more. She asks in perfect English what country I am from. Here it goes again. I tell her, and she asks very politely, "What are your opinions about the war?" "It is a horror, a disgrace." She relaxes, and tells me of the bodies of women and children that she saw on TV. I tell her that my friends, all of whom hate the war, have emailed me that they have not been shown the same film that the rest of the world has witnessed. "I am from San Francisco," I add. She congratulates me. "I watched the war protestors there. San Francisco seems to be one of your more intelligent cities."

I look at the book collection, left by not-so-intelligent people, and find nothing that I would choose. I end up with Barbara Walters' biography, even though I managed through all my stay-at-home years never to have watched her on TV. This is what happens to reading addicts. It's the equivalent of alcoholics who will resort to cooking-alcohol if there is nothing else around. I read with repulsed fascination about her friendships with Roy Cohn, Joe McCarthy, and Henry Kissinger. Other readers may be equally negative about her friendship with Fidel Castro. She is incredibly apolitical.

I recover from lovely idleness long enough to visit El Museo Regional de Ica, a small treasure house of ceramics and weavings, some 2,200 years old. Most are amazingly modernistic in design. The colors on the ceramics are so bright that they might have been painted and fired this week. A room of mummies shows the elongated heads, the hair woven into elaborate designs, some with added animal and human hair, similar to dreadlocks. Above some of these bodies are medical notes pointing out diseases that may have caused their deformities or deaths, such as arthritis, cancers, and tuberculosis. But a person can skip all that, and simply glory in the fine, very old tapestries.

Hotel Las Dunas, Ica ($100 - $200)

Lima. Reminding myself how much I do enjoy museums, I go back to Lima to be a museum glutton.

Las Americas and Swiss Hotel, chosen by our Amazon tour company, are fine at about $200 a night. Best Western is about $100. Family-run hotels are inexpensive and much more fun, I'm told.

After three very full museum days, I meet my friends, Ruth McClendon and Les Kadis, to begin our Amazon vacation. When I describe my yellow fever vaccination problems, Les, a physician, says,

"But don't you remember that you were vaccinated two years ago, before we went to Africa?" Big time duh. I remind myself that this is not necessarily a symptom of senility. I have never remembered medical details. School nurses used to complain because I didn't remember which daughter had which diseases, so each year I would make it up. One year Claudia was listed as having had measles, and the next year I listed Karen instead. Son David always knew exactly what he had had, so would advise me. School nurses like medical reports that are consistent.

The flight across the Andes, Lima to Iquitos, is clear and beautiful, with snow-white, sparkling mountains and then green jungle with the thick brown squiggles of the world's longest river, the Amazon. Other brown river-lines join it. The browns meander, turn, form half-circles, a lake, dots and dashes, the letter S backwards and forwards, as if a two-year-old god were having a fine time writing with a brown crayon on bright green paper.

We land in **Iquitos**, a dismal town strung along the Amazon, and go directly to our boat, the Amatista. It has three decks, is chunky, old fashioned, made of wood, a bit like the African Queen but larger. As soon as we are all aboard, the crew casts off and we start upstream. We'll be traveling briefly on the Amazon, then the Ucayali, the Maranon, and back to the Amazon. There are nineteen guests on board: four English couples who came on the trip together and rarely speak to the rest of us even to say "hello," plus seven Americans and four more British. Ruth McClendon, a family therapist professionally, manages to form the eleven of us into a close, fun, and very talkative group.

From the open top deck we gaze at the wide river and the jungle on either side. Though brown, the Amazon is as luminescent and many-colored as an abalone shell, and mirrors every cloud, tree, and passing dugout. The trees are lush, overgrown with vines, in a hundred shades and textures of living green. The air is so soft I feel it palpably on my skin. The boat glides slowly. Sunset turns the sky pink and gold, and is reflected on the water. We are treated to fine food and too loud music, as darkness encompasses us.

The wake-up bell rings every morning at 5:30 A.M., and by 6:00 A.M. we are in the launches for our first trip along tiny tributaries of the Amazon. We make three separate trips, early morning, late

153

morning, and sunset.

We see: *herons of all types, white necked, great blue, striated, capped, little blue; cormorants; vultures large and small; kites; hawks; eagles; a laughing falcon (and he does laugh insanely!) and other falcons; various curassows; kingfishers; and a zillion small birds.*

We spot six sloth, one so close that we can look into his vacuous eyes as he very slowly turns his head toward us and scratches his butt. It wouldn't be nice to be a sloth. A sloth has no friends. Even babies leave early, never to return. A sloth gets down from a tree every other day to defecate, changes trees perhaps once a week, eats leaves, and sleeps. When a sloth is dying, it may sink its claws so tightly into the bark of a tree that it will hang there until the fur dries and blows away, the quite minimal flesh is eaten, and only the skeleton remains, becoming part of the tree. When someone says, "Don't be a sloth," it shouldn't mean "Don't be lazy," but instead, "Don't be an isolate."

We see tiny spider monkeys, running along branches and making fantastic leaps from tree to tree. We cheer each time a monkey does not fall, and they never do. Tree iguanas lie like bumps on a branch. Pink river dolphins, who really are pink-gray, swim around our boat, diving and circling, then follow us upstream.

While we are in the launches or drinking beer on the top deck, the crew is working constantly, straightening our rooms each time we leave, cooking, waiting tables, cleaning up, and even providing the over-amplified band. A couple of the musicians play well, and gently teach the beginning drummer to keep the beat. They do all these jobs, early morning till late at night, with solicitude and cheerfulness. Although we pay a lot for this trip, the workers get very little of it.

We see monkeys with fine thick fur and long tails, like furry black cats. The highlight (for the birders) is a harpy eagle, a rare specimen that hadn't been seen by the guides for almost three years. I cheer its size and wingspan, because I can see it without binoculars. I look first with binoculars and then joyfully put them down, without feeling as if I am an anti-ornithology creep. I have trouble holding binoculars still and, besides, they tickle my eyelashes. The real birders are keeping binoculars glued to their eyes for almost half an hour, until the harpy eagle gives a shrug and flies away. Our guides, Tony and Adam, have been jumping up and down with pleasure! They spend lunch and dinnertime congratulating themselves on spotting it.

This is flood season, so the river has grown to be five miles wide. The tributaries are merely deeper paths of water amid a vast, tree-crammed sea. We can almost touch the plants, vines, and trees on either side of the launch. When the motor is turned off, we listen to bird songs, the whirr of invisible insects, the tapping of branches against each other, the crinkling of a leaf. Beauty is everywhere.

We visit an isolated, native village along the Ucayali. The guides choose a different village each week, so that the minimal goodies (this time writing pens for the school children) are passed around equally. Houses are built on poles six feet above the ground, and the ground under some of them is already a shallow lake. They need to build on land that floods, so that they will be close to the river and able to navigate during dry seasons. Chickens and pigs are kept on moored rafts beside the houses, and people go from house to house by dugout. Several children are carrying in their arms their pets: small monkeys, baby pigs, toucans, and guinea pigs. Others are carrying little brothers and sisters.

There are only a few people who appear to be over forty years old. There are fifteen married couples, who have a total of 120 children. Figure it! In spite of the birth rate, the population never increases in the village, because most of the adolescents leave for the city. The city is not a good solution, as no money is available for their schooling. Some boys learn a trade in the army, and many girls become prostitutes.

For those who remain on the river, there are celebrations in their village or in neighboring towns, where everyone eats pig meat and drinks masato, made from fermented yucca, spit, and seasonings. These fiestas give the young a chance to find partners. The village keeps in touch with the world by short wave radio and dugout travel. We are told that a public health nurse visits the village routinely to look for diseases, do first aid, and teach birth control. Obviously, the teaching of birth control has not been successful.

While we explore the village, Adam takes the children aside to plan a program. When they are ready, we are led to the community center, open-air with thatched roof and benches, on a slight hill and therefore dry. All adults in the village sit with us. Adam marches the children into the center, and directs an "Arms up," "Attention," "At ease" drill while they giggle wildly. He's taught them a song, "How are you, my friends?" to which we respond, "Muy bien, amigos," etc. The children and parents sing the Peruvian National Anthem. Adam asks if one of us has a song to sing, and one of the British does a fine "Teensy weensy spider," with Adam translating. Everyone cheers, and she does it for them several times. I find this a very sad afternoon, because of the overwhelming poverty and lack of a way to escape it.

In the early evening, the group goes again by launch for a four-hour trip to see more birds and monkeys. The Amatista will be traveling upstream, and I decide to spend the time on a lounge chair on the deck, reading and watching this green world go by. Dugouts drift downstream, sometimes with a single man or woman aboard, sometimes with whole families. Dead trees and branches drift by, a few with enough bright green, clinging vegetation to be floating islands.

I watch a bright red sun sink slowly, giving the river a sheen of red and gold. The sky is vast and full of activity. Downstream, lightning flashes and the sky is dark. Ahead is the sunset, while to the left, clouds hang softly, just barely tinted blue and lavender. The sun swells and is gone. All the clouds turn briefly pink, change to lavender, then purple. Lightning flashes jaggedly across more of the sky. A crewmember brings me a beer and asks if I'd like some fruit.

The group returns, and we have another of the cook's tasty dinners. He is very capable, managing to serve meat, a vegetarian dish, and freshly caught fish at every meal. Many of the vegetables, as well as the fish, are bought locally. There are always freshly squeezed local juices, often new to us. Desserts are pastries and ice cream. Crew members hover around me, because I speak to them in Spanish, and, most important, I'm the oldest person on board. Age counts!

The next morning we see: *a white headed eagle (who looks much like a bald eagle) and several species of bright macaws, plus six types of monkeys: capuchins, sake, spider, squirrel, titi, and my favorite from Costa Rica, the red howlers, who are so scrawny yet roar so loudly.* Caiman are lined up on the bank, and, big hurrah for this, we finally see a family of four capybaras, who look like baby hippos with their short legs and rounded heads. They are three to five feet long, the world's largest rodents. Their natural enemies are caiman and jaguars; all three, persecutors and prey, are most endangered by their common enemy, man. The jaguars have been hunted to extinction in these parts, and the locals kill both caiman and capybaras for food.

For some time now we have been advised that today is the day of the big Piranha Fishing Contest, and many of us have wavered. Do we want to fish? I fished with my father in childhood for sunfish, walleyed pike, bass, and catfish; twenty-five years later, I fished more reluctantly with my children; and twenty years after that, I waited riverside while Bob Goulding cast for trout. I am not interested in today's outing. One of the English agrees with me. He has never been fishing in his life, or played cricket or rugby, he says. I mention that some of the world's best trout streams are in England. "I was obviously born in the wrong country," he replies.

At least half of our group decides to stay on the Amatista, but at the last minute, amid sighs and complaints, we all go. After all, there is something about fishing for piranhas, we decide. A great rivalry has built up between our guides: Whose boat will bring in the most fish? Tony searches for the perfect spot, we drop anchor, and everyone is given a bamboo pole, line, and baited hook. We hear a roar from the other launch, "Got one!" They are cheering mightily.

I feel a fish on my hook, and instantly acquire a deep loathing for what I am doing. I've outgrown killing fish, which does not put me on a very high ethical plane, since I still eat them. I hold the pole quietly until there is no more movement, and bring up the line. The bait is gone and so is the fish, as I expected. I give back my pole, and watch the others.

More cheers from the other launch. Tony is upset. He beats the water hard and repeatedly, to get the fish to pay attention and look for the bait, which is not the way I was taught to fish. My father wouldn't even let us talk, for fear the fish would hear and swim away. If the piranhas would simply rise a bit in the water, Tony could beat them to death.

Ruth yells, "Come quick, hurry, you promised to help me!" as a piranha flies over our heads on the end of her line. Tony takes it off her hook. It's the size of a small sunfish but with two rows of deadly-looking teeth. Ruth suggests Tony throw the fish overboard, so it can live.

The other passengers in our boat have caught the fever. They try, lose their bait, try again, lose their bait again. And again. And again. Below us, the piranhas are having a fine meal of bait. Tony catches a catfish that looks just like a catfish anywhere. Nothing else of significance happens on our launch, as time drags by.

The cheers from the next boat continue. We find out later that they have a real fisherman aboard, who knows how to hook fish. He catches twelve. As the launches start back, pink dolphin frolic around us, circling our boats and leaping high into the air. One of their favorite foods is piranhas, which they eat teeth and all. I think they are getting ready for a feast.

The piranhas and catfish are served us for dinner. They are full of small, nasty bones and have almost no meat. Fortunately, that is not the only entree.

A BRIEF HISTORY OF THE AMAZON from the two guides: Viru (Peru) means "The land of riches" in Quechuan, the language of the Incas, who conquered all of Peru except for the Amazon region. Every time they advanced into the jungle, their warriors disappeared forever. In the Amazon there were over 500 separate tribes with their own languages, cultures, and their own rivers. Some mostly fished and others also hunted with poison spears. The Dubaros shrunk heads, by removing the scalp from the dead person, including the hair, and boiling it in a special solution of tannic acid and herbs. After the skin had shrunk sufficiently, they wrapped it around a stone and dried it in the shape of the stone.

Since they couldn't conquer the river tribes, the Incas adopted a policy of trade rather than war. They bartered gold, silver, and beautiful stones, such as jade, for monkeys, fruits, and feathers. The Nazca lines include a monkey, which was only indigenous to the jungle.

When the Spaniards conquered the Incas, the Incas lost their culture, their heritage, and were reduced to the status of slaves. They have never recovered their status and self-esteem. The Indians of the Amazon maintained their freedom for 300 additional years, even though the Spaniards sent thousands of soldiers, adventurers, outlaws, and priests to conquer them.

Missionaries arrived in Iquitos in the 1820s, and by 1824 the Spaniards had penetrated the rain forest. In 1872 rubber plantations sprang up, and Indians from all the tribes were enslaved. To terrify them into working harder, those who failed to meet their daily quota were tied to fire-ant hills, beaten, maimed, and killed in front of the rest of the slaves. This continued for forty years, until the market for Amazon rubber collapsed.

The British then used the Indians as slaves to harvest fine hardwoods, soft woods for making chlorine, and ivory palm for buttons. In 1970 the oil industry boomed, then collapsed in 1995. Most of the original indigenous population along the Amazon is now dead. Those in the Amazon villages today are mestizos, a mixture of Caucasian and Indian.

Tony wants us to know that of all the exploiters, the Spaniards were the most cruel. He will always hate them and their descendants.

In the morning we stop briefly to admire a bed of water lilies with extra-ordinary leaves over three feet in diameter, absolutely round, pea-green, with dark red, curled up edges. They resemble oversize, beautiful plates. In the water between these plates are the plants' white, luminous flowers. They are fertilized by small beetles that crawl inside the flowers and drink the nectar. In the evening the flowers close on them, and shower them with dust-like, male seeds. The next morning the beetles, still sprinkled with seeds, crawl to another flower and fertilize it. So says Tony. I like that story, even if it may lack scientific accuracy. For instance, can a flower be female by day and male by night? I think there are ramifications here that I will not dwell on.

We visit a local shaman and then a handicraft market. Tony translates with enthusiasm as the shaman explains his concoctions for various illnesses, acute and chronic. He gives himself the first dose and uses his own reactions to assess how it will affect a patient. He ends his lecture with a personal benediction for each, which is supposed to induce calmness and enrich our lives. One by one he blows tobacco smoke in our hair, does special incantations, and ends by making the sign of the cross. I find this entire ritual tedious. He strikes me as a charlatan. Especially, I don't want tobacco smoke in my hair.

The handicraft market is set up by a dozen people who are selling animal and bird carvings and beads. It's the first opportunity the passengers have had to buy, and they do. We go back to the Amatista and sail to the confluence of the three major rivers, Amazon, Maranon, and Ucayali, then head up the Maranon to a small town, Nauta, to see turtles. The town has TV. How do I know? Children ask where I am from, and then say bluntly, "You killed children and their mothers." I decide this is the last time I will admit my nationality. The turtles are large and turtley.

On the final day we visit a new lodge which Jungle Expeditions is opening in January. It's attractive, away from the flood zone, and has its own swimming lake with canoes and dugouts. Its major claim to fame is the "Canopy Walk," a swaying bridge, built in three long, separated segments. Unfortunately, fire ants have captured the railings, so we are told to walk very carefully. Each time the bridge sways, I am afraid of being thrown against these tiny dragons. This makes for a decidedly half-hearted love of the adventure, though the trees below us are beautiful. We see a snake and a bright red and green poisonous frog.

We leave for Lima. I wish I could stay aboard for a second trip. I'd skip the shaman, the villages, and sit like a queen watching the jungle go by. I would revisit happily all the birds and animals.

A GUIDE ON THE AMAZON

His name is Adam; he is an Indian, which he says is not a good word to use around here, as Indians are considered inferior by the mestizos who live in Iquitos. He is a member of a small tribe, the Witotos*, who live on a tiny tributary of the Amazon, the Tigres. There never were tigers in these parts, but it was the name given to black pumas that came to the village at night from time to time, when he was a child, to eat their dogs, chickens, and small pigs. He remembers seeing them only rarely in daylight.

His mother was raped by a married man who lived in the village. She was barely thirteen when he was born in 1971. His grandmother sent his mother to Iquitos to school, while she raised Adam. Life in the village was easy. Everyone was his friend. "We always had enough to eat and all of us had total freedom. I learned by experience what was safe and what was dangerous. When I saw a puma, I stood still - not afraid and we'd look at each other until it walked away." His pets included orphaned monkeys, dogs, baby pigs, toucans, and parrots. He especially loved birds. He became a bird watcher and began learning their Indian and Spanish names in early childhood.

He wore shorts, occasionally a shirt, never owned a pair of shoes, but had his own dugout canoe from the time he could walk. No one taught him to swim. "It's like walking, you just do it." He fished in the Tigres and helped plant and dig the local equivalent of sweet potatoes. In addition, they ate breadfruit, bananas, chickens, monkeys, and, on rare holiday occasions, pig. His mother came to visit as often as she could.

Usually, when Adam is working as a guide, he smiles and jokes a lot, and bounces like a child when he sees a rare bird. "There it is, oh there it is!" Laughing and pointing, he is genuinely enthusiastic.

Now his face is totally serious, as he waits to be sure I get everything down. He says he feels honored that I want to write about him. I tell him that I am fascinated by what he's telling me.

His mother has always been a very special person in his life. He admires her tremendously and went to live with her when it was time for him to go to high school. She has fine handwriting, the best in Iquitos, so was hired as a calligrapher even before she finished high school. This was important work, because documents had to be both written and signed perfectly. "She taught me calligraphy." He makes several capital letters to demonstrate. "This is the best I can do. If you could see her Fs you'd know I can never be as good as she is." He got his first pair of shoes to attend school in Iquitos. "I studied very hard. I concentrated on English and learned to speak and write it well. I always wanted to be an interpreter." He grins, shrugs, and says this is something he doesn't usually tell people. "Today is true confessions, isn't it?"

After high school, he enrolled in college in Lima to become an interpreter. He found Lima overcrowded, dirty, huge, and dangerous. It was a terribly hard life. "I was beaten up and robbed twice for less than a dollar. I was so poor, I couldn't afford to lose even that much." He kept going to school and looking unsuccessfully for work. "My personal crash came when the government crashed, in 1990, when I was nineteen. There was no work. I couldn't find anything to eat. For nineteen days at age nineteen I didn't eat. It was very strange. Each night I dreamed that heaven opened up and the angels gave me food. I honestly don't know if I was dreaming or hallucinating. All this time, I kept going to school and looking for work, and after the first days, I didn't feel hungry. I became very thin. On the twentieth day a friend told me there was a letter from my mother. I opened it and found money inside. She saved my life."

Adam went to a restaurant and was smart enough to order only a little, so that he wouldn't become sick. He still had a bit of money left when he found a job in a chicken-processing plant. He worked seven days a week from 6:00 P.M. to 10:00 A.M., went to classes after work, but kept falling asleep. He had no time to study. "I spent three years working like this, trying to support myself and graduate from college, but it wasn't possible."

An older friend visited him from Iquitos and told him to give up and come back with him. "He offered me a job with Jungle Expeditions and said he'd teach me to be a guide. I already knew English well, knew the names of the birds and butterflies, and all I had to do was memorize the English words for the plants and animals." He's been a guide now for eleven years and works seven days a week with only Saturday afternoons free. He has a wife he loves very much, a five-year-old son, and another baby is due next month. They live in Iquitos. Adam says he spends Saturday afternoons playing with his son and teaching him to identify birds and to speak English. He says he turns his teaching into a game, and his son loves it.

I make the mistake of assuming that this is a success story, that working on the Amazon is a happier and more rewarding life than being an interpreter in Lima.

He says, "True confessions? It's not the life I choose. It's the life I have."

Our interview is over, and he hurries off to get the launch ready for the group's last afternoon on the Amazon. He is smiling and singing to himself as we get on the launches. When he finds and shows us a fantastic red and green, very tiny, poisonous frog, he is as excited as ever.

*"For thirty years the Witotos were tortured ferociously under the direction of the Spanish rubber barons. Of 80,000 Witoto slaves, including families, 5,000 Witotos were still alive when the rubber plantations closed down in 1910." Davis, Wade, ONE RIVER, Simon and Shuster, 1996.

PUSSER'S CAY

solo

After two weeks of sailing with family, I stay at tiny Pusser's Marina Cay for one night before moving on. I have a king-size bed in a fine cabin high on a hill, overlooking the blue sea and the string of islands beyond. All around the cabin are flowers: bougainvillea, Scottish brush, frangipani, gardenia, oleander, and cacti in bloom. The beach is white sand.

The manager tells me that he grew up in Florida, "But there are too many rules there, rules for everything. So I came here and will never go back."

"Pusser" was the English sailors' pronunciation of purser, the most important man on any ship, in charge of the money on board and the daily ration of rum. Pusser's rum is still sold here. An American couple bought the island, wrote a book of their adventures, which was made into the movie, "Two On An Island," and then left after World War II started. The island was uninhabited for twenty years, until this small inn opened in 1960.

I sit on my balcony and watch the courtship dance of two brown ground lizards with speckled legs, and then decide to swim. In the shallow water around the island I watch two bands of minnows swim in formation, crisscrossing without ever touching. I take a boat across the channel to the reef, and drift along it. I see in a single enchanted afternoon: *parrot fish with golden eyelids and little turks with pea-green horns; fan coral, yellow, lavender, purple, pink, brown, and white; big-eyed squirrel fish; anemones like teeny Christmas trees that disappear the moment I wave my hand over them, and then pop up again. And more and more.*

At sunset, I return to my balcony to watch eight pelicans dive for fish. The sunset is a brilliant rose and orange. As the sky darkens, the tropical moon makes a highway of silver across the water. The pelicans are now diving into the brightness. The stucco cabins below me turn from reddish-brown to a dull orange, the roofs fade from red to pink, and the pea green trim remains exactly the same color as the horns of the truk fish.

I go to the outdoor bar, where a Caribbean cowboy sings, "Come back, girl, wipe the tears from my eyes." The air is soft. A few stars challenge the moon, popping into the sky quickly, and they remind me of the white anemone in the sea. A local woman says that on moonless nights the whole sky is alive with stars.

We have a beer together, and she tells me she wishes she could learn to swim. Boys, she says, just run out of their homes and jump into the water, but girls are protected, kept at home and watched over. She insists it is now too late to learn, and because I am leaving tomorrow I can't offer to teach her. I would guess she is about twenty years old. She says that next time I am in the area I should go to St. Vincent island, her home. "It is the best island of them all. There's more of everything. Flowers, fruit, fruit trees. And people are so friendly. You'd be part of the island from the day you arrive." Some day I will go there, I tell her.

Pusser's Cay, ($150 a night, Maximum 16 guests.) Yachts tie up in the harbor and tour boats bring customers for meals.

YUCATAN PENINSULA

solo

Valladolid. The air is soft and perfumed with gardenias. In the center of town is an old-fashioned, colonial style hotel beside a central plaza, where already this morning Mayan women have arranged colorful piles of lemons, tomatoes, eggplant, onions, and blouses and skirts just like the ones they are wearing, embroidered with bright flowers, birds, and geometric designs. These are the clothes Mayan women in this area have worn for centuries, different from the all white of Isla Mujeres. The fruit and vegetable shoppers are Mayan. Tourists like me admire the clothing. If a tourist prefers a blouse a seller is wearing, she takes it off, sells it, and dons another.

I hire a cab and go to the Ek Balaam ruins, named for the great Mayan leader who built this holy city about 1,000 years ago. The ruins are huge, awesome in the early morning. Already almost a hundred laborers, dressed in the white of Mayan men, are climbing over the ruins, using pulleys and their own strength to rebuild painstakingly the broken temple platforms and the giant pyramid. Others are using shears to hand-cut the grass that stretches between the platforms and the ancient ball court. Obviously, the government is putting money into a massive campaign to re-build and spruce-up Ek Balaam. I suppose it is hoped that soon it will be as over-touristed as Chichen Itza. I watch a group of workers attach a long plaster snake, which they have made and sun-dried, to the sides of a platform. Others are attaching new masks. I assume they are following someone's detailed instructions. I hate that they are doing this, putting phoniness on what is real. I wish they would leave the ruins alone, with their stones scattered and pillars lying on the ground. I climb the high pyramid and look out over soft green hills that are as-yet-covered ruins.

As the heat becomes intolerable, my driver and I flee Ek Balaam for the Dzipnup Zkekunthe cenote, (cenotes are freshwater wells, part of the massive freshwater river system that underlies most of the Yucatan). This cenote is a limestone cave with dripping stalactites, a natural skylight, and cool, clear, intensely blue water. It makes a fine indoor pool. I swim alone with a few tiny dark fish, some whiskered like catfish. When a bunch of swimming tourists arrive, I go back to the hotel for a late lunch: chopped eggs and tomatoes, wrapped inside a tortilla, and covered with a bright green sauce made of squash and wonderful hot peppers.

I pick up the local paper and see a tragedy. A truck carrying farm laborers collided head-on with a large bus, and seventeen laborers are dead. The truck driver was going irresponsibly fast and was on the wrong side of the road, says the newspaper. The men came from a nearby village that is not on any map I've seen. Their names combine Mayan and Catholic: Jesus Ek Cano, Felipe Pool Chuc, Jorge Iwit Ku. I assume they are distantly related to the famous Ek Balaam of the great ruins. I let myself mourn for them and the children I assume they left as their only legacy.

El Meson del Marques colonial ($50 with air-conditioning and fans.)

Travel Tips*: Look for the cenote Samula, which reputedly has Mayan drawings scratched into the ceiling. It should be open to the public in late 2005.*

In **Puerto Morelos** what does one do besides snorkel around the coral? "Do" is an over-valued word. Here I **do** nothing. I lie in a hammock under a palm tree over the whitest possible sand beside the bluest sea. I watch frigate birds soar and pelicans flap their wings with great energy. I read. I walk on this remarkably cool white sand, which comes from pulverized coral. I wander into the tiny town to see the leaning light house and eat lunch at a cafe beside the sea. Even the townspeople are laid back. There are tourist shops, of course, but salespeople don't urge you to buy. They smile, say "good morning, senora."

Brief History of a reef: *A coral reef begins as a free-swimming larva released into the water by its parent polyp. This microscopic animal may spend days seeking an appropriate place to settle, and may travel hundreds of miles in a search for the right site. If it survives, and few do, it will attach and metamorphose into a minute polyp, grow tentacles, and feed. It will secrete a limestone and make a skeleton beneath itself. Thus begins the structure of a coral colony. It will take centuries for a coral reef to develop. If a hurricane, a boat, or a careless person breaks off just one piece of coral, 100 years of growth may be destroyed. (Copied from a pamphlet I found in my hotel room.*

Author unlisted.)

Enrique takes me to the coral reefs in his motorboat. Hundreds of blue tang are swimming, packed together, and then suddenly dive to the coral and suck up food. They move as one, their bodies fluttering like blue butterflies, then swim again en masse. A single nurse shark is hunkered down in a small cave, as quiet as if he were dead. I am so surprised I gulp and choke on sea water. One large barracuda and two small ones swim silently by me, a turtle rises from the sand and swims to the surface to get its needed air. I drift across a dozen different bunches of coral with a million fingers, and head coral with bright worms in the cranial holes. Cute and black, they disappear, as anemone do, when I swim over them.

Women tourists stay at the Rancho Libertad to meditate, learn to make baskets, and beat the Caribbean drums. They explore the overheated jungle and visit a real Mayan village with a guide. They go to Xel Ha, a small bay filled with exotic fish and too many tourists. They visit ruins, small ones hidden away in the jungle and large, famous ones, Tolum and Copal. I choose not to go along. I am dedicated to the hammock and the nearby corals, which I visit daily. Next January, when it is cool, I will do the eco-tours. After a few days, I take a cab to Playa de Carmen and the boat to Cozumel.

Cozumel. This is the great dive capital of Mexico. I decide against diving, because I am leery of deep dives, currents, and the youth of the other divers. Young men and women like to dive fast and deep; I enjoy diving if I can be pampered by a dive master who likes old ladies. This doesn't seem the place for me. Instead, I spend the first day lazily swimming. I find a book about the conquest of the Yucatan peninsula. Cozumel was a sacred place, like Delos for the ancient Greeks, or Rome or Mecca today.

"Friday, May 6, 1518," writes the priest Juan de Grijalua about Cozumel, "We see fourteen white towers, one very large. A multitude of Indians were looking at our ship and made a great noise with their drums. The Commandant ordered 100 men to arm themselves. They embarked in the boats and landed, accompanied by a priest, expecting to be attacked, but they found no one. And in all the environs they did not see a single man. The commandant mounted the largest tower with the standard bearer, unfurled the flag, and planted it on the façade, and took possession in the name of the king." He reported that people

lived in stone houses *"so well constructed that we thought only Spaniards could have built them."*

The people wisely remained hidden in their underground passages until the ship sailed on. Nobody today seems to know where the passages are.

"In 1519 Cortez arrived to tell the Indians that they would go to hell for worshipping their idols. The people explained that they worshipped the same gods their ancestors worshipped, because these gods were kind to them. Cortez' soldiers destroyed the temples, baptized the people, and murdered them." Chalk up one more victory for the white man's God and international terrorism.

When the British travelers arrived in 1841 the island was overgrown and had not been occupied since the Spanish conquest. Today it swarms with people, who worship sun, warmth, and diving. I take a snorkel trip, drifting over the Palomar reef, seeing rocks, sand, and a few large puffers with beautiful black markings. I like the laziness of drifting with the current, so I sign up for an all-day snorkeling trip that includes three shallow reefs and an amazingly good lunch on a beach. Then I relax in a lounge chair on the grass beside the sea, and read Jostein Gaardner's THE SOLITAIRE MYSTERY. He says, "The reason most people just shuffle around the world, seeing nothing, is because the world has become a habit." That is sad. I am seeing so many wonders!

Plaza Las Glorias, ($125 with breakfast, excellent pool, large grass area with lounges, and easy access to deep water with interesting fish.

Travel tips*: Do not imprison yourself by paying in advance for meals and lodging in a hotel you have never visited except on internet. It may be a bargain, but what do you do if you don't like the place? On my snorkel trips, I heard horror tales from several unhappy, "trapped" tourists.*

Some people like to tour the swamps, rocky beaches on the windward side, the few uninteresting remains of old ruins, and what seems like miles of sand and brush. I did that long ago. Once is enough.

Playa Del Carmen is a great little tourist stop, with zillions of stores and restaurants. I stay at the big hotel right beside the ferry to Cozumel, and plan to find a better place in the morning. That night I get an email from my daughter Claudia, saying, "I am going to Alaska to buy an RV. Want to come with me?" This is not exactly a surprise, as she has been keeping me up-to-date on her negotiations with the owner. Now all is set. I say I will be back in California tomorrow, and go to the bus station to buy a ticket to the airport.

I like the bus station with its multitude of destinations from Aeropuerto to Zihuatenejo. Today, my last day in Mexico for now, I read the destinations longingly and promise myself I will return here to use Playa as a home base while branching out to the little towns whose names are unfamiliar. On the bus to the airport, they show us a movie of a plane crash. And they turn up the air-conditioning. Next time I will bring a sweater against the Arctic bus temperatures.

FAMILY, FRIENDS, AND DENTIST

I arrive at Claudia's home just in time for a "dental emergency." While eating a cheese sandwich, of all things, my front teeth fall out. My grand-daughter Ruth almost faints, not knowing two of the four teeth were already false. The other two simply broke off. I curse, take a quick side trip to my dentist in San Francisco, and then Claudia and I fly to Fairbanks, Alaska, a desolate, rather boring small city, where she buys an RV, names it Aurora, and we head south. We see one wolf, one bear, and a moose nursing her baby. It rains a lot. The super highway is so empty we could double u-turn anywhere without even looking. For long stretches there are no signs, no restaurants, not even a gas station. Finally, we spot a small Indian store and ask about the nearest restaurant. It's twenty-three miles south. "How late is it open?"

"I don't know. I've never been there."

We spend a day in Haines, a lovely little town surrounded by snow-capped mountains, and then take the ferry to Bellingham, Washington. It's a spectacular trip, with stops at all the interesting towns along the way. How clever of Claudia to plan this! After all, if she had bought her recreational vehicle from someone in Watsonville, we'd have missed Alaska entirely.

We spend the next week on Bainbridge Island at a family reunion to celebrate my sister Bette's seventy-fifth birthday. It is the first time all five sisters, Bette, Margaret, Diane, Laurie, and I, have been together since mother died in 1980. Two brothers-in-law, five daughters, two sons, and my grand-daughter Ruth keep the videos and flash cameras popping. I smile with my mouth tight shut, and the results are not good. To explain the closed mouth on a usually open-mouthed person: the temporary plate from my San Francisco dentist broke just as we arrived in Seattle.

The party is much fun. We eat, wander about town, swim in the condominium pool, and mostly talk. Three of us have lost our husbands. (I know that euphemism is not good. As a character in "The Importance Of Being Ernest," said, more or less, "losing one's loved ones sounds very careless.") I do not joke to my sisters about death,

171

believe me. Margaret came close to dying this year, from an aortic embolism. We pass around photos we have brought with us, and recall childhood memories. It's important to stick to family talk, because one of us is religious and Republican. Not I, of course.

The reunion is so fine that we have another in two months, at the home of our sister Laurie, who lives with twelve or more boats on the shores of a large lake in Montana. This time my son, one of her sons, and five more grandchildren attend, but only three of us old ladies get there. By then I have new teeth and a much flatter bank account.

Would you be interested in knowing what has been, so far, the most expensive trip I have every taken? To my dentist's office.

Claudia and I visit Karen in Colorado, and she takes us to **Indian Springs.** No one knows for how many centuries the Ute and Arapaho Indians soaked in the hot spring waters before white men arrived, seeking gold. A George Jackson wrote in his diary:

"Jan. 1. 1859. Clear day. My supply of grub short, so here goes for the head of the creek. Made eight miles and camped at a warm springs. Snow all gone around springs. Killed a mountain lion and a fat sheep. About 1,000 sheep in sight today; no scarcity of meat for myself and dogs." Later he found what he was seeking, a nugget of gold and some gold dust.

In 1863, two miners, tunneling for gold, struck only gushing hot water and, frustrated, sold their rights to a Dr. Cummings, who built a log and frame bathhouse near the "hot water mine," and started to charge the public for healthy bathing in the mineral springs. A resort was built in 1905, visited by the Teddy Roosevelts, Walt Whitman, Frank and Jesse James, the Vanderbilts, Sarah Bernhardt, and other famous or notorious men and women of the period. It has been re-modeled again but retains the rustic, stone caves and the stone baths scooped into the floor. The water is not just hot. It is the hottest spa I have ever tried to enter, except perhaps for Dogo Hot Springs in Japan.

When we can stand the heat no longer, we walk through the corridor of mud baths, which turn out to be gooey, cold, and very unpleasant. In Iceland, where the mud is the natural bottom of the hot lake, it was fine, but not here. Instead we go to the swimming pool in a lovely glass-domed greenhouse with palm trees, flowering plants, warm air, and music. We float languidly.

For $25 one can spend the day going back and forth between the hot spas and the warm pool. At nearby Idaho Springs, we have lunch and look in the antique stores. Karen always plans interesting excursions. Last time it was to visit moose and listen to the male's loud mating calls.

I return to San Francisco for a large party celebrating Reiko True's seventieth and visit more old friends, including members of OWL (Older Women's League). I head off to New York to visit friends there and revisit the Guggenheim and Metropolitan.

Travel Tips: *San Francisco is a marvelous city. If you are a woman over sixty and want to meet San Franciscans, phone OWL. Members have told me they love to show visitors the sights.*

There are dozens of walking tours: back streets of Chinatown, the Mexican district, the Gay area, murals done by Diego Rivera and others by school children, places made famous in movies. And don't miss the Palace of the Legion of Honor, an art museum overlooking the Golden Gate Bridge. Golden Gate Park is a wonderful hiking area, as is the Golden Gate Bridge . Everyone goes to the Sunday Farmers Market on the Embarcadero. etc, etc.

Hotel Stratford ($65 - $75) on Union Square, 415-397-7080.

OKINAWA

solo

I'm staying for a week on the island of **Zamami,** an hour's boat ride from Naha, the capital of Okinawa. I've come to snorkel, and am staying at a very inexpensive, delightful inn. As far as I can tell, no one on this island speaks English. A young graduate student, who speaks some English, brought me here by ferry, carried my luggage to my room, and labored over a note, "I am very happy to spend this time with you. I am sorry my English is so poor." He's a dear, and I want very much to hug him good-bye, but in Japan I hold back from touching people without their permission. Instead, I thank him for his note and his help.

I want to swim. The wife, who is co-owner of the inn, talks to me non-stop, even though I understand nothing. I say, "Where swim?" and make swimming gestures. I can't see the ocean from the inn. She continues her monologue in a high, tuneful, quite lovely voice. I wonder if she is giving me the complete history of Zamami or just tonight's menu.

Last week in San Francisco I saw the Russian movie, "Cuckoo" about a Finnish soldier, a Russian soldier, and a Lapland woman who befriends them. They have no words in common, but talk as rapidly as this woman, and totally mis-guess what the others are saying. When the co-owner pauses for breath, I say "Okay," bow, and go back to my room. I put on my swimming suit, pick up my mask and snorkel, and return to the front desk. She walks me to where I can see the beach.

It is wide and beautiful with white sand and very tiny islands in the distance. Half a dozen young men, probably scuba divers who have finished diving for the day, are sitting on mats and gazing seaward. I nod to them and walk into the warm, wonderful water. Patches of new coral, yellow, white, and white with pink flower-like tips, are beginning to grow from the white sand. The fish are colorful old friends. The warmer the sea, the brighter the fish. Here the parrot fish are almost obscene in their gaudiness.

The other guests at the Patio Inn are divers, young men and women in separate groups. At dinner they are very quiet and polite. Though most of them must have studied English at some point in their education, no one attempts to speak to me, except to say, "Good evening." They bow and smile. I imagine that refusal to attempt to converse is a symptom of their perfectionism. If they can't speak well, they hesitate to try. I may be making this up. Anyway, since I remember only how to say "Thank you" and "Good morning" in Japanese, I can't start a conversation.

The next day I am given a map of the area in English, with drawings of smiling snorkelers at a beach across town. When I point to it, the cook, who is also gardener, boat builder, husband, and co-owner, writes for me the time when the bus leaves for the trip to that beach. The beach is crowded with young people, plus families and children. Most rent large plastic inner tubes to ride on the water, and a few use life jackets. With rented mask and snorkel, they gaze at the fish from the safety of inner tube or jacket.

I see no one who is even slightly obese. I don't mean fat. There is no one with the slightest paunch, except me. It can't be just good genes. Last night's very fine dinner was raw fish, grilled fish, rice, green vegetables, and two tiny pieces of papaya. No sugar or processed food. I believe that is the healthy solution few overweight Caucasians will accept.

I rent a lounge chair and sun umbrella, and swim and read. The swimming is wonderful: huge rocks, coral, and outstanding fish. The new ones for me are a bright yellow gar three feet long, and a school of pale fish about twelve to fifteen inches long, whose heads shine as if covered in aluminum foil. Their large mouths are wide open as they swim in a tight pack; I imagine the bright heads attract plankton or whatever they strain out of the water.

I adopt a routine, one day at Ama beach next to the inn and the next day at the coral beach. In between I am finishing these chapters about my travel. I realize I have described tropical fish too often, but I can't bring myself to edit them out. In fact, here I am writing more:

Two yellow triggerfish come up to me, their lips a soft, sensuous, pale pink, their heads pink, their fins purple, and both fins and tails outlined in yellow. Pairs of black and yellow angel fish float almost motionlessly, while parrot fish in all possible bright pastels chomp at the coral. All around me tiny electric blues play tag and dive into the white coral to hide and eat. A small dark fish, quite unremarkable, kisses the glass of my mask right in front of my eyes.

Two days of rain and high winds, and I get a telephone call from Rishun, my friend who arranged for my coming to Okinawa. He says we are having a typhoon and hopes I am all right. I'm not, because I've finished the books I brought, and am stuck with only the Asian TIMES. That isn't what he was asking about, but he sends on the next ferry everything he has in English, a stack of psychotherapy magazines. Better than nothing, and I am grateful for his efforts.

I go swimming in big wind-made waves. The inn people have a fit, talking up a verbal storm when I return, but the waves are soft and the heart of the typhoon is elsewhere. In the afternoon I sneak out the back way, so that they won't see me. They are trying so hard to keep me safe and to feed me properly. They smile happily and nod their enthusiasm at my ability to use chopsticks. They peer to make sure I like the food, which is superb. They show me their papaya tree, and cut a fresh one each evening for dinner. But we never really communicate.

The rain and wind cease, and it is hot again. A huge turtle surfaces right in front of me, gulps air, dives, and swims leisurely away. A warm, luxurious final swim.

Naha. The workshop is attended by twenty young people, Rishun, who translates, and five now-retired therapists who were participants in the workshop Bob and I did here in 1988. I feel tearful seeing them again. In 1988 the Okinawans were still mourning their war dead. In their culture they hadn't talked about their losses or mourned openly. Using gestalt techniques, Bob and I had helped them say good-bye to husbands, sons, and other family members who were killed in World War II. It had been a very sad but important workshop. Our countries were adversaries, and in the workshop we united in our own private peace ceremony. I am deeply touched to meet five of them again. The young participants know World War II only as history.

One of the older women (and the only Christian in the group), states that in our earlier workshop she said good-bye to her father who died in the war. Today she asks to say good-bye to a sister who died recently. She imagines her sister as she was before her fatal heart attack, and tells her feelings she wishes she had expressed. She concludes, "We were taught not to say these things, but I want you to

176

know that I thought you were the most beautiful girl in the world. I was jealous of that, but I used to look at you and be glad you were my sister even if you got more attention than I did. You were very good to me and I think you cared about me more than our mother did. Your love saved my life and made me human." She then imagines herself at her sister's funeral and ends by singing in a very sweet, old, trembling voice, a Japanese version of "Amazing Grace."

The young have the problems I expect to hear at any workshop anywhere: writer's block, minor depression, public shyness, obsessive worrying, and disagreements with lovers or in-laws. They are a studious, successful group who have read translations of my books, use Redecision therapy in their practices, and are eager to work with me. For all of us, it's exciting.

The first evening we have dinner together in a lovely private room overlooking the sea. The second evening we have Okinawan specialties in a restaurant that features Okinawan folk dancing. The costumes are gorgeous, more vibrant than is typical in other parts of Japan, with sashes that are narrow rather than the wide, and bright red hats that resemble huge, overturned fish pots. The dancers keep their bodies rigid as they do intricate arm and leg movements. Their white-chalked faces are totally expressionless, and even in the courting dance there is no change in expression.

Throughout the evening we chatter by means of interpreters. The young make elaborate plans for "The next time you are here," as if I had a lifetime ahead of me. When the workshop ends, a group takes me to the famous local aquarium. In addition to the colored reef fish, there are whale sharks, giant rays, mantas, and huge barracudas. Nearby is a lovely orchid garden. They say that "next time" they'll take me to their local museums and promise to arrange even more exciting snorkeling than at Zamami.

Most Okinawan women of my generation don't swim, because they were brought up to believe that tanned skin is ugly. One of them says, "If you let your skin darken, the darkness will last your whole life," as if that were unthinkable. I give her a peek at my snow-white belly beside my tan arms and she gasps. "You could have been truly white if your family had taken better care of you!" Fortunately this was not a concern in my family. It was okay for me to look like a rice farmer's wife.

I fly to Tokyo to work hard for four days and reunite with dear, dear friends, some of whom have been attending our workshops since 1976.

Travel Tips: *I need more insulin and find that the Netherlands is not the only country in the world that refuses to sell it over the counter. I waste half a day and $50 seeing a Japanese physician. Bring the medicines you need.*

BELIZE

Laurie Barrett and solo

Six people, including the two of us, are on a small island, **Blackbird Cay**, enduring mosquitoes and "no-see-ums" as we prepare to count fish. That's right. We will lie in the water face down with mask, snorkel, and flippers, counting fish on the Caribbean barrier reef. We have been assigned parrot fish, damsels, snappers, and groupers, males and females, young and old. I thought I knew parrot fish, but their young are so unlike the parents that it would make any witted parent wonder. Also, it turns out that there are adults whose appearance is totally different from the clans I know. Damsels are damned near my undoing. I finally decide that any small round fish, black and yellow, dusky, blue spotted, or cocoa-colored is a damsel if it stays in one area and tries to fight off other fish. If it is friendly and willing to share the coral, it's something else. Hour after hour our research director, Wayne, shows us videos, slides, colored pictures in books, while we study with ever increasing anxiety.

We pay to do this. We share Spartan, cold-water cottages, though with lovely porches overlooking the Caribbean. The food is life-sustaining and sometimes tasty. We are studying very hard. I am amazed when I meet six other campers in adjoining cottages, who signed up for vacations of carefree snorkeling. They count no fish, and pay $500 less for doing nothing than we pay for being part of this research project. They can attend all our lectures if they choose, and snorkel as much as they want without a care in the world! Midway in our studies, I offer to give my place to one of them for FREE (a $500 bargain), and they laugh at me! "Why would we spoil our vacations worrying?" One of the happy campers predicts that we counters will all have nervous tics before the week is over.

We count in three-hour stretches, twice a day, on either side of fifty-meter tapes, by making marks on our underwater clipboards. This is not as easy as it may sound. The fish don't stay still. They hide in the coral. And they don't always look like the pictures of them. I finally know the parrot fish and damsels, but I am worrying about the snappers. Some have mahogany-tipped tails, some have four vertical stripes, and of course I recognize the common ones with one bright yellow horizontal stripe. But what are all these fish that suddenly appear with the yellow stripes and black tails? In desperation I count them, too, and end up with seventy-five more snappers than anyone has ever seen along the line. No, I don't get a prize for that. Just more time studying the books and videos of snappers, as I desperately wonder if the research project is being wrecked by my incompetence. Laurie is doing fine. This is her second year of counting fish and, besides, she is a certified public accountant, which should give her a leg up, right? CPAs are expected to count accurately.

On our last day of counting, the sky is dark, the rain is pouring down on us, and the waves are high. But at last I feel competent. I know the snappers, and count them. There are only a few damsels. I am able to identify and count every single parrot fish, including the little ones. We rarely see groupers, but today I find one, a rather dark, almost menacing fish. It stares straight at me and doesn't move. We finish and start back to the cay in our pitching, rolling boat.

I get seasick easily, so try to fight it off by planning an article on what I imagine is a major difference between Western and Eastern religions. This has nothing to do with fish or even with our imminent death. I have never heard a Hindu suggest that in absolute truth one of their gods did cut off his son's head and then, because his wife had such a fit about it, rush out and grab the first animal he saw, a baby elephant, decapitate it, and successfully replace the elephant's head for the boy's original one. That is about as unbelievable a story as the raising of Lazarus, and my Hindu friends know it. But my Christian friends accept the Lazarus story as true. What if all Christians and Jews adopted the Hindu attitude, and considered the Bible a collection of stories: happy, sad, triumphant, ridiculous, grand, shameful, dirty, loving, bloodthirsty, banal, disgusting, beautiful, without insisting that every story is literally true? (I know, the wafflers talk about "symbolic" truth, but still refuse to shake away that word "true") I am not getting less seasick, thinking about this.

The rain is icily torrential and drives straight at us, as if it were hail. We huddle together in windbreakers and soggy towels, freezing. The driver guns the boat to top speed and our sweet, young leader stands semi-naked (he keeps his trunks on) in the bow, staring ahead to protect the boat from the coral that now is scarcely visible. Knowing his love of coral, I assume he is more interested in protecting the coral from us than vice versa. I give up on religious thoughts, and instead remember that sailing ships, bringing gold to the king of Spain, used to sink regularly with all hands lost, right here on this barrier reef. That thought is not a good distraction, either. Fog descends and the driver loses his way. He does not lower his speed. We are all terrified, but in a few minutes the fog lifts enough to see our dock.

At dinner Laurie mentions the two groupers she counted. Hers had red spots. Mine didn't. I go back to the fish book, and find mine. Its name is Slippery Dick. I am not making this up. I assume the fish was named well before the days of Slippery Dick Nixon. The book says: "Slippery Dicks are sighted on deep rocky ledges well below safe diving limits." Mine was about eight feet below the surface. I decide it was obviously quite lost, and don't erase my mark. Anyway, somewhere along my tape there was probably a red-spotted one that I missed.

After dinner, the rain ceases, millions of stars appear, and, slathered in Deets (no other insecticide seems to work), we six watch the stars and brag about our day's work. We decide we are remarkably strong and capable, a fine belief for a gang of old men and women. The snorkeling was grand, we tell each other! The boat trip was exciting! And weren't we amazing, how well we counted those fish!

We are rewarded with a non-counting snorkel trip to three new sites, including the famous Blue Hole. Now that counting is behind me, I can appreciate the coral: *star and brain coral, fans, candelabra, sea plumes, yellow mustard coral, and the wonderful "purple corky fingers" that are brown until they withdraw their tentacles, and then are lavender.* Some coral is bleached, which is a warning that it is expelling algae. That's not healthy. A brown crust over the coral means it's dead. All over the world I have seen both bleached and dead coral, but here there is also a lot of gorgeous, healthy coral.

We go to a tiny island, **Half Moon Cay**, where frigates and red-footed boobies nest by the thousands on ziracote trees. (If I had talent, I'd write a song about Boobies in a Ziracote Tree.) We climb to a look-out and are on a level with the birds' nests. They grandly ignore us. A few horny frigate males are eager for sex, even though they are a couple of months early. Each has discovered what he hopes is the ideal nesting place, sits there, inflates his bright red balloon-like pouch, and trumpets his availability. Females fly overhead, evaluating them. When a male is chosen, he flies off to gather twigs, leaves, cloth and other sun-bleached rubbish, which the female sorts through to make their nest. Only then do they get to have sex and babies.

Frigates have a great wingspread compared to their bodies, but their feathers have no oil, so they can glide almost indefinitely but can't land on the water. They feed from the surface, catch young turtles on their journey from nest to sea, and practice kleptoparasitism, meaning that they catch adult boobies in the air, shake them until they vomit, then swoop down to swallow the vomit as it drops and bring it home for supper for their young. (I used to get a kick out of telling repellent facts. I was the oldest and could make my sisters go white or even rush to the bathroom, gagging,)

Several thousand red-footed boobies breed here. They are plump, awkward, adorable birds who look like stuffed playthings, the teddy bears of the bird world. Their babies are born without feathers, so a parent must sit continuously on the nest, covering them so that they won't become cold, sunburned, or be eaten by frigates. In spite of the kleptoparasitism and the baby-murdering by the frigates, the frigates and boobies make their nests on the same trees. They don't seem to have lasting animosity, which perhaps speaks to a certain stupidity in the boobies?

We return to Blackbird Cay and watch an eclipse of the moon, a dramatic sight.

If you want to count fish on Blackbird Cay, contact the Oceanic Society in San Francisco or Eldherhostel. This research project is sponsored by the Oceanic Society, a non-profit organization that conducts scientific research to promote environmental conservation and education. You can also sign up to count pink river dolphin.

Brief history of Belize:

1000 BCE: Archeological evidence of Mayan settlements.

250 BCE - 900 CE: Mayan culture flourishes, with a written language, calendar, numbering system including zero, vast, ornate buildings constructed without the use of metal tools or wheels, terraced agriculture, paved roads, elaborate religious beliefs and ceremonies, etc.

900 - 1000: Major Mayan sites abandoned.

1500s: Spaniards arrive, but don't settle.

1600s: British and Spanish do some logging of mahogany and other trees. Baymen (British pirates) use cays and mainland as ports.

1725: Baymen, who have given up pirating, arrive with African slaves, and begin logging.

1883: Britain bans slavery in all its possessions, including Belize, but it takes a few years before Baymen release theirs.

1962: Belize becomes independent.

1973: Name is changed from British Honduras to Belize.

Laurie and I go to the **San Ignacio** area in the highlands to stay at the Du Plooy Inn. In 1987 the Du Plooy family (the parents and their five daughters, then four to sixteen years old) left the United States, bought a large piece of land, and began building guest houses. They brought in hundreds of new plants and trees from the jungle, and established the first Belize Botanical Gardens on their property, two ponds for wild ducks, and a greenhouse for orchids from all over Central America. Because of the tropical weather and the fertility of the soil, everything grows with amazing speed. The tiny trees are now huge.

Laurie and I have a fine bedroom and screened porch, plus the magnificent luxury of hot-water showers, which we use immediately on arrival, then visit the gardens and go to the open bar, overlooking the jungle and the brown, flooded river. We are surrounded by huge, splendid trees and singing birds. Some of these trees are familiar houseplants at home.

Large black grasshoppers with bright yellow antennae flash brilliant red from the undersides of their wings as they jump nearby. Leaf-cutter ants march in single file, a bright green line of waving leaf bits. They harvest leaves and transport them to their nest, where the leaves somehow become a special fungus that is food for all of them. The queen lays the eggs. The tiniest ants tend the fungus gardens, the largest are soldiers who protect the colony, and the next largest are the ones I watch, bringing in the leaves. Not sheaves.

Laurie is sick, with what we first hope is merely tourista, but it turns into a sniffling, wheezing, coughing flu that leaves her without energy. At home there can be a positive side to illness, especially if you have sick leave. Our father, who grew up with the Scot Presbyterian prejudice against the use of alcohol except as medicine, would prop up his pillows, bring out his books, and enthusiastically put a glass of whiskey beside his bed. I know no positives in being ill when traveling.

We plan side trips, and Laurie struggles to go on some of them, including to Cahal Peck, a mediocre Mayan ruin in San Ignacio just half an hour away. The name means "place of the ticks," but we escape unscathed. There is a small museum with the requisite skeleton, lots of shade trees and green grass, and a few ruins that probably were ancient apartment dwellings. There are similar ruins throughout this area. Today, a hole broke through in the middle of a road and the road crew discovered a limestone ruin about twelve feet square under the hole. They simply threw in rocks to fill it up. They say that all of San Ignacio is built over ruins. We drive around the town, which is muddy from the previous week of rain, and see little besides laundry that is hanging hopefully, sopping wet, on everyone's lines. It has started to rain again.

Xunantunich is a major site. I go there without Laurie. My guide drives the minivan to the Copan river, parks it, and we cross on a raft with a wheel winch, cranked by hand. It's obviously hard work, but the guy in charge cons a young tourist into doing it for him. "Try it," he says. After a couple of turns, the young man wants to stop, but the driver insists, "You're doing fine! You're strong enough to get us across." (Note that everyone in Belize, even those with the poorest jobs, is multi-lingual.) The kid is sweating hard by the time the crossing is finished and the driver is smiling delightedly. I wonder if he manages to find a victim on every trip.

Travel tips: *Hire a taxi on the other side. It is a long, hard uphill hike from the river to the ruins. In fact, it is still a long hike from the entrance to the site, so I tell the ticket seller that I can't walk uphill, and he gives the taxi driver permission to drive me directly to the ruins. To get special privileges, ask for them.*

The ruins are a glorious, startling white against the lush green jungle. After the site was abandoned, the jungle grew over it, hiding everything except five white limestone pillars on the top of the temple-pyramid, 130 feet above the jungle floor. The descendants of the ancient Mayans considered this a sacred place, says my guide, who is a modern-day descendant. They came by dugout or on foot, bringing incense to light small fires to the gods, and ask permission to hunt at the base of the pyramid. No matter how scarce game might be elsewhere, there was always game here. A woman, as white as the limestone pillars, would appear beside the pillars to bless their hunt and then disappear into the stone. Or so they said. No one ever went away hungry. In honor of this woman, they named the site Zunantunich, "Stone Lady." The original Mayans called it Ka'atz Wit'z, "Supernatural Place."

Almost deserted today and surrounded by impenetrable jungle, the ruins seem hushed, truly supernatural. Even my guide speaks softly. So far only the temple and palace, have been excavated. The temple is built in tiers, pyramid style, with broad steps rising on four sides to the amazing friezes just below the pillars that crown the top. On the east frieze are carvings of the sun god, royalty kneeling in worship, and Chac with his long tongue. This is the side of the rising sun, of beginnings, of hope, says my guide. On the west side the sun god has the features of the jaguar with large ornate jaguar ears and the gaping mouth that signifies the entrance to the underworld. This is the side of disappearances, of endings. Beneath the western frieze a human skull is buried. Archeologists from UCLA have placed a fiberglass replica over the original carvings to protect them. I climb the temple stairs (very slowly; they are steep and there are lots of them), have a close-up look at the friezes, and then sit for awhile, looking out over the green hills, many of them unexplored ruins stretching to the horizon.

Across the wide plaza from the temple is the palace, where royalty supposedly lived. There are lots of rooms that once upon a time had murals. The nearby ball court is small and has a hole in the ground rather than the usual metal ring. No murals or carvings have been found that show how the game was played here, or if winners or losers were sacrificed. There used to be stele in front of the pyramid, and many beautiful jade pieces, brought here from faraway sites. This was a wealthy city, because it controlled lucrative trade along the Copan river.

The next day Laurie takes an excursion with me, along an impossibly rutted road, fording two frighteningly swift and deep rivers, to Barton Creek cave. At the entrance we get into a canoe and go downriver into a vast cave, in places as tall as a vaulted European cathedral, gleaming from silica and moist limestone. Stalagmites have grown into weirdly wonderful statues, strange altars, and pulpits. This cave was used by ancient Mayans for religious ceremonies, and replicas of their ceremonial pots (the real ones are in museums) stand on the altars. A skull is still embedded into one altar-like formation, and a few skeletons have been left in place. Huge stalactites hang down, glistening wet, with tiny drops of water gleaming like jewels in the beams of our flashlights.

We visit a butterfly farm, the Tropical Wings Nature Center, where butterfly lovers have built a very nice interactive museum for children, and are raising an incredible number of butterflies to supply living museums all over the world. The owners show us the eggs, larva, and pupa, and explain each step in the life cycle. We see two butterflies emerge from the pupa stage, and flutter their new, lovely wings to dry them.

On our final day we take a quick look at the famous zoo for injured and abandoned animals: jaguars, hyenas, caiman, turtles, various rare birds, and many others. Then we fly seventeen minutes, over a beautiful sea to Amergris Cay.

Travel tips: *There is much more to do, using the San Ignacio area as a base: hiking, horseback riding, canoeing, rafting or floating on inner tubes; exploring five more caves; visiting the Mennonite farms and United Nations refugee villages for Guatemalan Indians. Tikal is only two hours away. I suggest spending at least a week at DuPlooy's or a nearby inn.*

Du Plooy, (two-bed rooms are $117, or about $170 per person for cottage, food, and personal tours.)

Ambergris Cay and San Pedro. Talk about snorkeling! I have never seen bigger, more beautiful fish. The snappers here are over two feet long and the groupers so big I can pretend they are baby whales. Angels swim around us in twos, extra large and very beautiful, and the coral is grand. Our week at Blackbird paid off. In addition to the varieties we counted, we ended up able to identify many other species. After a fine swim with these fish, we go on to even bigger ones!

The boat anchors at a spot in the ocean that specializes in nurse sharks and huge rays with tails up to ten feet long. They congregate here, because this is where they are fed. Tour and snorkeling boats from Ambergris and the mainland arrive every few minutes, so the feeding is constant. I jump off our boat, the driver throws out a pail of fish, and over a dozen nurse sharks suddenly surround me, circling in a frenzy, so eager they bump me, and one even charges over my head, knocking my mask askew. Not to panic! Nurse sharks know what they want to eat and I am not it. The water is churning from their wild activity. I tip the water out of my mask, and back up a bit. The rays are like large black shadows below the sharks. From time to time, the driver jumps deep into the water to fight off the sharks and make sure the rays get their share.

In the afternoon we go to another exciting snorkeling site and do a long drift over sand, rock embedded with coral, and many fish. The current is perfect, strong enough to carry us while still sufficiently gentle that we can, when we choose, circle back to an interesting spot. The water is so clear I feel as if I'm Peter Pan, actually flying over a vast watery land. Four feet below and directly under me is a beautiful spotted eagle ray with a fierce, eagle-like head, gleaming eyes, and huge, dotted fins. We glide together until, with no observable effort, he speeds ahead.

That was a lot of swimming for one day, and Laurie is still obviously ill. We decide to spend the next day on land. San Pedro looks like a town from a century ago. Even the books in the public library are mostly from other eras: Fitzgerald, Hemingway, and Sinclair Lewis on front shelves, and then Dickens and Shakespeare. There are a few shelves of junk books that tourists have left. (I think a scathing dissertation could be written on the intellectual level of the tourist class, as demonstrated by the books they bring on vacation.) The painted wooden buildings are faded from the salty air, and filled with art and crafts shops, internet cafes, and restaurants, owned by people who immigrated here from Europe and the Americas. Their accents are Hungarian, German, Swedish, and English. The people here, locals and immigrants, are among the happiest, most gracious people I have ever met.

We rent a golf cart and drive south. I find a hotel where I will stay tomorrow after Laurie leaves. We then drive north past town to a river that splits the Cay in two, and take a small ferry-raft, powered by two men on either side of the river, who pull the ferry by hand from shore to shore, using a sturdy rope. The ferry is so small it holds one car or two golf carts plus a couple of foot passengers. Most people head north by boat. The road is impossible, as the ferrymen warn us. The potholes are filled with muddy water, so until we splash into one we have no idea how deep it is. After getting stuck twice, we give up. There is nothing of interest except expensive homes and a gaudy, multi-colored restaurant, The Sweet Basil. We have a lunch which I hope to duplicate when I am in California for Christmas: In the center of the plate, spaghetti tossed with pesto and good olive oil; on one side, roasted orange, red, green, and yellow sweet peppers; on the other side, chunks of lobster (or a substitute, of course).

On her last day in town Laurie goes to the main beach to try to buy carved wooden bowls from a local, but he hasn't opened by the time she must leave for the airport. Maybe he'll come dashing up as the plane is loading. There seems to be no security problem at the airport. People reach into the planes to sell bananas.

I have two days left in Ambergris and am having lunch at the Tropica hotel, lingering while listening to the Beatles. How innocent they were! "I want to hold your hand..." "...the lovely people, where do they all come from?" I ask the young waitress if she likes the music. "It's really boring," she tells me. Her preferences are rock bands I have never heard of. I am nostalgic for the Beatle era, when my children were young and we still had hope for racial equality and a peaceful country.

I swim from the beach, where the water is very warm and clear, and then sit on my second floor balcony and look down on the pool and beach. It's Sunday, and local children are jumping up and down in the shallow water. They throw fistfuls of sand into the sea, laughing so hard they fall down and roll into the water. Somewhere in the distance it is raining. A full, bright rainbow makes an arch over the sea. The next day I sign up for two more snorkeling trips before leaving Belize.

As I wait for my flight, a man comes by, selling cashew nuts for $2.50 Belizean or $1.25 US. I search my purse and pockets, and discover I have nothing smaller than $20 US. He has no change, either. He says, "OK, a present," and gives them to me. I am very touched.

Holiday Hotel, ($100, refrigerator, air-conditioning, and fans. Downtown, noisy.)

Tropica, ($75, south of town, swimming pool, nice grounds, fair restaurant.)

THREE BELIZEAN MEN

Current population of Belize:
41% Mestizo (Spanish and Mayan)
31% Creole (White and African)
10% Mayan (Yucatec, Mopan, and Kekchi)
7% Garifundi (Indian and African)
The rest are Europeans, Americans, Chinese, East Indians. There is a large Mennonite colony.

Randal is a twenty-one year-old Creole from Belize City, who has lived on Blackbird Cay since the Oceanic Society opened here four years ago. "I do cleaning, yard work, plumbing, and, when no one else is here, I am the guard. That means I stay here all alone during hurricane season. It's scary when there are storms, because I keep thinking that a hurricane could come and blow me into the sea, but really I would be evacuated before a hurricane arrived. I love this island. I love the cleanness and the tourists and the sea all around me. I love living here."

He has an opportunity to move to the United States. As he talks, he strokes his arms. "I am the wrong color for America." His girl friend is a white kindergarten teacher in Maryland, whom he met when she spent her vacation on Blackbird Cay. She bought him a plane ticket and last year he visited her. "She is very optimistic about what I can do. She says I can get a high school equivalency degree and then go to college in Maryland. She gave me this really big book so I can study. It's the biggest, thickest book you can imagine." When he laughs, his dimples show. I can understand her enthusiasm to have him with her. He's sweet and very endearing. "I am supposed to be studying for that exam. My girlfriend says that all I need is a push."

What did he like best about the United States? "The Orioles. We went to a game while I was there." What didn't he like? "When we were walking down the street together, people said bad things. Threats, dirty words. I didn't expect that. I watch American TV a lot, and it shows people getting along together. Black policemen are treated fine on TV. And on the news I see people my color in the US Army and they seem happy. I could get a job in America, that's not a problem. I don't like to be hated."

He attended school in Belize City until he was sixteen and then had to drop out because his mother was injured in a bus accident. "She's partly crippled now and can't work." He's her only child and feels very responsible for her. His father has eleven children by several women. "He's seventy-one and blind, but his other children support him, so I don't need to help him."

After the accident, Randal took a job loading sugar boats. "I worked from 5:00 A.M. TO 6:00 P.M. every day. I loaded the liquid brown sugar that goes to the US and Canada. Then a guy told me about the job here on Blackbird and I applied. It's really a good job." Again the dimples and the easy laugh. He spends his money supporting his mother and talking to his girl friend on the phone. On his days off, he visits his mother, occasionally visits his father, and plays basketball with his friends. "I wish my girl friend wanted to live here but she doesn't. I think she'll come to visit me soon and she wants me to visit her but I don't think I'll go to the United States again."

Sam, a local guide, trucker, and farmer, is a Mojan Indian from the village Xunantunich, next to the ruins. He speaks English, Spanish, his Mayan language, and Creole, but is illiterate. "Before I was five years old, I was working all day every day, picking up grapefruit for a fruit rancher, and then I had a job working with the sheep. I couldn't go to school because I had no father to support me." Sam is now fifty-four and has never stopped working. He says the constant labor has broken down his body. It is true that his back is bent and he looks as if he were at least seventy.

Against all odds, he is now a well-to-do man. He is the owner of a quite-new truck, a tourist van, a large home, and thirteen acres of land. I ask him how he accomplished so much.

"When I was seventeen, my first daughter was born. I applied for land." He explains that in Belize a citizen may lease unused land from the government. If the person builds on the property and makes it productive, he may buy it in twenty years for very little money, which he has done. He is now the owner of his original six acres, plus another seven acres of natural jungle. "As soon as I had my land, I made myself a wheel-barrow. Almost all my plants came from the jungle by wheelbarrow. That wheelbarrow and my short hoe wrecked my back. I sold my produce, went on working for the ranch, and saved

190

money until I could buy a horse. I made a cart the horse could pull." When an American bought the ranch where he worked, "I persuaded him I could be more effective with a big-wheeled motorcycle, so he bought me one. After a while, I traded the horse, cart, and motorcycle for a truck."

When his fifth daughter was born, his wife died. He raised the children himself, with help from his mother and an aunt. He is very proud that all of his daughters graduated from the eighth grade. Two of them have moved permanently to the US and two work in Belize City. One lives with her husband and two children on his ranch, but works as a waitress in San Ignacio. He is sorry that none of his daughters or sons-in-law is interested in working on his farm. "I'm worn out. I need someone who cares about the property." He wants to put guest cottages on the land and work full-time as a guide and inn-keeper.

He takes Laurie and me to see his farm. It has limes, avocados, grapefruit, several types of lemons, oranges, kumquats, bananas and plantains, mangoes, papayas, wild grapes, pineapples, and every flowering tree he has found in Belize. Bees produce honey, which he sells. Orange, yellow, black, dusky, striped, and dotted butterflies flutter about the trees. Birds are everywhere. There are over a dozen bright green parrots in one of his trees.

When we exclaim over its beauty, he agrees, then tells us, "My illiteracy is a handicap. If I could read, I could advertise my ranch and guide services on internet. I've got my first guest house almost finished, and I have enough land to put up as many houses as I can fill. I'm looking for someone to run a web site for me. Nobody in my family is interested. They don't have my ambition."

Although he is in physical pain much of the time, he keeps finding new goals and overworking to achieve them. He works constantly. That alone might keep his sons-in-law and daughters from joining him.

Philip, also a guide, is yucatecan, and a grandson of the famous curandero (medicine man), Don Elizo Panti, who died a few years ago at the age of 103. He had one of the largest and most splendid funerals ever held in Belize, attended by the prime minister, other heads of state, generals, and well over 1,000 of Don Elizo's friends and patients. I had been to the old man's herbal farm in 1995, when I ripped open my leg in an accident on a diving boat. The cuts were deep and beginning to fester. Antibiotic cream had not been sufficient. Don Elizo was retired, but one of his assistants put leaves in an oven until they were crisp, powdered them, and sprinkled them on my open wound. Then he wet other leaves, laid them over the dry ones, and bandaged my leg. I was a bit queasy about all this, but the next morning, when I peeked at the wound, the festering had stopped and the wound was healing. If I'd been in Belize when Don Elizo died, I'd have attended the funeral.

Naturally, I am delighted to meet Philip, and ask him about Don Elizo's life. He had been a chiclero (a man who slashed trees and collected sap for making chewing gum.) Chicleros worked in the jungles of Guatemala, Mexico, and Belize, and had no knowledge of national borders. They would be hired for six months, while their families were housed and fed at a base camp. When they returned to the camp at the end of six months, they would be told that their families had eaten too much and therefore they were in debt for another six months. If they tried to escape, they were beaten and imprisoned. This went on for a lifetime and was not labeled slavery. It reminds me of the stories of coal miners in the early 1900s in the US. ("St. Peter don't you call me, 'cause I can't go, I owe my soul to the company store." I was a child and very proud of Eleanor Roosevelt the day she was photographed in a coal mine with striking workers.)

When national borders became important in the jungle, chicleros were told which was their country. At the time, Don Elizo was working in Belize, so the family was told they were Belizean.

Before becoming a curandero, Don Elizo was already famous in the jungle for his treatment of chicleros' slash wounds. He was accepted as a "son" by an old yucatecan brujo (witch), when he faced down a jaguar without showing fear. That man taught him jungle medicine. Don Elizo became a curandero. His son, Philip's father, continued working as a chiclero.

When the chicle industry collapsed (chewing gum is now made of synthetic materials), Philip's father became a caretaker for an American rancher and Philip worked with him after school and on weekends.

Philip married at 18, and continued to work with his father and live in his parents' home. "When my fourth child was born, we needed more space, so I leased land from the government and built a house. My cousins and friends helped. If you are Mayan you never have to hire workers. We help each other. A home is built from the wood in the forest and rocks and clay from the earth, so it doesn't cost much.

My home is better than most, because it has running water and electricity. I pay five dollars a year for my land. I have built up a large medicinal garden from jungle herbs and medicines. I learned jungle medicine from Don Elizo and my father, but I keep quiet about it here.

Now, no one dares be a curandero, because the Pentecostals have taken over this area and convinced the people that all curanderos and brujos are Satan in disguise. No one is willing to oppose them. Even the Catholics seem to be afraid of the Pentecostals.

"Medical care in Belize is terrible. Belize doctors are not respected. Cuba sends us physicians who are good people, but they have hardly any medicines or laboratory equipment. I understand that Cuba supplies doctors and Belize is supposed to supply medicine and equipment, but we don't have it. Without a working laboratory or medicines, what good are doctors? Isn't jungle medicine better than no medicine?"

Philip and his wife now have seven children, a small number for Yucatecan families, he says. He's already built another house on is property, this one for his oldest daughter, who is fifteen. She has told her father, "I will only marry a man who wants to live here!" She has finished school, and will probably marry next year. His oldest son has moved to the United States. Philip plans to build a house for each child who wants to remain in Belize. "After I am dead, they will live in their homes and remember me." He says that is what life is all about, marrying, having children, and providing what you can for their future.

GUATEMALA

Tiredness
With all the weight
of a cut up tree,
a load of firewood
drips sap on my back.
The head strap turns to fire.
I stop for awhile
and my shadow, stretching himself out,
lies on the ground,
maybe more tired than I am.

     Humberto Ak'abal, translated by Miguel Rivera and Robert Bly

Central America Psychotherapy Conference and solo

I came to **Guatemala City** to be part of a therapy conference and am enjoying it very much. The panels and workshops are well run, interesting, and informative, and the audience is enthusiastic. I teach with the help of an old friend from the Dominican Republic, Ana, who translates for me. She was once a scholarship student in international affairs at a leading US university, where professors lectured about "third world" countries. Each time they said these words, she raised her hand to say, "Excuse me, professor, our countries have leading writers, artists, dancers, thinkers, scientists, philosophers. We are only *economically* Third World." Long ago, when I heard that story, I knew we would be friends.

When I am not presenting workshops or serving as a panel member, I am listening without a translator to the other presenters, which is good practice for me. My favorite speaker is a neo-Freudian, not for content but because he speaks slowly and clearly. I do not understand anything the existentialist says, but the Spanish-speaking audience tells me they don't understand him either. His sentences are long and erudite.

After the conference, six of us drive to **Lago de Atitlan.** It is one of the world's loveliest lakes, very large and deep, with many coves and islands, set in a valley surrounded by high hills and three perfect, cone-shaped volcanoes. We arrive at our hotel in Panajachel at sunset.

The sky is slashed with what I will remember as Guatemalan red, an extraordinarily rich scarlet. The lake reflects the color in bright red-tipped ripples. We sit on the beach, and a Guatemalan colleague sings in a beautiful soprano, first "Ave Maria" and then Guatemalan songs. The sun sets and a new moon makes a silver path across the water. The evening is magical.

In the morning we do some quick shopping in the local market. This is a tourist mecca, called gringoland by locals. If we had time, we could easily linger here all day. The women wear woven and embroidered blouses, black woven skirts, and many-colored ribbons braided into their dark hair. Children play all around us, the little girls dressed in miniature versions of their mothers' clothing. Men and women are selling food, bright ceramics, paintings, wood carvings, and the woven clothing.

Because one of our group has to catch a late afternoon flight to her home in Nicaragua, we hurry from the market to the town beach to rent a boat to go out on the lake. On all sides of us the mountains are reflected in the calm, dark water. Of the many little villages around the lake that we could visit, we choose one, San Antonio Palopo, where the Indians are harvesting scallions by the thousands. Their bright green fields are terraced in intricate squares running from the beach to the tops of the mountains. Men, women, and children are working together, pulling out the scallions and tying them into huge bundles. The children run down the hill at top speed, sliding and laughing, to bring fistfuls of scallions for us to buy. The air smells deeply of fresh onion and soil.

We visit their local weaving center to watch men card the wool, dye it, and twist it into long strands for weaving. Centuries before the Spaniards arrived, Mayan women were in charge of clothing. They raised cotton, harvested it, and wove the cloth. When the Spaniards arrived with sheep, the care of the sheep and the making of wool into cloth became man's work. This division still exists. We watch half a dozen boys at large looms, weaving black wool into skirts. Some skirts are pure black, and others have strands of red and gold woven into them.

This town is also well known for its ceramics, a very delicate, embossed pottery in soft colors. I yearn to buy a plate with a thin, green lizard and one tiny, pink blossom on a gnarled branch, but don't want that extra weight in my suitcase, so I'll carry it in my mind. We return to Panajachel. One car leaves for the airport, while three of us spend the afternoon walking along the lake and eating lunch in the hotel garden. The garden is filled with blooming trees, and the lake below us changes from deep blue to light, sun-specked, to dark again, as clouds appear and disappear. Lake Atitlan is one of the most beautiful and peaceful places I have ever seen.

Monterrey Hotel ($30, waterfront.) Beautiful garden and fine breakfasts.

Next year I am returning, to stay at this hotel and visit each of the small villages by boat. I know exactly what I will do:

Go to Tecpan and the Iximche ruins, then on to Lago Atitlan.

Swim in the thermal waters by the shore at any one of several places. Take a boat to San Lucas Toliman at the foot of the massive volcano and stay there a day or two at an inexpensive hostel or the new expensive hotel with a swimming pool. I'll visit Santiago Atitlan, where the women wear and sell wonderful huipiles (long blouses), see the parade for the local god Maximon, and visit the church with the saints dressed in native clothing. It is in this church that the death squad murdered the Indian's beloved priest in 1981. I may spend a week in Jaibilito, a tiny town accessible only by boat.

Tikal is the greatest of the Mayan ruins. I fly to Flores and overnight in Remate, a nothing town of half a dozen hotels and a cluster of wood-working shops. These shops are important, because selling beautiful bowls and carvings to tourists is ecologically far superior to selling the trees as lumber. I am staying, on the recommendation of a Dutch couple I met somewhere, at Casa de Don David. After supper, a group of us begin chatting, and Don David joins in. At the moment he is in a bad mood because his computer isn't working. I offer heartfelt sympathy. Malfunction must be doubly horrible in a place where you can't just call your local repair person. Others at the table offer to help and go with him to his office, but don't succeed in starting it. They all come back to drink beer and chat. A young US couple, both physicians, want to leave the US permanently, and are looking for a country they like. Another couple, also young, has started a business buying small amounts of hardwood for musical instruments.

They care about the ecology of Central America, so choose trees carefully and plant "three for one." They live in Belize, and return to

196

the US only on business. Don David says he left the US thirty years ago, married a Guatemalan, and built this hotel. He says he's never regretted his move, "except when the damned computer goes out!" Mostly, we talk politics and the adventures involved in living abroad.

Travel Tips: *Do NOT believe the guide books that tell you loneliness is inevitable when you travel alone. I don't mention this often enough, because much of the time I want to be alone. LONELINESS IS NEVER INEVITABLE. When you want company, look for it. You will meet serious adventurers, first-time travelers, and lots of liberals. If your politics is the opposite of mine, you might choose somewhat classier hotels, where I imagine there are more Republicans. Everywhere there are local people who want to practice English by conversing with you. There are singing groups, birders, Elks, religious societies. When traveling alone, you have the world to make friends with!*

Hotel Don David ($15 - $25) Clean. Good food. A real bargain.

I want to see Tikal early, when birds and animals awaken, so I take the 5:00 A.M. bus. The other passengers are hikers, who immediately outdistance me, leaving me alone on the kilometer-and-a-half trail to the Tikal plaza. I go slowly, relishing every moment. The jungle is alive with bird calls and roars of howler monkeys. Trees, huge ferns, plants, and vines grow so thickly that it would be impossible to stray off the path. It is like the jungle surrounding Xunantunich in Belize. A green parrot flashes by, and a very plump, possibly pregnant coati waddles down the path and disappears. Finally, the white roof-combs of the largest pyramid appear above the green. The grand plaza is a huge green square, flanked by two tall pyramids, the tallest as big as a fifteen to twenty story building. In front of them are small, carved altars, like stone pillows two feet high, and stele etched with drawings of kings and dates of conquests. To one side is a sprawling, one-story palace with several dozen rooms, and on the other side is the so-called north acropolis, covering more than an acre of land. Luminescent peacocks, their bodies the size of large turkeys, pick at insects in the grass.

I sit on a low shelf of the acropolis, and look and listen.

Brief history of Tikal:

20,000 - 2,000 BCE: Hunters and gathers in this area.
2,000 - 800 BCE: Preclassic period, farming and fishing.

700 BCE: Tikal settled, flint tools used for carving early buildings. Already a trade center.

500 BCE: Ceremonial sites constructed.

200 BCE: Huge complex, important religious, cultural, trading center. The pyramids are built of limestone blocks over rubble.

500 CE: Population over 100,000.

600 - 900 CE: Height of classical period.

900 CE: Downfall of Tikal and exodus of the people.

The first non-Mayans to see this site were Father Avendano and his companions in 1695. The priest wrote that they were lost in the jungle and starving, when they saw "old buildings - and though they were very high and my strength was little, I climbed up them, though with trouble."

When new all of the buildings were decorated with stucco facades and painted in brilliant colors. The taller pyramid was a tomb for a ruler named Hasaw Cha' an K' awil, built by his son who succeeded him in 734. Inside the tomb were found beautiful vases and bowls, 180 pieces of carved jade, Mexican pearls, shells, long bones etched with the religious history of the people, and the king's sting ray spines which he used to pierce his penis for ritual blood-letting.

The palace rooms are stucco with vaulted roofs and raised concrete slabs for sitting or sleeping. Today they seem as bare as prison cells, but the Mayans decorated the walls with bright murals and flowing curtains, and the slabs were covered in tapestry pillows and soft jaguar skins. The elite lounged on the pillows and skins, and were served from beautiful jade and pottery dishes, while orchestras of string and wind instruments played in the background. With dinner, they might have alcohol or an hallucinogenic enema. How is this known? It can all be seen on surviving polychrome pottery.

I climb the north acropolis to the huge masks attached to the walls, and then find the ball court. In addition to this area, there are six other pyramids, more acropolises, and an estimated 3,000 square stone bases for individual thatched huts grouped around their own plazas. To see it all, I would have to walk ten miles. I walk as long as I can, climb more than I thought I could, and know that, like Father Avendano, "my strength is little."

At the Tikal museum, I buy a book on the Mayans. I learn that the causes of the fall of the Mayan civilization were warfare, overpopulation, and exploitation of the land. They used no form of birth control. They made war almost constantly, to capture royal subjects for sacrifice and to enslave the common people. They over-farmed and carried out massive deforestation. Erosion ensued, followed by years of terrible drought. They fled their grand cities and lived in small farming groups or roamed as nomads.

The Spanish conquest brought terrible diseases, cruel subjugation of the people, and poverty which has never eased. During the recent Guatemalan Civil War between Marxist and government troops (1970 - 1996), 200,000 non-political Mayans were killed or "disappeared." Their villages were burned, they were forced into model villages (a move suggested by the US military, who did the same in Vietnam,) and thousands fled to Honduras, Mexico, and Belize.

Now the war is over and many have returned, still poor, illiterate, and marginalized. Over half of the Mayan men and almost all the woman are illiterate. I am told by white Guatemalans that Mayan men do not want their wives and daughters to attend school. (This is very different from what Belizean Mayans and a Guatemalan cab driver, who is Mayan, tell me.)

In Watsonville, California, a local group heard about a Mayan village that was dispossessed and destroyed by a wealthy Guatemalan in order to give the land to his son as a wedding present. Watsonville people collected money to buy the Mayans new land and material to build homes. Anyone could contribute money for a door, a sack of nails, shelving material, a window frame, or an entire house for $750. Bob and I decided we'd never again be able to buy a house for so little money, so we gave a house. Others went to help with the building, but we skipped that part.

In spite of oppression, the Mayan population continues to grow, as they continue to raise huge families. The present Mayan population in southern Mexico and Central American is estimated to be 7,500,000.

I take the bus to **Flores**, about an hour from Tikal, to rest and write for a few days. Flores is a colorful town with cobblestone streets and freshly painted, many-colored buildings. I'm sitting at an orange and green table in the Casona de la Isla hotel, above lovely Lake Peten Itza', as large as Lake Atitlan but without volcanoes. It's a gorgeous morning, not hot, and I am watching two large, white, long-legged egrets step daintily along the grassy shore. Dugouts and motorized water taxis pass by.

Hearing firecrackers, I rush to the street. A marimba band is playing outside the hotel and twelve-foot puppets (people on stilts) dance around it. The air is acrid with the smell of old-fashioned firecrackers, the kind we exploded when I was a child. I ask what the festival is about. "Nothing. Just local," a man says. A woman explains, "It's December. Christmas is coming." Everyone is clapping in time to the music and laughing.

When the mini-fiesta ceases, I ask a taxi driver my usual question, "What is interesting here?" I know from the guide book what he'll say, but hope I'll get lucky and hear of something wildly wonderful. I don't get lucky. He tells me of the nearby Cave of the Serpents, so named either because very poisonous snakes live in rocks outside the exit no one uses, or because some of the interior rocks have markings that look vaguely like serpent trails that might have been made a million years ago when the rocks were soft. Whatever, I agree to be taken there. Inside the cave are rock formations that the locals say resemble sharks' teeth, elephants' feet, a Mayan profile, a jaguar. It is dark and slippery, I totter, and the taxi driver holds my arm. I feel old and clumsy, and don't stay long.

The driver's name is Oscar. He tells me that he and his wife are thirty years old, have been married twelve years, and have seven children. The last six are girls. His son is in school, but the girls' classes start later this morning. Would I like to meet them, since they live only a few minutes away? Of course, I would. They are beautiful, adorable children, back-eyed and round-faced with dimples. Each is dressed in a starched, happy-colored, flared skirt and blouse. I think of the children in "Sound of Music," and believe these six would be darling in a movie or TV show. They say, "Hola," "Mucho gusto," giggle, and the littlest raises her skirt to show me her new, embroidered panties.

Her big sisters go off to school and she runs next door to their mother's dress shop. I chat with the mother and am amazed that anyone with so many children can be so calm. She sees nothing unusual in having so big a family and doesn't find it difficult to keep them healthy and well-dressed. They take care of each other, she says, and are no problem. She likes making their clothes and seems to like her life. She says it will be difficult to educate them past primary school, which is free, "but if any of the children want to continue in school, God will help us find a way."

Her store is small and caters to locals. She is sewing ribbon on a large tan dress as she talks. She says that white Guatemalans are wrong to believe Mayans don't want to learn in school. All her children except the youngest can already read and write. Women do try to teach each other and their older children, in order to avoid tuition. It is harder for men and women who need to work as porters, carrying heavy loads of wood or water. "Some of them are very young. They have no one to help them because everyone in the family is poor." She adds, "We do not know the white people and they don't know us. We are like two countries on the same land."

Hotel Casona de la Isla ($33 with lake view and swimming pool.)

I'm back in **Guatemala City** for two days, before returning to California for a conference. Most guide books suggest skipping Guatemala City and going straight to Antigua. Antigua has its volcanoes, ruins, cathedral, and an over-abundance of tourists. The narrow, cobblestone streets aren't made for vans, and the zillion tourist buses make the city horribly-congested. I find Antigua oppressive. I was invited to spend today there with some psychotherapists from Antigua, but I prefer wandering by myself in Guatemala City. The layout of avenues and streets here is easy to understand. Even I don't get lost. Sunday is a happy day at the Plaza Mayor, with lots of families wandering about or sitting on benches, chatting. I taxi to the large park, Minerva, even more crowded. There is an amusement park at one end, and lots of nice walking paths, plus the famous, very large relief map of the entire country. Little signs attached to the map give the names of towns, lakes, rivers, harbors, and major ruins. I locate each place I have been, while fantasizing where I will travel next time.

In the Christmas market I buy presents like crazy: weavings, little clay doves, small mirrors, purses, and shirts. Locals are buying ornaments and other holiday decorations. Outdoor lights are selling big. Christmas songs play loudly over loud speakers, including "Rudolph" and "White Christmas" in Spanish.

I find the best weavings in the store that is part of the Ixchel museum. It's a pleasant little museum of Mayan weavings and designs through the centuries. Across the street is another small museum, Popul Vuh, which has an interesting collection of pottery, whistles, and urns.

Tonight local therapists are giving a big party for me. Because I have to get up at 5:00 A.M. to get to the airport, I ask for an early party, but they are late picking me up, and dinner isn't served until almost midnight. Oh, well. I have the rest of my life for sleeping. They sing, I listen, and we all eat well.

A GUATEMALAN PSYCHIATRIST

Rolando is a happy man. He smiles, laughs, teaches beautifully, is fascinated with new ideas, and his students obviously adore him. I ask him, "Why are you so happy?" and he tells me about his wife, who is a successful business woman, a teacher of a type of movement therapy called bio-dance, and a soprano in the Guatemalan national choir. He tells me about his four grown children and his one grandson. And he says, "God is good to me."

As a therapist, I know that sad children usually become sad adults. The fearful stay fearful, the worriers keep worrying, and the stoics not only suppress their feelings but acquire more disasters to face with stoicism. Rolando knows this, too.

"So what kept you happy in your childhood?"

"I was the first son, first nephew, first grandchild. Everybody loved me. I was raised by four women and each of them gave me something important. My mother was a nurse-specialist in the care of premature infants. She taught me to work hard and to love my work. From her I learned to choose my profession carefully and do it well.

"My grandmother loved people. She surrounded herself with friends, and valued them. She taught me the importance of people in my life. My mother's oldest sister, my aunt, must have started choosing books for me on the day I was born, and she never stopped giving me books and discussing them with me. She taught me to love reading and learning. I don't think there has been a day in my adult life when I have not read. My younger aunt was a professor of physical education. She bought me my first basketball and taught me to play. I became a member of our national basketball team that played in the Olympics.

"The men in my family were absent. My grandfather was a distant person. My father was a Panamanian, whom my mother left after my birth. I met him when I was fifteen. I didn't miss having a father, because my life was full. However, I liked him when I met him.

"I teach students and patients to be active, to play with the cards they are dealt, not to focus on what they didn't get or wait for someone to give them something better. That is how I live my life."

A BROKEN HIP and A DEATH POSTPONED

This is the beginning of my third year of full-time travel. First stop, Isla Mujeres, for the eleventh gathering of mostly-retired women psychotherapists. There have been changes. Flo Olivier is dead. Three members are now too old to travel, and others have taken their places. We stay, as always, at the twelve-bedroom Hotel Garafon de Castillo, every room facing the warm, wonderful sea.

After breakfast, we meet to share our lives. Our Mexican member recounts her thrill at receiving the 2003 award for the best research in the social sciences in Mexico. Her research is on female co-dependency, its social, cultural and familial causes, and new ideas for treatment. A member, who grew up in Japan, reports having a private luncheon with the Empress of Japan. The Empress is very interested in her work with trauma victims in post-earthquake Kobe. Tragically, one of our first members, an internationally known psychotherapist and writer, announces with consummate courage, "I have been diagnosed with Alzheimer's. I have difficulties in my thinking, especially at night. But please treat me as you always have. I am still me." As we listen to her, we are weeping and offering what help we can.

Our oldest member, eighty-nine, quite deaf and almost blind, swims daily, even when the wind is high and the waves strong. The two youngest, forty-four and fifty-four, swim with her. During our years together, all have lost loved friends and family members; this year is no different. We laugh and cry and cheer together, and prove the healing power of empathic listening and love. On the fourth evening, we have a party honoring two members who are celebrating their 50th anniversary of living together.

Travel tips: *pack a skirt, toga, dress, or sari. You just never know when you might break a hip. And you really don't want to pull pants down and up when you have to pee.*

It happened. **Thursday** night, February 5. After two years of traveling without an accident and a lifetime with only minor injuries, at the final party for the Women's Workshop, I fall hard and break my hip. The pain is horrendous. I am taken by stretcher, ambulance, and

204

launch to Cancun for X-rays. A naval doctor, who accompanies me, rubs my stomach very softly and sings me a children's song in Spanish about a little turtle with a hurt tail who, if he doesn't get well today, will get well tomorrow.

X-rays show a crack in the neck of the femur. There is no displacement, so perhaps it isn't too important. I'm told not to try to walk; the hip may heal slowly and naturally without surgery. Others urge that I take the first plane back to California, where I'll receive excellent surgery and physical therapy paid for by Medicare. I don't consider this option, because I'm scheduled for two weeks of workshop-seminars in Redecision therapy in Cuba, and will be introducing a child psychiatrist from Mexico who will teach with me. Also, six other women are coming to Cuba at my invitation and I don't want to dump them on their own. I am sure I can manage with a wheelchair. The night at the Hyatt is long and painful.

Friday: In the morning I phone my friend Adrienne in Cuba to tell her of my accident. She says, "An orthopedic surgeon from Canada happens to be visiting me and is in my living room right now. Hold on." She is back on the line. "Don't worry about a thing. We'll meet you at the airport with a wheel chair." The trip to Cuba turns out to be the most terrible in my life. We get to the Cancun airport at 2:00P.M. for the 4:00P.M. flight. There is no place to lie down. The quite-new airport, like so many others, is equipped with hard plastic seats and hard plastic, immobile arm rests to guarantee that all passengers remain erect. The departure is delayed. Finally, I am moved by special wheelchair onto the plane, and have to get my body from wheelchair to seat. I am literally screaming from pain. Thirty minutes later we are told that there are "mechanical difficulties," and we must return to the lobby. We finally arrive in Havana about midnight. Even the slightest movement is agony. As I greet my friends, my face is slimy with tears. The Canadian surgeon gives me an immediate shot of morphine and decides to spend the night in the room next to mine. (After the Cuban people won the revolution in 1959, wealthy Cuban physicians and surgeons fled. This orthopedic surgeon from Canada came to Cuba to establish a first-class school of orthopedic surgery. Now retired, he returns yearly to vacation and visit friends.)

Saturday: Rivas, my psychiatrist friend, the Canadian surgeon, and the chief of orthopedic surgery at a huge teaching hospital in La

Habana all look at my X-rays and decide I need immediate surgery. They want to hospitalize me now, to make sure I don't compound the fracture, but I refuse. I want to do my workshops here! Finally they agree to postpone the decision about surgery until after the workshops, and see what happens.

I move to Celeste's apartment, where I have lived on previous visits. She has hired a full time practical nurse, Lili, who knows how to cook very special vegetarian food. During the day I have to scream, really scream, to get her not to help me in and out of a wheelchair, but she is very cheerful and does cook well. Her fee is ten US dollars a day.

I phone my daughter Karen to tell her the news. She tells me to come home, but I assure her I am doing well. "I will be fine."

Sunday: At my request, Rivas emails therapists in Peru and Ecuador for me, to cancel my workshops scheduled there next month. Celeste hobbles about, much more crippled than last year. She, too, is scheduled for hip surgery, hers due to arthritis and subsequent hip deterioration, but she must get rid of her kidney infection first. We try to laugh about our troubles, and do enjoy each other very much. She suggests I move to Cuba permanently and live with her. I tell her I would love to, but my entire family is in the US.

Monday, Tuesday, Wednesday, and Thursday: The long, difficult treks, about forty feet from bedroom to bathroom to living room by wheel chair, are painful. I still believe I'll be okay in a couple of weeks, but Juan Pablo Hecheverria, my laserpuncturist and healer, is especially pessimistic. He wants me to have surgery before it gets worse, and says there is really nothing he can do that substitutes for surgery. After surgery, laserpuncture would speed the healing process, he says.

Every day I have visitors, American, Mexican, Canadian, and Cuban. My Mexican co-therapist and I work with our translator, to see if she can handle the job of translating two languages simultaneously. My co-therapist wants to speak only in Spanish, which I'll need translated in order to keep up with what she is saying. The translator isn't that proficient, so all three of us will have to cooperate on the translations. It won't be smooth. I'm becoming worn out from pain and morphine even in large doses doesn't help much.

Dr. Hecheverria comes every afternoon, exuding simultaneously energy and beautiful calmness. On Thursday he is quite serious. He is feeling my hip very carefully, and saying little. He spends more than half an hour slowly moving his hand over my hip and leg. He puts the laser on new areas of my body and right leg, all the time cupping his large hand over my broken left hip. He doesn't quite touch it but I feel his heat. The pain disappears and I sense a deep relaxation. He packs up his machine, kisses me goodbye, and leaves. I sleep from 5:30P.M. to almost 6:00A.M, my first night without pain. But when I wake, the pain is there with fresh intensity. I am being given morphine regularly and benedryl for the hives the morphine causes. Then Lili brings me pills from a friend of a friend. For me they are better than morphine, although they are only ibuprofen. I'm eating very little and have stopped giving myself insulin.

Friday: More friends drop by. This is the week of the Book Fair, held annually at the huge fortress, built between 1589 and 1630 on the high limestone hills at the entrance to the harbor, across the bay from Old Habana. It cost the king of Spain so much in gold, silver, and manpower that he reportedly said, "For that price it should be high enough for me to see it from Madrid." In 1762 the British captured the fort by attacking on the landward side and building a tunnel into it. So ended the usefulness of many fortresses and Great Walls.

Cubans love to read, which makes the Book Fair an immensely successful annual event, attended by thousands. Last year I attended, and enjoyed the excitement and the presentations tremendously. There is one room dedicated to Che, which is especially moving. I am sorry to miss this year's festivities, but there is no way I can even leave the apartment. Rivas has been coming to Celeste's each night to tell me what I have missed. Two days ago he described for me the launching of a new psychiatry text. Today is the launching of Adrienne's book, SEVEN WOMEN OF THE REVOLUTION, a story of seven very rich women who decided to stay in Cuba after the country became Communist. They lost their sugar refineries, private railroads, and tobacco corporations, but were allowed to keep their palace-like homes. The launching is grand, Rivas tells me. A major poet gives a speech in praise of the book, and the five of the women who are still alive introduce themselves and their families, and autograph copies. Hundreds of people crowd in to buy the books at fifty cents each, priced so that Cubans can afford them. The printing was subsidized by foreign contributions and the Cuban government.

Saturday: Adrienne spends much of the afternoon with me. I tell myself I am feeling a bit better. Celeste and Lili fix a lovely lobster dinner for eight of us. We have a lively, bilingual evening.

Sunday: It is time to be moved to the Censam Rehabilitation Center for the first week's workshop. The van is high and my hip hurts a great deal. I can't seem to maneuver myself well. As I let people try to help, my hip displaces. I hear the cracking, and the pain is more intense than I ever believed possible.

Monday: I begin the workshop, but can't continue. My co-therapist finishes this first day of work, and the rest is canceled. I go to the hospital for new X-rays that show huge damage. Even I am frightened by the pictures. The orthopedic surgeon would operate immediately without charge, and I would recuperate for two months at their beautiful modern hospital, where I would receive daily laserpuncture from my friend, special massage, and top notch physical therapy. The best of Eastern and Western medicine is combined in post-surgical treatment. I wish we offered the same quality of free care in the United States. Bitterly, I tell my friends we could, if we weren't spending our money on wars.

I act as if I don't know what to do, but in truth I have already decided. I have completed everything I have planned for this life. There is always more, of course, but I am old. Dying seems increasingly pleasant. I bring up the subject with two friends. "Do you have ethical problems with suicide?" One is so horrified she won't even speak about it. My Mexican co-therapist, about ten years younger than I am and in excellent health, understands. She says she has always believed that the timing of death should be an intensely personal decision.

"What if I told you it is my decision?"

"I'd understand."

"Well, let's lighten up a bit. Call it death by chocolate."

We both smile briefly. She is a physician, so knows, as I do, that this is considered an easy death for diabetics. I try to think about my options to the extent that I can through the pain and the morphine that confuses me but is not sufficiently potent against the pain.

Tips for everybody: *Much later, I learn that as many as five per cent of people do not respond positively to morphine. To subdue their*

208

pain, something needs to be developed.

I've pretty much stopped eating, and haven't used insulin since Saturday, so I believe my body decided even before my mind became fully aware of my decision. I ask my friend to arrange our flight to Mexico. I phone my children to tell them my hip has displaced and I am flying to Mexico. It's almost impossible to communicate because telephones between Cuba and the US are jammed. From Cuba people phone all over the world easily, except to the US.

Tuesday: The Cuban doctors give me morphine for the plane trip. I am sad to be leaving, especially as I don't plan to see them again and don't want to tell them this. On the plane I think about being dead and ask my Mexican friend if she would be willing to stay with me while I die. She says she will. We go to the Hyatt in Cancun, but can get a room for only one night, because it is Fiesta Week.

My life has been such a good one. I am one of the luckiest people I know - in my vocation, family, friends, lifetime opportunities. I have always planned to die before I am old and fragile, and now I am both. At the hotel I consider injecting myself with a full bottle of insulin, which would make my heart stop, but I read in the Hemlock society literature that this is not a pleasant way. Much more pleasant, but slower, is simply to die of lack of insulin. Without insulin and with sugar, I will eventually slip into an irreversible coma. That first night in Cancun, I am propped up on the bed, facing the glorious blue sea, as I eat a full-size chocolate cake, piece by piece. I've thrown away my insulin paraphernalia. I am very peaceful and it seems as if I am hurting less. The freedom to die may be hypnotic, or perhaps the sugar takes me out of myself. I am in pain but somehow beyond it. It doesn't really touch me any more. I seem to be enveloped in a soft whiteness. I don't think or plan or talk. I don't feel.

Wednesday: I phone my son David to tell him I am in Mexico, am going back to Isla Mujeres, and I am planning to die there. I'd like him and his sisters to come to say good-bye if they choose. I remember to tell him to bring his mask and snorkel, because the swimming is wonderful. Almost immediately I receive a call from Claudia. I am very confused, and think I am talking to Karen. She is crying very hard. In my confused state I believe she is only a little girl, maybe six years old. How did it happen she has stayed so young, while everyone else is grown? I speak very gently to her, "I would be dying soon anyway, honey. What difference does a year or two make?" She keeps repeating "I'm not ready for you to die!" I don't know how the conversation ends, but eventually we hang up. I am unable to contact Karen. So I lie back, and eat chocolate creams. Sometimes I seem to be only semi-conscious, which feels lovely.

David: *I phone Claudia, and she arranges a one-week emergency leave from her hospital. We meet at her home half an hour later. I ignore Mother's request to keep this secret, because I want her sister Laurie to come to Mexico with us. We need her support. She agrees. Claudia also tells two people, our family physicians, who write her prescriptions for whatever she thinks she'll need in Mexico for Mother's comfort and pain relief. We are shocked and, of course, very sad, and I certainly plan to bring Mother back to California if at all possible. The first tickets we can get are for Friday. Claudia and I spend Thursday buying drugs and packing. Laurie will fly to Texas and go with us from there.*

Thursday: We are taking the launch back in Isla Mujeres, and I am crazy with pain. The men at the hotel carry me in my wheelchair down the long stairway to a first-floor room. I have known some of these men for more than twenty years; some were babies when I first arrived. I tell them my family is coming, and they assure me they will make room for any who arrive, "even if we have to evict other guests." They help me to bed, and then one of them brings me a huge, home-made orange and chocolate cake. He, of course, has no idea that the cake is for the purpose of my dying. I eat it piece by piece, in between passing out. The air becomes a soft, palpable whiteness and I am wrapped in it. It buoys me somewhere above myself, then merges into a dusk that comes and goes. I am not sensing movement around me or in me. I simply am, in this white, sweet light that tastes of sugar and chocolate. Dusk darkens and fades, blending with the light.

Friday and Saturday: David, Claudia, and Laurie arrive. As soon as I see them, I rouse myself enough to tell them, "If you've come to take me back, you may as well turn around and go home." I think everyone is crying. They assure me they are here to make me comfortable and to be with me. By now I'm not totally sane, but I know what I want.

(Karen keeps in touch through the hotel phone in the office, as there are no phones in the rooms. She plans to come to Isla with another of my sisters and my friend Felipe, if I don't come back to the US.)

Claudia writes in her notebook: *Mommy's worse than we could have imagined. Bruised, dehydrated, jaundiced, and still without adequate pain relief. I give her a large dose of morphine and put on a fentanyl patch, which helps a lot. She doesn't respond well to morphine. Much of the time she isn't fully conscious. Her Mexican friend explains that the Cuban doctors tried very hard to persuade her to have surgery. All of us believe she made a bad choice when she refused surgery there, but do we really know what is best for anyone? She's lived courageously, and traveled where not many women go alone. We've all had exciting, happy times with her and our lives are better for it. She has taken excellent care of us and of herself, kept her mind active, and continued writing and working with amazing wit and productivity until this accident. She is also willful and controlling, and perhaps we won't be able to change the path she is on. She says she's on her last voyage and it is beautiful. I can't sleep, so I sit by the beach and watch the lights from Cancun.*

Mommy's Mexican friend is patient and loving. Today she and I go to town to get more supplies. It's carnival day, and the plaza is full of dancers. We walk past them, carrying a commode and stacks of diapers. It turns out that even the commode is impossible for her to use as the pain is too great, so I insert a catheter, and find her urine to be red and jelly-like, possibly from a crush injury? Mommy doesn't seem to realize anything that I am doing, but even so I tell her and get permission for each procedure. I disimpact her bowels. I truly want her to have time to make an informed decision, which she won't have without fluid, insulin, and the patches. I may be too late. She's not responding well.

I am very worried, so decide we must involve a physician. I find one who speaks English and is a dear. He drives right back to the hotel with me, then drives me around town to collect IV fluid, needles, benedryl for itching, and other supplies, which I can't get without him. Medical supplies are sparse here. The tape I need is sold by the inch and wrapped around a popsicle stick. The pharmacies don't sell a syringe for mixing fluids, so the doctor gets his only one from a trunk in his own office, and drives me back to the hotel. I have to put saline, sugar, vitamins into the IV all at once, because there is only one needle on the island. It clots and I have to take it out and aspirate it with the syringe. We stack end tables and tie the IV bag to the top, using the string from Mommy's glasses. What I am doing, for the first time in my life, is third-world medicine. I feel as if I am working with Doctors without Borders.

My sister Laurie lies beside me on my bed, whispering to me how much she loves me and how important I was to her when she was little. I was fourteen when she was born. "You must not die now. I want to travel with you now that I am free to go any time. Stay alive! Please don't die." I hear her and am very touched, but don't have the strength to answer.

David is mostly silent, but always present. He strokes my hair, pats my face, and is with me all the time. I know Claudia is my loving, beautiful nurse. I am profoundly grateful that she has made much of the pain go away. I am surrounded by their incredible love, but am also still somewhere beyond them all. I am eating ice cream.

Claudia: *The doctor visits several times, and, because no pharmacy sells blood glucose meters, he tests her blood for sugar. It is over 600, which is frightening. He understands her desire not to have surgery. He says he knows many old people who prefer to stay home to die rather than have surgery, and this is a legitimate choice at Mommy's age. He thinks she can last here only another two weeks.*

Sunday I wake up early, and there, lying in my bed, his face only inches from mine, is my smiling grandson, Brian, who left his job to be with me. Last night he missed the final launch, so slept on the concrete pier until early morning. He keeps smiling at me, I smile back at him, and he yells out, "Grammy's going to be all right!" We stay just as we are on the bed, grinning at each other.

A few hours later, Claudia says, "How about going back to California with us?'

I say, "Sure," as if that is what has always been planned. They immediately make the arrangements. Laurie leaves first.

Tuesday, February 24: Brian stays until I am on the first plane home. The long trip to California is terrible, but mostly I am out of it. They have me wrapped in a sheet and blanket from the hotel, which they use like a stretcher. My friend, Claudia, and David literally carry me up the plane steps and put me in the first seats of first class, which the plane personnel give them without extra charge. Between planes,

American Airlines has stretchers waiting, and I am taken easily through customs. I have only scattered memories of the trip, and for the next two days, before and after surgery, I know my name (people in the hospital keep asking), but don't know where I am. I think I am in Cuba, but my Cuban friends are not with me, so I believe the anti-Cubans have invaded and destroyed the country. I need somehow to get out of bed and hide. I keep asking where is Rivas and am afraid he is dead. David or Claudia is beside me every minute, day and night. If I am crying or agitated, they are stroking my face and holding my hand.

The next day, quite suddenly, I know I am in Watsonville, California. My body and self have reunited. Two large, Black, very strong nurses are lifting me so gently I scarcely feel it. They remind me of Hecheverria, but they are not Cuban. During the next few days, the nurses who come into my room are from Southeast Asia, China, the Philippines, Mexico, and even two plump, blonde older women who look just like my German grandmother. With each of these nurses I feel as if I am still traveling. I like all of them. They are amazed at my travel stories and hang around my bed, asking for more. My left leg lies motionless, a strange, dead animal in the bed with me, but gradually it begins to come back to life. I am still in pain, because no one understands that morphine doesn't help me. I get hives from it.

My daughter Karen arrives from Colorado with a huge bouquet of flowers and a pair of fancy ski socks "because you've left the tropics, Mommy." I am delighted that she is with me. My friend Felipe has come from Texas, and fixes us a Mexican banquet to celebrate my leaving the hospital. Brian is back at his job in Mexico, but the other three grandchildren are here in Watsonville. Ruth, an undergraduate in biology, is very loving and helpful. Chandra and John, in high school, tell me about their track and volleyball teams. All my visitors are jubilant that I am back. I know it is harder to say good-bye than to be the one who leaves, so I understand their joy but don't totally participate in it.

I am exhausted and without zest. I think I may be satisfied with being alive. But not entirely. Dying was a friendly state, and now in my private alone time, when the others are not beside me, I mourn its loss. Some day I will move again consciously toward death, slowly and peacefully, in a leisurely fashion, surrounded by family who with great good luck will finally be ready to say good-bye. Or I'll find a lovely place to die alone by the sea. I'll die of chocolate and giggle as I go. That date is in the future and now I have to start exercising in order to walk again.

A month later, while walking with a cane, my right leg buckles and I fall to the sidewalk. My right hip is fractured. There is no romance in my hospital stay. With my first broken hip, I was an interesting character who'd been in Mexico and Cuba. The staff wanted to hear all about it. This time I am just another boring old lady.

I manage to escape on the third day, back to Claudia's, a happy place full of dogs, birds, fish, and all her reminders of past trips: Asian dolls, a ceramic Sicilian vender of cheese and bread, a tapestry from Brugge, her framed photographs from Italy, Spain, Paris, Austria, and Mexico. We are having a good time, but I am embarrassed that I am also a burden. Besides working full time, she has to take care of me.

I am afraid, very afraid of falling. I have osteoporosis. What bone is next? If I still had my apartment, I'd be tempted to go back to it. Just lie about, rent movies, visit my wonderful family and friends. And quietly eat chocolate and ice cream and sugary drinks when I am ready. I want a gradual lessening of life at my own speed in a place of my choice, watching my last sunrises or sunsets. I want to be in charge of my own comas with nobody fussing me. I just figured that out. I love traveling alone, and this will be the final travel.

In my first chapter I wrote cheerfully; "If I find out I do not like being homeless, I am one of the lucky people. I can change my mind." That's no longer quite true. An evil man, the only truly evil man I have ever known personally, Bob's eldest son-in-law, has entered my life and found a way to steal my money legally. He won't stop my traveling but he may have left me with too little money to return to the US in comfort. We'll see. But soon it will be time to figure out what to do next, me and my walker.

PUERTO VALLARTA TO IXTAPA

Solo, and a week with family

It's May, six weeks after my second surgery and I can barely walk even with my new walker. Thomas Jefferson wrote to John Adams in 1812: "Our machines have now been running seventy to eighty years, and we must expect that, worn as they are, here a pivot, there a wheel, now a pinion, next a spring, will be giving way, and however we may tinker with them for awhile all will at last cease motion." Adams responded, "I am sometimes afraid that my machine will not surcease motion soon enough, for I dread nothing so much as dying at the top."

For the first time in my life I'm afraid of traveling alone, so I must prove to myself that I can do it. In June some of my family is vacationing at Club Med Ixtapa, where grandson Brian is working. I decide to fly to Puerto Vallarta and take first-class buses down the coast, stopping at small towns on the way to Ixtapa. I'm comfortable in Mexico, because I've loved it for so long, and Mexican taxi drivers always take good care of me. I decide to test out the west coast of Mexico to see if my walker and I can manage. I buy a duffel bag that will fit on the seat of my walker, plus a light backpack for my pillow and medicines. It turns out that a backpack won't do. I can't carry weight. So it goes on top of the duffel bag. I've packed very lightly, just essentials and my feather pillow that I take everywhere.

Travel tips: *Packing depends on the purpose of the trip. Romance, potential or actual, and conferences demand more clothing and bigger suitcases than plain old solitary travel. For this trip I take: two swimming suits; two pairs of lightweight slacks and one long-sleeved shirt for sun protection; a pair of shorts; three light T shirts (that sell three for ten dollars in San Francisco); and a Mexican mumu from past trips, which I bring so that I won't be tempted to buy another; pills and vitamins sorted into plastic sandwich bags to save weight and space; lotions and sun protectors; beach shoes; underpants; my pillow; and three books, which I'll exchange in used book stores along the way. I carry a sweater, so as not to freeze in the super-air-conditioned, Arctic climate produced on first class Mexican buses.*

Fortunately, I gave up bras in the bra-burning era and haven't worn one since. For the non-handicapped, this is easy carry-on luggage. I have to use check-in, but I avoid the long lines by ordering a wheelchair when I buy my tickets. Since wheel-chair pushers need to work swiftly, I am always waved to the front of the lines.

In 1944 I went by second class bus from Mexico City to Acapulco, the only non-Indian aboard. In those days Indians still dressed traditionally, the women and girls in long skirts, embroidered blouses, shawls, and strips of bright cotton woven into their dark braids; the men and boys wore the all-white shirts and pants of the campesino. They all gawked at me. White skin on a second class bus obviously was not a common sight. This was years before the hippies. The women turned around in their seats or leaned forward to ask me questions, and giggled wildly into their shawls when I responded. I don't think they had ever before heard anyone speak Spanish so badly. I didn't mind their giggles. It was fun. After a couple of hours, the bus stopped beside a cornfield. All the females except me got off, crouched, and peed. Obviously none wore underpants. I sat on the bus alone with the males, red faced and as humiliated as an eighteen-year-old can be. I decided that the first thing I would do in Acapulco was to buy myself a long skirt and eliminate underpants from my traveling outfit. When the women got back on the bus, the men got off, formed a straight line, backs to the bus, and peed.

By the time we got to a second-class bus station, I was desperate. Leaping from the bus, I ran to the toilet. When I stood up, there were the men, crowded around the toilet booth, staring down at me. My first experience with a unisex restroom was not a happy one. Acapulco was wonderful. I paid only one dollar a day room and board. I thought I had found the Garden of Eden.

I found Puerto Vallarta in the sixties, right after Elizabeth Taylor and Richard Burton made it famous. Donkeys carried their loads along cobble-stoned streets, and cows wandered by. Dead Men's beach (playa de los muertos) was fantastic. The waves were ideal for body surfing and swimming, the sand soft and smooth, and one could spend entire days lazing under a coconut tree, watching the venders who formed a steady parade, their trinkets, blankets, and blouses piled high on their heads. Every day at sunset I drank a coco loco and nibbled the liquored-up coconut meat. By the eighties Puerto Vallarta was crowded with Gringos, and that's when I began doing workshops in Akumal and Isla Mujeres. I already know that P.V. is touristy, but I don't care.

I fly to **Puerto Vallarta** and tell the cab driver that I want an inexpensive hotel with a good swimming pool and a ground floor bedroom with an ocean view. I suggest Tropicana, where I used to stay.

"It's been fancied up and has lots of stairs. It would be very hard for you." He thinks about the problem. "El Arco is better." He's right. It's just what I want. I rent a large room on the ground floor, with picture windows overlooking the water. I unpack, put on a swimming suit, and lather up with sun block. There are two swimming pools, one for everyone and one for adults only, so I don't have to fear a child jumping on me. Lots of people are in the pools, mostly Mexican families. I'm timid about getting in and out, as I've been land bound since my accident in Isla Mujeres.

I decide to try the beach first, but find that the walker wheels are worthless in the soft sand. Not to worry. I have help from the young man who rents lounge chairs and beach umbrellas. He waves his friends over, and four of them push-pull me to a front row spot beside the water. I settle into a lounge chair and, because this is a special occasion, order a rum and diet coke. Around me, mariachis are playing. A young man from Zacatecas, who is studying alternative medicine, offers me a massage for very little money. I let him do my shoulders but am afraid to have him touch my hips or legs. We chat awhile about his studies. A beach salesman offers silver jewelry from Taxco at a "very special price for you, senora." He laughs when I ask if it will be specially high or low. Do I want a needle-less tattoo? The young tattoo-seller grins charmingly. We both know I am two generations past tattoos, but he shows me his designs anyway, and I pretend to admire them. Although the next salesman can see I am wearing dark glasses, he thinks I might want a second pair, "very cheap, senora." Behind me six college age young people, four men and two women, perhaps from Guadalajara, are playing beach volleyball quite well.

The launch, Princess Yelapa, passes. I've ridden it many times in the past, south to the coves and hotels that are inaccessible by road. Once I jumped off the Princess as soon as it was anchored, and swam the distance to Yelapa instead of waiting for the small boats that take passengers ashore. I'm nostalgic, remembering these trips.

Wispy clouds float past. I watch pelicans, seagulls, and four of the largest frigate birds I have ever seen. A brightly colored parachute high in the sky is towed by a small motorboat, while the girl aboard kicks her legs in a carefree way. Obviously she has no fear of heights. I should have taken that ride long ago, right here on Dead Men's beach. But it doesn't matter. I am too old to debate should of/could of with myself. Now I **can't**, so I'll just enjoy the fearless female high above me. It's calming to know that such frightening activities are not options any more.

People all around me are sunning, reading, and sleeping. The parachute lands only a few feet from me, and the young woman climbs out to join the volley ball players. A man and his tiny daughter are playing in the waves. She screeches joyously as he dips her in and out. I buy a necklace with blue and silver beads, to give to my sister for her birthday, and then shut my eyes and nap a bit. When I wake up, I'm hungry, so have a late lunch of barbequed shrimp right here on the beach. I think my soul is smiling. I love Puerto Vallarta. And, guess what, I'm glad I'm alive to have this day.

From my bedroom I watch the sun go down over the sea, hazy and only vaguely orange. During the week I'll probably see a spectrum of sunset colors. I push my way slowly to Olas de Cafe, only a block away, but it is the farthest I can go. My wrists hurt from leaning on the walker, and my right hip is sore. The enchilada and chile relleno are worth the trip.

The next day I get up the nerve to go in the pool. I push the walker to the edge, feeling frightened and incapable, set the brakes, and immediately a man comes to help me down the steps into the water. I begin to swim and am ecstatic to discover that I swim as well as ever! I do a fine crawl, roll over into a back stroke, surface dive and bounce back up, float, dog paddle. There is nothing I can't do! I'm laughing under water, as I watch the bubbles rise. All day I alternate between a poolside lounge chair and the glory of swimming. A couple of old ladies (probably a bit younger than I) tell me that I swim like a dolphin. I thank them, and wonder why they are not swimming. I suppose they never learned how, poor things.

Tips for everyone: Make sure your children learn to swim when they are young. I believe it is a civic duty for all school districts to teach both swimming and a second language in every elementary school. Remember Iceland, that freezing place, where everyone has access to a warm public pool. People who learn to swim as adults are forever awkward in the water, just as adults who learn another language never get it quite right.

I wish our government would discard its obsession with test passing, and instead offer art, music, dancing, swimming, languages, and creative writing. Reading, writing, history, science, and arithmetic can be woven into these other courses. Oh well, my wish list for the US is volumes long and begins with: stop making war.

I've been here in Puerto Vallarta a week, swimming in the pool, relaxing on the beach, walking to nearby restaurants, reading, and lying on the beach. I could easily spend another week or two alone here, but I want to visit other towns on the way to Ixtapa.

Hotel Los Arcos ($88 with tax) is located near Old Town, within a block or two of excellent seafood restaurants, Olas de Cafe for Mexican food, cafes specializing in good coffee and spectacular fruit, an internet cafe, and a used book store. For those not walkingly-challenged, the beautiful church with the tiled roof, the main plaza, and the malecon are nearby.

Melaque is dusty and shabby, an uninteresting town. At this time of year there are almost no tourists, though Canadians fill it during the winter months. The town is like a somewhat inferior sister, just not pretty or interesting compared to glamorous Puerto Vallarta. It doesn't have the beautiful church, winding river, lovely hills, Gringo Gulch. It has no scandalous past. Elizabeth Taylor and Richard Burton never made love in this town. Yet I imagine that this is a more comfortable place to spend a winter. I'd like it better. There are no sirens, crowded streets, or incredibly expensive hotels, no plastic pretentiousness. What Melaque does have is a long, beautiful stretch of sandy beach, nice waves, cheap hotels, and Las Palomas, a very special retreat.

A Canadian couple, Richard and Nancy Lennie, moved to Hawaii, found it too cold for their liking, and came here. They have been building and decorating studio apartments ever since. There are now ten suites of various sizes, built randomly between trees and beautiful gardens. Unfortunately for me, only second floor suites have ocean views, but I have my own private garden with a wildly green fountain, hand painted tiles, hibiscus everywhere, and palm fronds shading my private hammock. A table and chairs for eating outdoors is under a huge tropical tree. My one-room suite is decorated with Nancy's art, plus bright, exquisitely crafted Mexican ceramics. Each suite is uniquely decorated. Nancy gives art classes to guests who come from everywhere to attend. Private and group Spanish lessons are available from a woman who lives across the street. Another neighbor cooks and serves dinner to guests who don't want to eat in town. Other locals offer manicures and massages.

The swimming pool is beside the beach, with flowers and a large ceramic iguana. This is a happy place because the staff and the Lennies are happy people. She says they have had the same staff for nine years, which must mean they pay well and are good bosses. I count about twelve people, from bricklayers to the Spanish teacher, to whom they have given employment. They manage all this without learning Spanish themselves. Instead, they surround a Spanish word or two with lots of English. "How much longer trabaja with the jack hammer? It is mucho noise." "Mary wants her comida at siete." Everyone seems to have learned to translate what she says. In response, they speak slowly, simply and clearly. After two days here, I almost believe my grasp of Spanish is perfecto. When I go downtown for lunch and internet, reality rushes in.

After school, boys bring their sand boards to the beach, jump on them and scoot across sand and shallow water up the mountainous face of a high wave. Timed correctly, board and rider reach the crest just as the wave crashes. The rider does a back flip with the board still somehow on his feet, spins in the air, and rides triumphantly the short distance back to shore. The unlucky are tossed high, arms and legs flailing, and come down like rag dolls. Even less lucky are those smashed into the sand and whirled about, scratched and bleeding. Triumphant or bleeding, all collect their boards from wherever they land, and ride out again into the waves. These waves are dumpers, never used by surfers. Some of the boys look to be about seven or eight years old. Boys dare, while girls sit on the sand, tending babies and watching.

Once, about forty-two years ago in Puerto Vallarta, I got dumped while body surfing, and tore some ligaments in my shoulder. My three children and I were returning to California the next day, so a local doctor in Puerto Vallarta taped me up and airport personnel wheeled me to the plane. The kids walked proudly beside me, dragging luggage, while piled high on my lap were their three huge pinatas. If I hadn't needed the wheelchair, I don't know how we'd have carried all our stuff.

Las Palomas ($50 - $200), depending on size of the room and the season. Within walking distance of town, for those who can manage to walk on rough roads.

The bus from Melaque to **Manzanillo** is a one-hour trip past deserted, tan-colored beaches on the ocean side. On the other side are rolling hills, fruit trees, bright green palm trees, a few small houses, and stretches of desert with twisted leafless trees, framed by the distant pale purple and gray mountains. Inside the bus, the Mexican music is deafening, as it competes with the noisy air-conditioning.

Again a cab driver chooses well for me. Marbella hotel has clean rooms with views of the Pacific across a very wide malecon. The steps to and from the pool area are impossible to manage alone. Everyone offers a hand, which I think would be dangerous. If I fell, so would they. So I suggest one person carry my very light-weight walker up and down the stairs, while I balance by holding onto railings. It works. I am new to the world of cripples, (handicapped, walkingly-challenged, whatever.) I make sure to praise myself several times a day for my pluck in traveling alone in this condition. I need my praise. Truth is, it's not dangerous or difficult, because people help. I am learning that it is okay to depend on them, but I do wonder why my hip is not healing.

The pool is cool and clean, and full of Guadalajara families who come weekends to picnic and swim. One very small boy is screaming hysterically as his mother tries to calm him and to get him to enjoy the water. He doesn't want calming. He wants out. I decide to intervene, which is rare for me. I duck under the water and come up spouting into the air. Twice. On the third spout, he giggles. When his mother mouths, "gracias," I assume I have permission to continue. We splash downward to make bubbles, the child and I, but never splash each other. I spout, he claps, we splash.

That night at dinner I meet a Gringo from Watsonville, where Bob and I ran our institute for twenty-two years. He came here "to fish and be alone. I was a loner." He says he was a very shy man, but then he met his wife and together they run this restaurant. "I married

Magdalena, her parents, this restaurant, and more cousins than you could count. I'm never alone any more. If I take time off to go fishing, a cousin is always along. I'm not griping about that." He doesn't miss the United States at all and has no reason to return. Between seating clients and taking orders, his wife comes over and joins the conversation. She's charming, gregarious, and happy. Their ten-year old daughter is sitting beside us, doing her homework. She's obviously heard their story too many times, so puts in some sighs and eye rolling. When she leaves, she hugs them both.

The next evening, I take a cab to the Jardin del Malecon, (erroneously called the Zocalo in many guidebooks), for the evening concert. The garden is several blocks long. On the town side are yellow, green, and tan stores: pharmacy, dry goods, women's clothing, photo shop, ice cream parlor, and cafes. On the ocean side are a Navy ship and several freighters at anchor. At one narrow end is a white Catholic church and some nondescript municipal buildings, and at the other end two budget hotels and a restaurant. In the garden are beds of roses in all colors, iron benches painted white, and a bright blue sailfish at least three stories high, to honor the fish that brings in tourist dollars. Nearby is a statue, probably of Zapata, who stands so erect it seems he must fall over backwards. He is Noah size, compared to the whale-sized sailfish.

Hundreds of black birds are swirling through the sky to grab pieces of bread thrown by sailors. The black birds and white-uniformed sailors fill the middle of the park, with children running between them, flapping their arms at the birds to scare them briefly away. Men carry huge bouquets of balloons in all the rainbow colors. It is a lovely, cool evening after a hot day. An old man asks, "What happened to you? Did you break your leg?" I tell him, he nods seriously, and then says, "What do you call that machine that helps you walk? It's a good thing to have."

Dozens of plastic chairs are being brought in by truck and placed in front of the bandstand. An announcer repeats by means of a horrendously amplified and distorted sound system that the program will begin with folklorico dancers from Baja California, followed by their own, much loved singer, senorita something or other, and then the local band. Families arrive in groups, and soon all seats are taken. Everyone is well-dressed and very formal. Rarely do families greet other families, which surprises me. This is a small town, so they must know each other. I compare it to Cuba, where the whole crowd would be kissing, hugging, and laughing together.

The dancing is mediocre and the local woman is almost drowned out by the sound system's background music. The band, muy Mexicana, plays more loudly than well.

In the 1930s I spent many summer Sundays in the park in Litchfield, Minnesota, with my grandmother and aunts, listening to the local band play. The Litchfield band wasn't very good either, but my grandmother would say, "Clap loudly. The boys are doing the best they can."

Marbella Hotel $35

I veer a bit off course see **Colima,** the volcanoes and the old city, which has been shaken by eruptions, toppled by earthquakes, and rebuilt countless times. Colima was the third city of the Spanish conquest, after Vera Cruz and Mexico City. When the Spaniards arrived in this area, the Capache Indians became their allies and very quickly learned they'd jumped from frying pan to fire.

I plan to stay at the main plaza in the famous old Colonial hotel, Ceballo, so drag my walker, with my two small suitcases propped on it, into the spacious, colonial lobby only to discover there are no elevators and no guest rooms on the ground floor. The second floor is reached by climbing twenty-one stairs! Worse, there is a convention in town so the receptionists tell me there are no vacancies anywhere.

Travel Tips: *When other options fail, believe in serendipity and give it a nudge.*

I repeat politely, "What can you do to help me?" The question, repeated to each person behind the reception desk, gets me Gilles, owner of Volcano Tours.

He tells me by phone, "This is my day off. I'll be there in an hour. Don't worry about a room. I'll find you one."

I dump my luggage and spend the hour walking around the central plaza. There's a traditional Cathedral, last rebuilt after the 1941 earthquake, which I don't bother with. Inside the government palace are murals of the history of Mexico and especially of Father Miguel Hidalgo, the revolutionary hero who was once a local priest. As my grandmother would say, "Clap. He did the best he could." Next is a regional museum, closed for the lunch hour. I take the hint, and lunch at an outdoor cafe.

Gilles is French, young, has collected three master's degrees, traveled almost everywhere, and found himself a wife in Colima. He now teaches natural science and ecology at the local college and runs his touring company. His specialties are mountain climbing, rappelling into the center of an extinct volcano and down a waterfall, and motorcycle tours. We may not seem a good match, but he is one of my luckiest encounters. As he drives me out of town to a hotel without stairs, he tells me of his ninety-year-old grandmother in France. The second day after her hip operation, she tried to get out of bed. She explained to her nurse that she had to practice walking, because she was going to Mexico to visit her grandson. "I am her favorite person," he says. He planned "perfect trips" to El Volcan del Fuego (Fire Volcano) that she could handle. He'll do a one-day version for me. See how serendipity works?

We start at 7 A.M. in order to reach Volcan de Fuego before the clouds gather. The drive is glorious, past palm forests and bright blue lagoons, deep canyons, and small villages. Along the way, he stops the jeep to show me views of the volcano. He tells me it is the most active in Mexico, more active, it seems, than my favorite Popocateptl. The road ends, he parks, and we walk only a few feet to where the volcano shines directly ahead of us. It stands alone, rising dramatically like Mount Fujiyama in Japan, a high, perfect cone with wisps of smoke, angry rumblings, and bursts of fire erupting from the top. Truly, the mountain is awesome. We sit quietly in this splendor, with colorful songbirds trilling around us, for almost an hour, until the fog covers both trees and El Volcan.

We make a pit stop at a coffee plantation. Their coffee is rich and dark. The next stop is the small village of **Suchitlan**, with the workshop of the Candelario brothers, mask makers. In a land of mask makers, these two men are special. The masks are beautifully carved, winsome, magical animal heads in intricate primary colors. One brother is carving an owl face from a short log, as the chips fly around him. The other shows us a photograph album of their work. I buy a shiny white coyote mask with bright blue and yellow ears pointed straight up, black eyes and nose tip, and red, yellow, blue and black dots in elaborate scrolls, like tattoos, on his cheeks. Even though I have no wall of my own, I am sure someone in the family will hang it

224

for me.

The Alejandro Rangel museum in the next town down the road, **Comala**, has the artist's water colors, doll-like Indians with intricately colored clothing, and lots of fruit, birds, and butterflies around them. Many of the paintings were donated to UNESCO and sell as Christmas cards. All are very sweet but I am not excited by sweetness, especially Mary, Joseph and Babe surrounded by plant and animal lushness that has never been seen in arid Bethlehem. I like the story of the artist. His father was a wealthy businessman and the family naturally expected he would work in his father's business or choose a prestigious career such as lawyer or doctor. But from the time he started grade school, he announced to everyone that he was going to be an artist. He began painting flowers and birds and children early in life, and never stopped or changed the subject matter much. In another room of the museum is his collection of local artifacts, round-bellied dogs and figurines. We finish the day eating tapas and listening to mariachis at an outdoor restaurant. Then Gilles drives me to a bus, and I am off to Cuyutlan.

To reach Gilles: Volcano tours: www.colimamagic.com

Cuyutlan is a dumpy beachside town with inexpensive hotels. I choose the San Rafael, because it was the only one with a large, well scrubbed swimming pool, and swim for an hour or so. Then I sit on the wide porch and watch the sea. The waves are huge, with an eerie, almost transparent greenness, which is visible only from April to June. Supposedly scientists don't know what causes the color. As I watch, the green fades to gray and the air grows oppressive. Suddenly a "tormenta" (storm) strikes. Rain sloshes down, kicking up sand, lightning flashes, and thunder increases to a mighty roar. After an hour or two, the rain ceases, the sun comes out, and the waves are again the strange translucent green. People appear from their hiding places in restaurants to walk on the gleaming, wet sand.

I start to rewrite God Bless America, to make it all-inclusive:

> God bless our precious world,
> World that we love.
> Stand beside us and guide us
> Through the night with the light from above.
> God bless our precious world,
> Our home sweet home.

Hotel San Rafael $30

The next day it is pouring rain, so I decide to take the bus all the way to **Ixtapa.** I arrive during a break period, while Brian is playing volley ball in the huge Club Med pool. He leaps out, we hug, and he goes back to the game. Two days later, the rest of the family arrives. With six strong adults in our gang I can easily get in and out of the ocean. Hurrah! It is like a rebirth to be able to swim in the waves.

I've done enough traveling for now, so simply kick back, enjoy the buffet food, the darling young counselors, and swim in both pool and sea. I go down the road to **Zihuatenejo,** where Mexicans live and sell cheap souvenirs to tourists only once, to get my reading glasses fixed.

If your idea of a fun vacation doesn't involve vacationing with 300 kids between 4 months and 17 years, Club Med Ixtapa might not be the place for you. It is known for its Mini-Clubs for kids, that begins at 9A.M. every morning except Saturdays. This is the kid version of the popular TV show Survivor. During the week they hook up with others their age and run the gauntlet of activities. They learn kayaking, roller-blading, putting, tennis, ping pong, water and hard court basketball, sailing, hard court, beach and water volley ball, and all sorts of high trapeze acts. In the late afternoon they give trapeze shows to family and friends. In addition to regular buffet dining, the bar is open for all the free pizza, spaghetti and coke the kids can consume. Alcoholic drinks and snacks are available for adults.

Maybe you're worried that your children won't like organized activities. If not, they can stay with you. Those over twelve can sign in and out of activities, perhaps to grab a Virgin Pina Colada and sit under a palm tree, watching the others sweat. Children can major in ceramics or face painting (their own). Most stay in their own groups, because the activities and counselors are exceedingly popular. We scarcely saw our teenagers and the younger kids followed the counselors like little ducks with their mamas. Evenings, adults and teenagers put on wild shows and dances to music not meant for old ladies.

I fly back to California, see my surgeon, and find out my second surgery was not a success. I need a complete hip replacement. I refuse, and leave for Europe.

IRELAND AND NORTH IRELAND

Tour

I decide to go to Ireland. Why? Because I've never been there and I have a chunk of time before I'm expected in Romania and the Ukraine. Why take a tour in a country that would be more fun to do solo? My sister Margaret loves Ireland and goes alone quite often. Just a month ago, I did the west coast of Mexico alone, so Ireland should be easy. The problem: I feel older than before Mexico. I am angry that the operation was unsuccessful and the idea of more surgery is appalling. I know I really am not all that safe pretending I can walk well enough to travel alone. I hear myself say, "I need someone to watch over me." I can crumple into self pity or I can go on. I let my fingers do the traveling through internet, find a tour company with an email address, get friendly with the agent who responds, and here I am on a plane to Ireland.

What is the worst airline in the world? You know the answer: the one you are on. Almost always. British Airlines has seats so close together that when a passenger leans back, the one behind can barely breathe. I am sitting beside a fat man who lapses over the entire arm rest. The food is miserable. I change to Aer Lingus for the flight from London to Dublin, and on arriving in **Dublin**, the red cap refuses to do what every red cap always does, wheel me to baggage while I carry my walker on my lap. Instead, he grabs the walker from me and, as I scream at him to stop, throws it down a chute that ends in baggage. When we get to baggage to recover it, the poor thing is smashed beyond repair. I don't just feel helpless, I am helpless. If I weren't, I imagine I would knock the man down and jump all over him. Now, that would be a first!)

Airline personnel apologize and say they will pay for a replacement, even though the behavior of porters is the responsibility of the airport that hires them. I am wheeled to a taxi. Fortunately, the hotel has an emergency wheelchair, so I am wheeled to my room, where I am trapped until the next day, when a taxi takes me on a long drive to the only medical supply store in Dublin. It has one style of collapsible walker, tacky, for twice the price I paid in San Francisco. I accept it and am no longer helpless. I miss the national museum, where I had planned to spend the morning. The Ireland tour begins immediately after lunch.

Travel tips: *Arrive at least a day early for all tours to avoid problems with late or canceled flights, lost luggage, or crazy porters who smash your belongings. On a more positive note, early arrival lets you feel rested when your tour begins.*

We are an interesting group, middle-aged and older, from Australia, Canada, England, New Zealand, Israel, and four of us from the United States. We start with a quickie tour of the city: row on row of large, brick Georgian houses, all exactly alike, as if they were welfare housing rather than top of the line from the seventeenth century. A wealthy duke bought a huge block of pasture land, put up his own house, and then built the rest for sale to others who could afford them. The cost of each depended on its nearness to his home. Occasionally an owner changed the color or decoration of his front door. Otherwise, they are identical. The first floor was divided into a huge living room and equally huge dining room. The second floor had another living room, called a sitting room, a master bedroom, and a bedroom for guests. The third floor was for children, with a playroom and as many beds as were needed. The fourth floor was shabby , with low ceilings and tiny windows, for the servants. The toilets and baths were ceramic, emptied outside by servants. I never found out where the kitchen was, outside or in the servants' quarters.

There is almost no space between houses, but each group of about a dozen homes had its own locked park, with trees, flowers, ball courts, swings, slides, and walking trails. These lovely parks still exist, some locked and private, others open to the public. The homes are now divided into apartments and offices.

We pass tree-lined boulevards, churches, and grand cathedrals, as we drive along the river that divides the city. There are lots of statues, including one recently built to commemorate the millennium. It is a very tall, skinny, naked gray pole, a flag pole without a flag, which cost Ireland four and a half million dollars to erect. Our guide says apologetically that Dubliners hate it and are furious at the cost. I understand. San Francisco has even more dreadful modern art. In fact, we almost had a bare foot, really huge, planted on the waterfront, but this time the people were able to fight back successfully. The art commission said the foot was in honor of our Asian immigrants. Our Asian-American population wasn't pleased. As my friend Reiko said, "I don't believe a single one of us arrived barefoot." But it was our Gays who ultimately triumphed in blocking the statue. They said, "How wonderful! We'll paint the toenails magenta and string ankle bracelets in honor of our Gay Asians."

Next morning our group sets off to see Ireland and North Ireland in eight days. The sky is pearl-colored, misty, quite lovely actually, and the grass is the greenest I have ever seen. Each small field is enclosed by stone fences or dark green hedges, making an immense green patchwork quilt miles long, decorated with sheep and their little lambs, bright white with black faces; and white, brown, black, and marbled cows. I've never thought of cows as pretty, but these are. Their hair is soft and luminous, supposedly because they eat only fresh, new grass.

The mist turns to rain, fog, and back to mist, while we drive through the Boyne valley and cross the border into north Ireland. Throughout the day our guide explains the history that led to the recent wars and the division of the island. Ireland is part of the European Union, uses euros, and has its own Irish Catholic church. North Ireland is part of the British Empire, uses pounds, and supports the Church of England. That's official, but in each area there are large opposing minorities.

In **Belfast** I go alone to the famous Crown Pub, hoping to meet people who will tell me of their lives in North Ireland. The pub is beautiful, over 100 years old, with two ornately carved wooden bars and lots of gleaming copper. This is a craicing place (pronounced "cracking," meaning happy and convivial). A soccer game is on the many TVs, every barstool and table is occupied, the music too loud, and the cigarette smoke makes my eyes burn. I leave.

Both Ireland and North Ireland are more prosperous than I'd expected. People are well dressed and there are almost no beggars on the streets. Unlike in the United States, no one is left homeless. Homes are newly painted and much new construction is going on. Our guide says that for the first time immigration is being reversed, as the American Irish find work and good housing in both Ireland and North Ireland.

We drive around the city, see the university, city hall, and a church or two. While the group does a walking tour, I have a diet coke in an outdoor cafe. The people are truly friendly and eager to chat, after they find out that I, too, hate Bush and his war. I assure them I did not and will not vote for the man. They ask about San Francisco, which they know from television. They ask about my ancestry and I tell them that one side of my family came from North Ireland, which is partly true. One of my aunts told me that the McClures were among a group of Protestant troublemakers sent by the English in the early 1700s to Ireland from Scotland. They stayed in Ireland a few years before sailing to Pennsylvania, where the Quakers had established friendly, peaceful relationships with the Indians. The Scots made trouble with both groups, stealing from the Quakers and murdering the Indians, but I don't explain that.

A bit of history:

150000 BCE: The Ice Age begins to thaw. Dense forests grow and giant deer roam in the grasslands. No one knows exactly when the smaller, dark people arrive or "from whence they came."

6,000 BCE: Celts cross from Scotland to Ireland. They place huge stones upright in a circle, and build stone-lined crypts for their dead.

3,500 BCE: The people grow grain, keep domesticated animals for food, make stone axes, and pottery.

1800 BCE: They mine copper and import tin from Cornwall and Spain to use in making bronze. The aborigines have disappeared. Perhaps they were the "little people," the leprechauns of Irish mythology.

432 CE: Saint Patrick arrives, and supposedly rids Ireland of snakes. Monasteries begin to flourish all over the land.

795: Vikings arrive, to steal and murder. Some remain and establish colonies.

900 – 1000: Monks build high towers. When the enemies arrive, they go to their towers, pull up their ladders, and are safe.

1169: The Normans invade. Within five years they have subjugated the country, establishing the feudal system and land tenure. Internal and external feuds and wars are constant.

1533: Henry VIII of England breaks with the Pope and forms the Church of England. Fearing that the Irish might join the Pope and invade England, the English do the preemptive strike thing (like Bush) and attack and repress the Irish.

1641: Oliver Cromwell comes to power in England and, with God on his side, slaughters the Irish, razes their monasteries, and brings in the Scots. Guerilla warfare escalates.

1695: Repressive anti-Irish and anti-Catholic laws are forced on the people.

1798: Insurrection is occurring all over Ireland.

1845 – 1851: Potato famine. Ireland loses one-fourth of its people to starvation and emigration.

1919: The IRA (Irish Republic Army) is established, and the fighting goes on.

1920: Government of Ireland Act is passed. North Ireland comes into existence. And the fighting goes on.

1940-45: Republic of Ireland remains neutral in World War II, withdraws from the Commonwealth, and declines to join NATO.

1998: Good Friday Act: The people vote to accept peace in both parts of Ireland.

We drive north to the coast and past the splendid basalt columns that rise from the sea. I am becoming quite sick. Fortunately, we are spending tonight and tomorrow night in **Londonderry**, so I go to bed, skip meals, and sleep a lot. No pain or nausea, but a feeling of being "dumbed down," not quite sure where I am or why. I suspect a stroke but say nothing. When we start out for **Castlebar**, I listen to our guide read Yeat's poetry in her beautifully melodious voice, and begin to feel better. She gives us the history of this part of Ireland, but I don't take it in. I have vague impressions of bogs, yellow fields, distant mountains, the sea, islands, dark, craggy rocks, and greenness.

By **Galway** I am well. So much for dire predictions of strokes! I change to my mother's usual diagnosis, "A bug of some kind." I spend a lovely afternoon with a favorite niece, who lives here. She and her lover work from their home, using internet. Their apartment is light and airy, with views of fields on two sides. The rent is almost nothing compared to rent in California.

The next day we go south via **Ennis** to **Limerick**, and see more Cathedrals, Castles, and the Treaty Stone. Ennis is a pretty town that winds around low hills and the river Fergus. Limerick is a city, crowded and unattractive, at the mouth of the river Shannon. It was originally a Viking settlement. The Normans moved in, expanded the town, and built the huge fortifications that became King John's Castle, another of those high ruins I cannot visit. The local people fought hard against Cromwell, but finally capitulated in 1691, because they were promised religious freedom and property rights. The agreement was signed on the large Treaty Stone. Two months later the British reneged and enforced even more oppressive laws than before the treaty. The Treaty Stone stands today, as a symbol of all that was hateful in England's rule over Ireland.

Limerick is now known to Americans chiefly because Frank McCourt grew up there. It is the home of his ANGELA'S ASHES. To set the record straight, Limerick has changed. When the film company arrived to make the movie of McCourt's book, they couldn't find anywhere in the city that looked sufficiently underprivileged and poverty-stricken, so the scenes of poverty were shot in Dublin and Cork.

We drive to **Adair** to admire the thatched cottages, and then go on to **Kilarney**. The scenery is spectacular, with plunging cliffs, islands, mountains, lush greenery, and beautiful lakes. In the distance are Ireland's highest mountains. On this beautiful drive, we finally have warmth and sunshine. There are special sights along the way, such as the Ladies' View, named for Queen Victoria and her ladies-in-waiting, who, like thousands of tourists ever since, admired the vista of blue lakes, green shrubs and trees, and the soft purple of the highest mountains.

When I was young, I was fascinated by words, and one of my favorites was Inishmore: "Oh, to go to Inishmore..." We see the island Inishmore, a rocky dot seven miles long.

We go to Blarney, so that the hardiest (or most determined) of our group can struggle up the high hill to reach yet another castle and kiss the Blarney Stone. How did this foolishness get started? The castle in the town of Blarney was owned by a man named Cormac MacCarthy, a garrulous person who kept inventing excuses for not paying Queen Elizabeth I the goods or tithes or whatever she was trying to extract from him. She lost patience, and said angrily "his blather is blarney." From then on, people were led to believe they could inherit his gift of gab by kissing a stone in his castle. Not just any stone. You must pay to climb to the top and then let yourself be hung by your heels, upside down, in order to kiss that germy blarney stone. I think MacCarthy was a very clever man. For over four hundred years tourists have been paying to climb and kiss.

We finish the day at the Waterford corporation, where crystal costs so much I don't even dare pick it up. Once upon a time I inherited some Waterford from my mother and grandmother. I wasn't very interested in cut glass then. The kids and I broke most of it. Now, seeing the prices, I can't believe I was so careless.

Our last stop before Dublin is the medieval city, **Kilkenny**, dominated by its Norman Castle and Cathedral. Then we have a final dinner at a cabaret in Dublin, with music, dancing, and jokes. It is pleasantly nostalgic to listen to a tenor sing the songs I've known since childhood, when we played them on my grandmother McClure's wind-up phonograph.

In Dublin I learn via email that the Ukrainian Transactional Analysis group can find no ground floor room for my workshop. The beautiful apartment, where I worked two years ago, is on the fourth floor, and I just can't manage that. My hip hurts a great deal and my walking is worse. The river boat, Marshall Rybalko, where two Ukrainians and I were to vacation before the workshop, has very steep steps without railings. The Rumanian workshop rooms are equally inaccessible. I have to cancel both. With time to spare, I book at the last minute two more tours, one English and one French.

Travel tips: *What I would do if I went back to Ireland on my own: use the Eireann Express. It has over 50 routes linking cities and towns, so travelers can map out their own private trips from Shannon airport throughout southern Ireland. I'd include the twenty minute ferry ride between Killimer and Tarbert, to watch the dolphins play.*

A PEACEFUL LIFE

Valerie is a plump, pastel woman, with light hair, very blue eyes, a round face, and naturally pink cheeks. Although she says she is a monotone and therefore can't sing, her laugh is melodious and she reads aloud beautifully. She says I won't really want to put her life in my book, because readers would consider her boring. She is an Irish tour guide.

"I was a wanted child. That is the most important fact of my childhood. My mother was well-educated, and a national leader in the Irish Country Women's Association. For ten years she suffered miscarriages before she had me, so you can imagine how important I was to her. My father felt the same way. I was his companion. He had a large farm, where he bred horses and sheep. Horses were his passion. He took me with him to horse shows and races, and when he was buying and selling horses, I was right there beside him. I grew up loving horses almost as much as he did. He wasn't aggressive. His prices were fair and everyone knew it, so I don't remember any arguments. Selling a horse was exciting but a bit sad for me, as if a part of our family was moving to another home. It wasn't just business, you see. The races and shows were thrilling.

"In the winter Mother made my new dresses, which were very fancy, with lots of embroidery and smocking. At the same time, I made new dresses for my dolls. We all dressed up and had lovely tea parties for ourselves and the dolls. What else? I didn't want to play outside. I never was athletic. I went to a primitive country school, with outdoor toilets. We froze in winter, but that was how it was. None of us knew it could have been different. School was simple. I don't remember homework, but I read a great deal. That was our winter.

"Spring brought lambs and every year one or two lambs were rejected by their mothers, so I got to bottle feed them and treat them as if they were my own. I waited so eagerly for at least one to be rejected! When there were two, I was thrilled, because then I had twins to care for. Each year I mourned when they grew up and had to be sold, but there would always be more.

"Summer the farm workers came, so there were lots of people and huge, merry picnics.

"Autumn began with haying season. The men were working from daylight to dark, and the women were cooking for everyone. I was watching, and sometimes helping in the fields and sometimes in the kitchen. But I didn't neglect my babies, the dolls and the growing lambs I had adopted. After haying was finished, all the workers left, and school opened again.

"It was such a good life. I never had to ask for anything. Life flowed, season to season. I honestly can't remember frustrations or unhappiness. I was content, then and now. When I meet American women, I am amazed at their aggressiveness. They decide exactly what they want that they don't have, and go after it. Maybe it's only a hotel room with a view, or maybe it's a new career. They tell the world the direction they are heading. I sit back and let life happen. So, you see why I believe my story is boring."

Valerie is married and has two children in college in Dublin. Her parents, now in their nineties, still live on the farm. Valerie and her family live in Dublin, but she visits her parents every week. She is working only part time now, in order to be available when they need her. I ask if her children are like her.

"When my daughter had a ring put in her tongue, I cried for three days. I would never have done such a thing." She thought a minute, and then said, "They are more like the Americans I meet. They make things happen. I believe their lives are happy. Mine is, too."

ENGLAND

solo and tour

London is an old friend I haven't visited in years. I arrive in the late afternoon, too late for my favorite pastime, museums, so check into the hotel the tour group uses, and go to the London Eye. I first heard of the Eye on the day 1999 became 2000. My daughter Karen was visiting me in San Francisco. Remember, lots of people were sure there would be a world-wide catastrophe that day, and had loaded up on canned stew and gallons of water, which may still be on their basement shelves. Karen and I turned on the television early, for the report from the first country to announce the New Year. "No Problems!" We cheered together, and she phoned her colleagues at Sun Microsystems to cheer with them as each time zone announced that the world was not going to end on their watch. By the time the New Year arrived in London, we learned of the only glitch in the entire world, the London Eye wasn't ready for the Grand Occasion. They had a rousing good celebration anyway. We got to see the Queen looking vastly uncomfortable as she backed away from linking arms with her son and Tony Blair for the singing of Olde Lang Syne.

That was when I learned of the existence of this London Eye. It is a giant Ferris wheel with each glassed-in, bullet-shaped car holding twenty people. Today, four and a half years later, there are still long lines of people waiting to ride it, but as an "incapacitated" person, I am ushered to the front and into a next car. If you like Ferris wheels, let me tell you that this one is BORING, in spite of nice views of Westminster Abbey, Big Ben, and a couple of bridges.

I find an Italian restaurant just down the street from the Eye. The owner claims that their beer is from a secret recipe made by their family in Italy for over 1,000 years. Of course, I order it, and it's very good. So is the food.

I devote the next morning to impressionism, post impressionism, and dozens of English children. First, I go to the National Gallery and the joy of Modigliani, Gauguin, Seurat, Matisse, and Van Gogh. Then to the Somerset house, once lived in by Sir Walter Raleigh, The courtyard is a huge bricked plaza with a fountain made of over 100 spigots that shoot jets of water into the air. Though it is a typical cold English summer day, sopping wet children are playing in the fountain, jumping over the jets of water, dancing around them, squatting over them, running in and out, and laughing wildly. When a child is stark blue and shivering, an adult comes with a towel.

Around the fountain are children's activities: plastic pennants to be painted and hung on lines all around the plaza, drums and home-made flutes to be played, bits of twisted pipe cleaners, twigs, and colored paper to be made into miniature sculptures, and finger paints. Suddenly the fountain erupts twelve feet into the air, and the children drop their art and music to dash into the water. This is a multi-racial, multi-ethnic group of Londoners, children, parents, and nannies, all seeming to enjoy each other.

My grand finale for today is an afternoon at the British Museum, with the Ancient Egyptians and Greeks.

Victoria Park Plaza (Rooms from 65 pounds.) A block from Victoria Station. New, clean, very good food.

The tour begins with a drive to **Oxford** and a much-too-brief stop at Balliol, the oldest of Oxford's colleges: Brick buildings, ivy-walled, with steep slate roofs, just as I have always pictured it. This is how a real college should look, medieval and wonderful. I've never cared much for colleges with modern buildings. I think of Oxford as a place for quiet scholarship, in spite of a sign proclaiming the rules for Graduation Day: "There is a fine of 90 pounds for throwing food or drink. You may carry with you unopened champagne. Afterwards you may release balloons and confetti only."

Bath is a glorious town. Every building in the downtown area is a treasure. I'm eating an egg salad and cheese sandwich on the plaza beside one of the world's fanciest Cathedrals, with turrets and long, spiked towers, stained glass, and stone statues of saints and famous non-saints, and an especially large statue of God at the top. On the street a boy on a unicycle is juggling flaming torches, and another is playing and singing English ballads. In front of me are the Roman baths.

During the Stone Age, hunters gathered around the hot springs, which must have seemed a mysterious place, marshy, hot, with willows and elders growing in profusion. Next, the Celts came here to worship their god, Sulis, and found a village. Romans invaded the area in 53 CE, and within twelve years were building these baths. They had hot and cold baths, saunas, and three swimming pools, one over twenty yards long. All were exquisitely tiled and decorated with statuary. The Romans built a large temple dedicated to Minerva, and called the complex the Minerva Sulis baths, probably to harmonize Roman and Celtic beliefs. When the Romans left, the baths were never again used. As our guide said, "Our ancestors never bathed. They just stank."

Little remains today: only the broken-off head of Minerva, two tile floors with fish and sea monster designs, and some columns. A monk, an Eighth Century tourist, wrote in the English of his day, which is translated:

> "Wondrous is this masonry shattered by the fates.
> The fortifications have given way,
> The buildings raised by the giants are crumbling.
> The roofs have collapsed. The towers are in ruins.
> Owners and builders are perished and gone."

The modern baths, here in Bath, are being renovated. New and super luxurious, they will open in 2006 for all who can afford $300 - $500 a day. It will be much more for Americans, if the value of the dollar continues to drop.

All hail the good people of **Glastonbury**, who bought motorized scooters to rent to those who cannot walk through the ruins of the Abbey of Glastonbury! In all my travels, I have never before encountered this loving gesture. I get aboard my scooter, thrilled to be mobile among the acres of paths that crisscross in all directions. There are ancient walls, arches and remains of arches, burial sites of saints and of long ago people, who paid vast sums to be buried near the saints, ruins of the monks' cells, and an old kitchen restored to show what kitchens were like in the tenth century. In the distance is the tor (hill) with the ruins of a monks' tower.

This is a place of history and legends.

Legends: Modern women, who love the idea of female goddesses, believe that in the beginning this land was ruled by an earth goddess whose followers held fertility rites here. They swear they feel "a surge of energy" from this old goddess. Others say they feel these surges, but believe them to come from the martyred monks. Some say the early Celts are still hanging around, sending vibrations.

At one time the whole area was under water, except for the tor, which was an island in a sea. Gradually the water receded. In about 300 BCE the Celts built a small village here, where land met sea. They believed that here was the place their newly dead passed into the underworld ruled by the god Avalloc. The monks arrived about 200 CE and built the first church on the grounds. It grew to become one of the largest monasteries in England. Its most famous legend: King Arthur is buried here. Edward 1 believed this and paid for a new Great Church to be built in honor of King Arthur. In 1278, it was finished, and Arthur's bones were put inside.

In 1539 the Protestants took over England, and in a burst of frenzied Christian passion, they hung the abbot and two of his monks from the tower on the tor, then totally destroyed all the buildings. King Arthur's bones were lost in the rubble. But, lo and behold, in 1934 the bones were again discovered! They were re-buried, this time on the ground next to the rubble of the Grand Church. We visitors can read the stone proclaiming that here lies King Arthur. However, the word "legendary" has been added. There is no proof that Arthur, Lancelot, and the rest of the Knights of the Round Table ever existed. During Medieval times, romantic folk tales were told about them, and when books began to be printed, these stories were most popular. Maybe they are true.

I spend an enchanting couple of hours riding around the grounds. I feel a definite surge of energy, which I ascribe to being able to drive a scooter after all these months of hobbling.

Next, we visit Devon, Plymouth, and drive along the Cornish coast. St. Ives, an artists' colony built perpendicularly down to the sea, has delightful homes and art galleries, but I can't manage the cobblestones or the steep streets. Ditto Michael's Mount and Land's End, and the ruined castle of Tintagel, where the legendary King Arthur was born. I do wish scooters were for rent everywhere. Mostly, the terrain is too steep even for wheelchairs, though I do see long-suffering companions valiantly pushing their friends.

There is so much more to see in England, but my tour of France awaits me.

FRANCE

tour

I arrive in **Paris** in the early evening, to discover that my tour company, Trafalgar, picked the type of hotel hyped for business executives, swanky, impersonal, a $20 cab ride to the left bank, the Opera district, or anywhere else worth seeing. The group has already left for a tour of Paris by night.

How many times have I warned people to get to their destinations early!

I have a mediocre dinner in the hotel and watch a very fat couple smile at each other as they hold hands across the table. At the next table three business women seem to be vying to outdo each other in their laughter at anecdotes the man of the table is telling. Two men are together at a table and talk at great length on their cells phones as they ignore each other. I leave a note for the tour guide and go to bed.

Very early the next morning we head to Beaune, (pronounced more or less like "bone") on the way to Lyon. Our guide, Bart, plays French opera, and talks about the climate of France. We are in the northern Atlantic climate. The other two climates are Mediterranean and Alpine. We are passing fields of drying sun flowers, dull brown and boring compared with last year's vibrant yellow during my summer train trip from Arles to Paris. In the distance, the hills are a muted green and blue, merging into a deep purple near the horizon. We pass small forests, meadows with white cattle, and villages where the houses are wood and stone with reddish tile roofs. The churches are thirteenth century stone. There are chateaus, abandoned, made into hotels and inns, or remodeled into homes for the super rich. Vineyards appear, and our guide gives an impassioned talk on how to taste wine and how to cook snails.

Wine: Observe the color, smell the aroma slowly, swish the wine in the glass and observe the "tears" (streaks on the glass). If there are no tears, the wine hasn't aged properly. Again, inhale deeply, let a few drops of wine enter your mouth and, as the bouquet opens, fill your senses with the joy of wine. Swallowing is not necessary to your enjoyment. (Oh, yeah?)

Snails: Wash, dry carefully, soak, remove from shells, wash and dry again, cook in wine and herbs for four hours. Cook shells forty-five minutes. Put back in shells, douse with burgundy butter, and bake for forty-five more minutes. Serve with your favorite burgundy. Disclaimer: I may have left out a couple of steps in the cooking of snails, so consult your favorite French cook book. If you plan to use snails from your own backyard, don't. You need a corn meal snail cage plus care of snails for at least three months to decontaminate them.

Wine and snails have been specialties of this area for almost 2000 years. In the early centuries, monks arrived from Rome with the grape roots, and kept their vineyards alive throughout the middle Ages. They wanted the finest wine possible to celebrate their Lord Jesus Christ. I hope for their sake that they celebrated often.

Bart reads from the writings of a twelfth century monk, "I do not see Him with my eyes because He has no color, nor by my ears because He makes no sound. Perhaps God did not come to me, but was in me from my beginning."

We pass more cows, trees, round bales of hay, and grape vines, then see a large stone gate, put up to welcome Louis XIV to **Beaune**, a lovely old town full of flowers and medieval buildings.

We stop to visit Hotel Dieu, (in French "hotel" used to mean hospital), built in 1443, the year the Hundred Year War ended. The town, ruled by the Duke and Duchess of Burgundy, was very poor. People were hungry, ill, and without supplies for the future. The Duke and Duchess decided to build a charity hospital, the first in all of France. They gave wood for the buildings from their private land and paid the locals to do the construction. Then they persuaded the government of the time to exempt these buildings from taxes. They hired famous artists and weavers to decorate the interior, and endowed the hospital with a perpetual income to cover the needs of the sick. They gave the town ownership of a vineyard plus salt mines, so that the town would have its own industries.

The hospital, now a museum, is amazing. Within the huge buildings, each single bed is enclosed on three sides by six-foot tall wooden walls, for privacy. Beside each bed: a small table and chair; pewter dishes for food, water, and blood-letting, the standard medical treatment of the time; a beautifully polished chest for the patient's clothes; and a shelf for religious and other personal mementos. Each bed has a warm, bright red, hand-woven blanket. The major walls are covered in rich tapestries and paintings. The hospital is famous for its painting of Revelations, originally placed so that all patients could see it from their beds. The painting, made to look three-dimensional, shows the naked, newly dead rising from their coffins to be welcomed by God and his angels into a glorious temple or dragged into the fires of hell. It is enough to make any dying person do whatever was still possible to avoid the latter.

In the kitchen are pots and pans, large ovens, and a steel spit over an open fire, now turned mechanically by a little robot dressed in medieval clothing. The Holy sisters took care of the sick and cooked for them. They also made bread for any of the poor who waited each morning by the gates.

If Marie Antoinette had been so thoughtfully, beautifully charitable, giving art, bread, and medical care to the poor, there would have been no need for a Revolution. When the industrial revolution arrived, townspeople would already have had a tradition of group ownership of mines and vineyards, free medical care and basic food for all.

If our government, so much more powerful and capable than the Duke and Duchess of Burgundy, gave hospitals and work and food to the poor and sick in Iraq, we'd be friends today rather than enemies. Read Howard Zinn's A PEOPLE'S HISTORY OF THE UNITED STATES to realize how many times we've done it wrong.

Our tour group gathers for wine-tasting at the Musee du Vin, and rushes on. The town is small, quiet, with lots to see. When I return to France, I plan to spend a week here.

Lyon is a beautiful city. The Rhone pours down from the Alps, clear and rapid flowing to meet the darker Saone. Along the Saone, the buildings on one side are yellow, pink, and stone gray, and on the other there is a romantic trail with benches, green grass, flowers, and beautiful, twisted cypress. Today couples are walking together along the Saone, many holding hands, as if to verify the belief that the Saone is the romantic river. Our group climbs to the huge cathedral in the sky, by stairs, escalator, and then funicular. I stay below, enjoying the splendid river views from the Bonaparte Bridge, and then have a beer at an outdoor cafe where I talk with two German tourists. It is getting redundant to hear from everyone how much they hate George Bush and our war, but it seems we always have to get through this before going on to other topics.

The Musee de Beaux Artes, once a Benedictine convent, has the second largest collection of world art after the Louvre. Musee de Tissues displays beautiful tapestries and silks. Musee des Artes Decoratifs is also considered top notch. I'm sorry we whiz through without time for museums. I will come back to Lyon and stay awhile.

We drive through the Loire Valley, with its fields of olive trees, brought here by the Greeks 2500 years ago. The sunshine is gorgeous. I can image the Greeks coming ashore with the small trees in their boats, as well as their other produce: tomatoes, eggplant, garlic, and summer squash, to mix with the olives for ratatouille. Our guide talks of these Greeks, and also gives a capsule history of the region from the Middle Ages through World War II.

A bit of history according to Bart and a little pamphlet I picked up:

1100 - 500 BCE: The Celts settle in what today is France. Greeks colonize in the Loire valley.

58 - 51 BCE: The King of Gaul, with an intriguing name, Cercingetorix, capitulates to Julius Caesar and his armies. Many Romans stay on.

800 CE: Charlemagne is crowned in Rome by the Pope. Next come more rulers whose names I enjoy: Louis the Pius, Charles the Bold, Robert the Pius, Louis the Large, Louis the Young, Louis the Lion, Philip the Bold, Philip the Fair, Jean the Posthumous (?), Philip the Long, Philip the Fair, Jean the Good, Charles the Wise, Charles the Mad, Charles the Victorious, and an assorted few with ordinary names.

1589 – 1793: The Bourbon Kings rule.

1792: The First Republic is proclaimed. The French Revolution begins.

1793: Luis XVI and Marie Antoinette are guillotined.

1804: Napoleon has himself proclaimed Emperor

1814: The Bourbons make a brief comeback.

1830: Another revolution and one more king.

1848: Napoleon III becomes president of the Second Republic

1870: Another war (Franco-German). The Third Republic is formed.

1914 – 1918: World War I

1940: Germany invades France. Charles de Gaulle heads the French resistance. Philippe Petain establishes the Vichy government that collaborates with the Germans.

1944: Allies land. The Germans are defeated and World War 11 is over. The new government is headed by Charles de Gaulle.

On to **Monte Carlo** and **Monaco**, passing en route the craggy mountain that Paul Cézanne painted seventy-four times. The coastline is glorious. In Monaco you know you are a nobody unless you truly are that top one percent that gets the tax breaks in the United States and probably all over the world. Las Vegas and Monaco are very different. Las Vegas' goal is constant expansion, with ever more people arriving to gamble, so there are games and slot machines for rich and poor. Monaco's goal is to keep away all but the elite. It costs us nobodies ten dollars to have a short peek at the luxurious gambling tables, but don't think for that paltry sum you can linger, take photos, or gamble. You can't even use a bathroom in the place. I am not wasting ten dollars where I can neither participate nor pee. The Principality of Monaco is a tiny country that consists of two huge rocks, with a palace and a cathedral on one; Monte Carlo, exclusive stores, and palace-like homes on the other. Some of the world's most expensive yachts are harbored below.

Nice comes from the Greek word Nike, meaning victory. Now I know why the sport shoes are called Nike. The city was Greek first, then Roman, then Barbarian, then Italian. Wealthy English travelers came and built the beautiful promenade along the Mediterranean. Wealthy Russians built the Opera House, where Wagner, Verdi, and Puccini conducted. France got Nice from the Italians in 1860, but you can still see retired Italian men playing bocce ball and Italian women hanging their laundries from the elegant balconies. After World War I the artists came; after World War 11, the film makers. The climate is Mediterranean, with palm trees, scents of wonderful blossoms, and soft, moist air. Elegant hotels border the promenade. Between the promenade and the blue sea is a long beach, consisting of sharp stones. Give me Mexico or Hawaii, where the sand is smooth.

The next day is "free," so I spend my time at the Musee Chagall, a wonderful place. I never tire of Chagall. There are twelve large paintings illustrating Genesis and Exodus: creation of man, Adam and

Eve, Noah's ark, Moses and the burning bush, Sacrifice of Isaac, and a gorgeous Paradise, full of flowers, animals, and love. It is his love of life and love of love that shines through all his work. He said, "In art as in life, everything is possible so long as it is based on love." A two-story mosaic reflects in a fountain. There are beautiful depiction's of Jesus as a Jew, much more creditable than the blonde, bland Jesus of European artists. (I was just as delighted with the Catholic churches in Irian Jaya, where the Holy Family is native, like the artists, and pigs are the animals that snuggle up contentedly against the Babe.) It would take a minimum of a week to see all of Nice. With only a day here, I skip the contemporary art museum (mostly Andy Warhol, I was told) and the Musee Matiste (with mostly sketches of paintings hung elsewhere.) I sit awhile on a bench beside the promenade, and watch the sea and read a lovely, illustrated book of Chagall.

We drive to the ancient hill town of **St. Paul de Vence,** where you truly need to be ambulatory to enjoy its cobbled steepness. Halfway down the hill is the world-famous Fragonard perfumery where some in our group buy armloads of soap, lotions, and perfumes to bring home to friends. We stop at the top of another hill where we can see three countries: France, Monaco, and Italy.

For dinner we park on a hilltop and walk downhill through the citadel, a long, steep trek, but do-able. Dark, gloomy stone surrounds us until the light at the end of the tunnel is the Mediterranean in all its bright beauty. There beside the sea is a wooden village so small and quaint that it looks like a facade for a movie set, **Villefranche sur Mer**. We dine at a rustic restaurant, long wooden tables, bright tablecloths, an unlimited supply of wonderful fresh fish and red wine, plus an accordionist who asks where we are from and then plays for us Waltzing Matilda, When Irish Eyes Are Smiling, O Solo Mio, My Bonny Lies Over The Ocean, and Yankee Doodle. With unlimited wine, it is delightful. Because the uphill walk to the bus is impossible, Bart orders a cab for me. The cab is too small for my walker, so he decides to push it. When the group gets to the bus, they are all laughing. They tell me that a member of another group saw him with the walker and said, "Wouldn't you think Trafalgar could afford a healthier guide?"

We stop at **Cannes** only long enough to see a statue of Joan of Arc beside a little sand beach, and the homes and hotels of the rich and famous. Then on we drive past corn fields and small pine forests. A few olive trees have run away from their rigid rows to hide in the forest with the pines or scatter themselves between corn stalks. We pass a mammoth pedestal for a long gone statue to Caesar Augustus and the Pax Romana. In **Nimes** we climb around the amphitheater built at the end of the first century, see the three-tiered Roman aqueduct, and visit the city gardens. And on we go, past vines, vines, vines and another quaint little town, **Longuedoc**.

We reach **Avignon**, where a couple of Popes, Clement V and VI, built massive ramparts and a fortress, Palais des Papas, over both sides of the Rhone. This was the site of the Papal government. In 1407 Gregory VII moved the Papal government back to Rome. While our group goes up countless steps to see the empty fortress-palace, I stay below to examine about 100 dolls before choosing a goose girl for Claudia's collection. Music is being played in the square, and people are singing and laughing together. I have my best lunch so far, rare salmon on warm, delicately herbed bread. A disadvantage for tour groups is that any large group, eating at the same time, turns even many-starred restaurants into mediocrity. This is another town worth exploring, with whole streets of extravagantly large stone houses, churches, and museums.

Camarque: rice fields and cattle, with wetlands that are a bird sanctuary. We see the Alps in the distance, and get close enough to Arles to stop at the Pont Van Gogh, with a copy of his painting tacked beside it. I missed the bridge when I was in Arles, but saw the original in the Kroller-Muller Museum in the Netherlands. What a world traveler I have become!

We stop above the walled city of **Carcassonne**, where the Cathars were put to death by the Catholic Church to keep them from the sin of suicide. It is a strange story. The Cathars were a rapidly growing Catholic group who believed in vegetarianism, celibacy, self-abnegation, prayer, and the life-long striving for perfection. The ultimate perfection was self-death and re-incarnation, which they preached in song and oratory. The Pope decided they must be exterminated, and chose the Dominicans to hire knights to do the job. The Dominicans were already running the heresy trials, so one might say they were professionals at killing for God. Cathar was smashed and every Cathar inside the walls was murdered. The few survivors outside the city, their religion silenced, became wandering troubadours and poets. They sang about lovers whose love was never consummated. Over time, they changed their original passion for the divine into stories of extra-marital yet chaste romantic passion. All this is told us by our guide, who knows many histories of France and tells them well. He doesn't just tell, he makes history into romance, sometimes beautiful, sometimes tragic. He tells of the Greeks, the Roman soldiers who retired in France after conquering Gaul, the Crusades, the kings and queens, the divided France during World War II. (See next chapter.)

A massive fortress was built on the ruins of Cathar. Its walls, seen from below, appear endless, high and wide, with sharp corners, an impregnable gate, and many huge turrets. In the evening, the fortress is spot-lighted softly, and becomes a pale white, dreamlike, awesome ghost against the deep gray sky. Standing below, I imagine the troubadours still singing songs of love.

Lourdes is incredibly tacky. People buy cheap plastic bottles decorated with pseudo-gold Bernadettes. These are filled with holy water to bring home to family and friends. Dozens of stores sell cheap crucifixes, Madonnas, and Bernadettes. It would be slightly more tolerable if the stores didn't charge so much for their shoddy souvenirs. Supposedly 200,000,000 people have come here to drink the holy water and pray for a medical miracle.

The Catholic Church, with the help of leading internationally-respected physicians, has established forty-seven spontaneous cures which may be miracles, says the Church. Those are not exciting odds. I am one of the 199,999,953 who got no cure. I still limp. Of course, I did not visit the shrine, drink the water, or pray. I feel miserable, seeing people on crutches, in wheelchairs, gaunt and dying, obviously hoping for a miracle when the odds were less than 1 in forty million! Andrew Weil, SPONTANEOUS HEALING, and lots of others do better than that.

The history of Lourdes: Bernadette, a local child, saw the Virgin in a nearby cave, who told her to build a shrine there. When Bernadette told church and civil officials, she was not well received, but common people arrived in droves. Poor Bernadette fled to a nunnery, where she died young and in terrible pain from some unknown disease. In my prejudiced opinion she'd have done better to have kept her visions to herself.

While our group is visiting the grotto and drinking holy water, I am in a local hotel, using internet. People here are very sweet to anyone who they see as in need of a miracle. Since I am using a walker, they hold doors open for me, and don't even charge me for sending emails.

We leave this afternoon on our way to Biarritz. The farm houses have gray slate roofs and all the cattle are beige. Each area in France presents a slightly different scene, always interesting. After the dowdiness of Lourdes, **Biarritz** is just what I want! The Atlantic is wild today, with huge waves roaring endlessly. When it was a wealthy whaling port, Biarritz citizens built sumptuous stone homes and villas, put in green-green grass and zillions of flowers along hedges and in planter boxes. The newer, plainer wooden houses are all painted in gay colors, and they too are alive with flowers.

I spend the next day on the beach behind the large casino. The sea has calmed a bit, and in front of me are surfers riding perfect waves. I tried once, long ago, to learn to surf but never lasted "on board" more than a second or two. I quit when I broke my front tooth. But I used to body surf and ride boogie boards. I go to the beach café for lunch, and keep on watching the young, bronzed, beautiful athletes. This is a wonderful town, and I hope someday I can return to spend at least a week in a hotel by the sea. I'll keep an eye on internet, hoping for a time when the $500 - $1000 per day rooms are reduced at least two-thirds.

Travel tips for the handicapped: *Joining a tour group is a good way to get "the lay of the land" before venturing alone. By the end of this trip, I'll know exactly where I want to spend time in Ireland, southern England, and France. Because the Trafalgar guides are excellent and lecture only while we drive, I don't have to waste time in classrooms, as in some "educational" tour groups.*

Bordeaux has long been a wealthy wine area, with museums, a theater decorated with statues of the Muses, and classic old homes along the waterfront. It had been allowed to deteriorate through the years, its buildings growing dark and filthy from toxins. About five years ago the new mayor began a cleaning and restoration campaign. Many buildings now sparkle, roads are being repaved, but some areas are still torn apart, so the city looks like a war zone in places. In a largely torn up plaza there is a gargantuan statue to liberty, with spouting fountains and sculptures with the spirit of liberty breaking free above them. Beside the fountain, people sell sticky candies and other carnival goodies. The weather is perfect, warm, sunny, with bright blue and marshmallow skies. I buy an English paper to learn that Bush is bragging senselessly, Clinton is being prepared for surgery, and Russian parents are grieving for their dead and maimed children.

In the evening we "dine with the troglodytes." Another one of those wonderful words, to me it sounds as if ugly little dwarfs will be eating with us. Turns out, the troglodytes are swiss-cheese like caves in chalky cliffs along the river. The French use the caves for ovens, wine storage, growing mushrooms, and for restaurants. Here, I dine on the most exquisite snails I have ever eaten. Gorge is a better word, because on both sides of me and across the table are people who have never eaten snails and refuse to try them. Lucky me.

The **Limoges** area consists of tranquil green hills dotted with old churches, castles, cattle, sheep, and a famous ceramic "must stop" factory, full of tour groups. The landscape is worth the drive, even though I am past the stage of trying to carry ceramics home.

The first close-up view of **Mont St. Michel** is awesome, alone and gigantic against the sky. Most travelers can identify it from French brochures or postcards from vacationing friends ("Wish you were here"). If the friends are more chatty, they brag on the postcards that they climbed 300 steps to reach the top.

A bit of history of Mont St. Michel:

Legend says three tiny islands arose suddenly from a giant tidal wave.

708 CE: Archangel Michael appears on one of the islands and announces to the local bishop that God wants a place of worship built on it. Never mind how difficult it might be to reach the island with all the men and tools need for building. The bishop lays the foundation, using four huge crypts.

966: King Richard I sent Benedictine monks to the site to build a chapel and, I suppose, living quarters for the Benedictines. Religious pilgrims, the first tourists, arrive in ever increasing numbers.

1099: Crusaders, having seen the gothic arch on Moslem buildings, bring home the know-how for building them. Gothic arches are added to enhance the monastery.

1200s: Mont St. Michel becomes a major center for learning, as well as a pilgrimage site.

1400s: Huge ramparts are built to keep the monastery safe from the British.

1789: French Revolution. Mont St. Michel is turned into a national prison, holding 14,000 prisoners including all the Benedictines who had been living there.

1863: The prison is closed.

1897: The place is cleaned up, new spires and a fancy statue of St Michael are added, and pilgrims and other tourists return.

The rest of the group climbs to the top and says the view is wonderful. I stay below, looking at stores and having lunch.

The **Bayeux** tapestry museum on the way to the Normandy beaches is a first class must-see. The tapestry is seventy meters long, with fifty-eight scenes all richly embroidered in colored wool and silk, and still as beautiful as when it was woven 900 years ago. The first scene begins in 1064, when old King Edward, knowing he was dying, sends his brother-in-law Harold to offer the English crown to William of France. Harold swears an oath of allegiance to William, but as soon as the old man dies, Harold grabs the throne. In the next scene William hears the news, and immediately begins building ships and amassing an army. They set sail for England in boats packed with arms, men, and horses, plus pigs and chickens to feed the army. The fighting begins, with foot soldiers, archers, and knights on horseback. The English troops are all hairy, to distinguish them from the clean-shaven French.

Between battle scenes are local rural scenes of cattle-breeding, land cultivation by donkeys yoked to plows, ship building, and religious life. Finally, poor Harold is stabbed through one eye with a huge spear. The war ends, the ships return to France, and William is the new king. As we walk the seventy meters, we wear headphones which tell the story.

Normandy got its name from the Norsemen who arrived in the ninth century, sacked and pillaged, and eventually settled down in the area. It's a lovely, pastoral part of France.

On June 6, 1944, seventeen boats filled with 135,000 British, Canadian, and American soldiers landed on Normandy beaches. The Americans landed on the one called Omaha beach. I walk along it silently, staggered by the horror of thousands dying in the ocean and thousands more dying as they struggle up the hill into enemy fire. It was a terrible tragedy.

Next we go to the cemetery, which overlooks both Omaha beach and the sea. There are acres of green grass with row after row of white crosses and stars of David. We arrive at sunset, as taps are being played and a giant American flag is lowered, folded, and marched away. I think of Joan Baez' plaintive plea of the Vietnam War, "Someday they will call a war and no one will come." How I wish she were right.

We return to Paris by way of Monet's beautiful gardens in Giverney, and the group disbands. The next day I meet Felipe here in Paris.

BART

Bart, our guide, is a difficult man to describe, because he is much more interested in talking about history, art, philosophy, politics, or historically important people than he is in talking about himself. He is from the Netherlands. He claims not to be a romantic, not to be an actor, but listen to him! He describes Paris of 150 years ago. "Awful, just awful! There are no sewers. Human waste is thrown from the upstairs windows or pushed into troughs in the streets or thrown in the Seine, which is nothing but an especially large open sewer. Thousands of horses and dogs shit in the streets, pigs are driven to the slaughter houses in the center of town, and the slaughter-house mess goes into the streets. When it rains the narrow streets turn into ankle-deep sewerage. People wear excessive perfume against the stench, hold perfumed hankies over their noses, and faint in their fancy liveries. Summer heat makes it totally unbearable. The rich flee to their summer homes. It is terrible for the rich. Think for a moment how much worse it is for the poor, without summer homes, carriages, and perfumes as they wade through garbage and shit. No one is ever clean!"

"Finally, a king took action. Area by area he had every building torn down, and below them was constructed a first-class underground sewerage system (which you can read about in LES MISERABLES.) After the sewers were ready, he rebuilt the narrow streets into glorious boulevards, and lined them with the famous plane and chestnut trees to let in light and enrich the beauty. "Spacious homes were built, first along the Seine in the area of the Louvre. Look on either side of you. How wonderful they are!"

Or about our General Marshall, who inaugurated the Marshall Plan for Europe: "He saved us. We had no food, our cities were bombed out. We had a two-thousand year history of murdering each other. Gen. Marshall developed a reconstruction plan that he insisted be based on a free trade zone and cooperation. For the first time, Luxembourg, Belgium, Holland, England, France, and Germany began to live in peace and prospered legally."

He teaches us French history, talks of the French Revolution, of Petain and De Gaulle, and reads us love letters between Abelard and Heloise. He tells in detail the life of the king who married a super-ugly Medici woman for her money, and describes happy and unhappy artists and their loves. He describes architecture as a stage for human encounter: the grand buildings are stages for weddings and coronations, Versailles is a stage for world politics, side walk cafes are stages for philosophers, writers, and other intellectuals.

Bart is fifty-eight and holds degrees in sociology, philosophy, and art history. In college he was "a seeker of truth," who liked to question what is relevant in life. While in school, he owned a school of judo and he worked part time as a tour guide. "My students were good at judo, and I'd take the whole gang to contests. They needed uniforms; I needed bus fare for them. So I earned the money to keep the school top notch by also being a tour guide. I already knew quite a few languages.

"I thought a degree in sociology would be meaningful, but I soon realized the impotence of theorizing. I received a scholarship to the prestigious New School for Social Research in New York, and wrote my dissertation on the holocaust. The holocaust is different from wars based primarily on gaining land or hating opponents. It is cold-blooded, assembly-line killing, like assembly-line killing of chickens. Mass murder is accomplished as cheaply and efficiently as possible and no one feels shame. 'My job was to make certain the trains were running on time.' 'My job was to keep an accurate census.'" He thinks there will be other holocausts. "We'll run out of oil. That may not bring assembly-line slaughter, but what about when we run short of water? Which people will we kill quickly and efficiently, without guilt or shame?"

He has given up his judo school. "I used to have a lot of fun showing off to the kids, but I got older. Now my degree in art allows me to be a professor in a Netherlands college for adults."

He has loved the same woman for over twenty years and has two stepchildren whom he also loves. He met his wife when her sons attended his judo classes. He and his wife married only recently. "I saw no reason to involve the state in our private lives." She wanted them to marry, because she was feeling increasingly embarrassed when she had to fill out forms asking "married or single."

Two years ago, he says, "I finally heard her." They decided, "Since we are going to do this, we are going to do it big." They invited every friend and every business or professional colleague either had ever had. The list was huge. Several hundred people attended their wedding and the party afterwards. "And now I know the importance of ceremony. This day was the most significant in my life. It was a very special testament about our love."

I ask him how he would sum up his life. "In my personal life, I am happy. But I am a failure. I have accomplished nothing." I dispute that.

He says, "People are incapable of a true peace. We blame, we insist on having an enemy. Perhaps we lived in peace after the war only because we had the communists to hate. And now you have brought us the Moslems as a substitute for communists. You insist we hate them, too." He says about the Netherlands, "I used to be proud of our tolerance and open-mindedness, beginning with Erasmus. During the war, we had much to praise and much to be ashamed of. Now, like all of Europe, we are sliding to the right. We pretend we are decent just because we haven't yet joined your war. I am ashamed of the increase in prejudice I see in Holland."

We are two people who once hoped we were helping to make the world a more decent place. And we both thought that through our learning and our teaching we could nudge the world toward decency. I told him how Bob always said he taught psychotherapy to teach the world to love instead of hate. "And look at it now," Bart says.

PARIS, STOCKHOLM, AND HERRADURA

The tours are over. Before going back to California and surgery, I'll visit some friends; first, Felipe Garcia, right here in Paris. He arrives from a conference in India, with a big smile and a white linen pants suit he picked up for me there. We go to our favorite funky hotel, Louisiane. The assistant manager greets us like royalty and helps me into a hotel room off the only hall wide enough to accommodate my walker. (The Lousiane has the world's narrowest halls. During the years John Paul Sartre lived here, I wonder if he even noticed.) Felipe picks for himself a corner room full of windows. Late at night and in the early morning he watches the bakers across the street as they make pastries and croissants. In the early evening he watches people gather at the popular outdoor cafe across the street. He can see all the way to the Seine from his room. When I visit him there, I need to leave the walker beside the elevator and brace myself against both walls as I move slowly down the corridor to enjoy our fresh fruit, cheese, and wine that we stash by his windows. We sip together and watch the crowds, then go downstairs for a late dinner. We eat in a different ethnic restaurant each night, and thereby escape the immense expense which can result from our ever-declining US dollars. Indian, Thai, Chinese, and Italian are all tasty, cheap, and nearby.

We do the museums again. Whenever we meet in Paris, they are on our agenda, but this time we borrow a wheelchair at each museum. In France people in wheelchairs and their pushers pay no museum fee and never have to wait in line. In the Louvre guides motion us past the long, almost motionless lines. I am like a queen on a royal wheel chair, decked in Indian linen as I pass the plebian crowds, and suddenly we are less than six inches from Mona Lisa.

When Felipe leaves, I stay on a few days to see how well I can manage Paris without a tour guide or a friend. I have a hard time. I can't use the metros, because there are no elevators to the stations. Buses don't want cripples. They stop just long enough to load, and no one offers to help. In London all taxis are large enough to accommodate my walker, but most trunks in Paris are too small. Of course, the walker could fit nicely in the back seat, with me in front, but that is unheard of! Upholstery may be scratched, the French drivers explain in huge gestures. Or they simply signal their eloquent "No!" and stamp on the gas. But if there is a line of taxis, which very occasionally occurs at taxi stops, the first driver in line will spend ten minutes trying to jam my walker into his trunk before reluctantly letting a larger taxi have the fare.

I fly to **Stockholm,** a beautiful city surrounded by water. I'm here to visit an old friend, Graham Barnes. It's been years since we've had a quiet time together. If I hadn't gone to Stockholm, I never would have known how successful his life has become. His condo is beautiful, full of windows and light, and on the walls are five Dali prints I love, a Degas, a Warhol, and modern art I don't know. He has beautiful modern furniture, sleek marble walls, nice old wood floors, throw rugs, and, best of all, a partner of twenty years, Stephano, who spins rapidly between art expert, psychotherapist, lover, charmer, brat, superb cook, and loudly argumentative Greek. He keeps us animated.

Graham and I watch the Democratic convention together, while Stephano complains, "Graham has lived here twenty years and you've left the US, too, and you both constantly complain about your government. Underneath, you are the two most American people I have ever met!" We explain that we were fortunate enough to have grown up under Franklin and Eleanor, and nobody since then has been worth much. Or were they so fine because we were so young? Truth is, I heard Norman Thomas speak on socialism when I was about twelve, and have been a Thomas-type socialist ever since.

Graham loans me a computer copy of a novel he has written, his first. It's American Southern, heavy and anguished, and very good. Graham grew up in the South.

Stockholm is a clean air city. Everything sparkles. We take a boat trip around the harbor, go through two locks from bay to lake and back, and see gardens in full bloom. Some little cottages behind the flowers were given by the government to landless poor, whose families continue to live in them through lots of generations. We see parliament, other old, impressive buildings, and have lunch at the Grand Hotel, which has been grand through, I believe, over a century. We are seated with a view of the water, as we dine on avocado soup, asparagus with splendid dipping sauces, and smoked salmon. We shop and, by great luck, I find a $750 US dress reduced to $75.

Next, I visit friends, Carlos and Conchita in their summer home overlooking the Mediterranean and the small town called **Herradura** which means horseshoe, the shape of the bay. Carlos is a business man and Conchita one of the best therapists in Europe. Their house is beautiful and comfortable, though we spend most of our time outdoors. The garden is a joy. Thick green grass is surrounded by flowers, and below us the incredibly blue sea blends into blue sky. Nothing intrudes, not a house nor even the sound of cars. We are alone, just garden and sea and occasional white gulls. In the distance are a few tiny white sailboats. Behind the garden is a cool, blue-bottomed swimming pool. I hear myself laughing, and realize I am laughing for the first time in months. I laugh more, and don't turn it into a need to cry. I think that may be a miracle.

We are within a short drive of the great Alhambra, a wonder of the world that I should want to revisit. We could visit any of the lovely coastal cities. Instead, we laze. We make our own lunches from fresh asparagus, chilled giant shrimp, tomatoes, onions, shelled corn, garbanzos, home-made mayonnaise, and greens. Every night, between ten and midnight, which is dinner time in Spain, we drive to town for fresh seafood, usually at a restaurant beside the sea.

One Christmas, Carlos and Conchita stayed with us at Western Institute, along with our huge family: Bobs three sons and four daughters plus my son and two daughters, and all the spouses and children. The fact that Conchita and Carlos tolerated all of us is amazing, but they did more than that. They let each of our offspring feel special, and they said they had a wonderful time.

Then came Bob's illness and the 1989 earthquake that destroyed our home and institute, and took all the money we'd saved just to rebuild it. Bob died in 1992, my son David finished the rebuilding, and I put the property on the market. Three years later there were still no takers, and I was struggling to pay off the debts from the re-building. I'd been offered a plane ticket to Europe to work a week in Germany, but I was running out of money. As if she had extra-sensory perception, Conchita insisted I come live in this same wonderful vacation home, with their cook and housekeeper for the entire summer at their expense. I sublet my San Francisco apartment and left for Spain. All summer I walked the mile down to Herradura, swam in the

Mediterranean, then bought vegetables and fruit for dinner. That Fall the property finally sold.

Now there is no possibility of swimming in the sea. I don't care. The pool, the flowers, the house, and their company are enough! One afternoon Conchita and I go to town to a shop that sells wonderfully bright clothing, imported from India. I buy a dress with all the colors of the rainbow, and more. Somehow, I forget the rules of third world dyes. I put it, my super-sale dress from Stockholm, and the linen pant suit from Felipe into the same washer. The dress spread its brilliance horribly into the pale linen outfits. They are ruined. But the Spanish dress lives on, bright as ever. I am learning to say "Ni modo" (so what) when minor catastrophes occur.

I fly to California and have my hip replacement. My daughter and her daughter Ruth nurse me.

WHERE TO GO AND HOW TO TRAVEL SPLENDIDLY

My friends want me to write how I choose where to go and how I keep my expenses down. First, I keep expenses down by not having a home or apartment. I know that most people are nesters, so this would not be emotionally feasible. However, I save enough to travel full time. I have none of the usual expenses of insurance, repairs, maintenance, or monthly rent. I have no car so no car insurance, repairs, or garage rentals. It is not a sacrifice. Without encumbrances, I feel free. I'm fortunate to have a daughter with a home, who loans me a closet for extra clothes, a couple of shelves for books, and this year has had the kindness to take care of me after surgeries. You can keep expenses down by traveling where the dollar goes farther: Central and South America, and almost anywhere that does not use euros or pounds. Check prices and exchange rates on the internet, and look for bargains.

Plane travel is the most frustrating and expensive part of every trip. Airports almost everywhere are dreadful. A minor silliness is being forced to go barefoot through security because one crazy man once smuggled an incendiary in his shoes. I am glad no one so far has tried to smuggle an incendiary in his underpants, or we all might be marching naked through security. Lately I have avoided the intolerable lines for boarding passes and security checks by requesting a wheelchair when I make reservations. I'm not in the airport to shop, so I dislike the miles of shopping malls on the way to the boarding gates. Airport chairs are the ultimate in discomfort. What is so wrong with giving passengers soft chairs and even a place to lie down? Many airlines, especially British Airways in my experience, crowd the seats on the planes to the point of acute physical distress. Long plane rides aren't healthy for seniors, but it is impossibly expensive to break the trip. I yearn for an airline that offers fares to Europe, Asia, or South America with no extra charge for stopovers on our East and West coasts. It would be an incredibly generous gift if mileage "freebies" offered this. My motto: Bite the bullet and go. Travel is worth the discomfort.

On arrival, I look for an inexpensive hotel, inn, or private home. At my age I must have a private bathroom, and I pay extra at times for a large, clean swimming pool, especially in the tropics. As I have often written, I ask taxi drivers for recommendations. I read internet and travel books, and write down names and addresses of "wonderful bargains." Unfortunately, everybody else has also read of these bargains, and I find they don't stay bargains long. If you will be arriving in the evening or after a long trip, make a reservation for the first night. Later, if you like the area, you may find within a block or two of these bargains there are others equally as nice and less expensive. These are the places that don't use internet or get into travel books. Sometimes they are run by a couple who is new at the game and enthusiastic.

I stay at international hotels only during conferences, in order to be with friends. Otherwise, they are much too expensive. Besides, hundreds of white faces are monotonous, as is American English when spoken by everyone. Once in a while I do have an unquenchable yearning for a special hotel, a castle somewhere, for example, and I'm willing to pay for that luxury.

As for how I choose where to travel: whim, opportunity, blind luck, desire. Luck got me to the San Blas islands, opportunity to work got me to the Ukraine and Cuba, whim sent me to the Isle of Capri, but usually I go to places that I have always wanted to see. The world is so large and interesting that the real question is how much can I crowd into a lifetime? I've only written about my travels since January 2002, so you've missed much of what I've seen. Here are some of my earlier favorites:

Bhutan: I went on a tour, because only tour groups were allowed in the country at that time. Now I believe you can go on your own. I love the mountains, the clothing people wear, their adoration of their king, the emphasis on Buddhism in government and private life. Be sure to watch basketball and archery tournaments, even if you don't watch them at home. I think basketball is much more exciting in a country where no one is tall enough to slam dunk. Archery is a national sport. Archers use huge bows and are incredibly skillful. Visit local dance festivals, especially those that include children. When I was in Bhutan, there was no television, so the people were isolated from so-called civilization. Now, with television and more tourists, Bhutan may be becoming part of the homogenized world.

Cambodia: Ankor Wat is the most exciting archeological site I know: huge faces carved in stone, one on top of the other, magnificent by morning and evening light; carved walls of tiny figures in battle and in daily life; huge carved buildings with wonderful statues. My sister Bette and I flew directly from Bangkok to Phnom Penh when the Khmer Rouge was still nearby.

One night they were firing tracer bullets beside our window and there was also gun fire. We learned later that the Khmer Rouge was intimidating local people in order to influence an election. Tour groups evacuated the hotel at top speed, while my sister and I, plus a next-door French tourist watched them. We stayed in the hotel, because it seemed safer than the streets. In the midst of the evacuation, someone screamed, "Where's Roger?" The cry was taken up hysterically by that entire group. Finally they left without him. Instead of being frightened, the three of us stood in the corridor giggling about where Roger might be. Bette and I hired a marvelous local guide by pretending to be archeology professors who required the most knowledgeable guide available.

Vietnam and **Laos** are both wonderful. I suggest going alone or, if you insist, in a very small group and being open to all the people who want to practice speaking to you in English. These are safe and interesting countries to visit without an itinerary or time limit. When you find a town you like, stay awhile.

Bali has changed drastically for the worse due to over-invasion of tourists. When Bob and I first visited, there were only one or two hotels, and no one spoke English, but we were escorted to dances, ceremonies, and burials, and had the time of our lives.

If you want to visit an unknown world, take a trip into the back country of **Irian Jaya**, away from the areas that US mining companies and the Indonesian government are trying to destroy. Also, avoid the villages where the Dutch Evangelists are converting stone-age villages. To make them good Christians, the evangelists insist that breasts be covered, long pants instead of penis gourds be worn by men, and no one may use body paint. Sing alongs are now Bible songs. I spent two days in such a village and everyone, including the missionaries, seemed depressed. Catholic priests are more lenient with their clientele (there never were penis gourds in this part of Irian Jaya), and the churches are decorated beautifully with Mary, Jesus, Joseph, and the saints all carved as Irian Jayans. The tragedy here is that the priests oppose birth control yet don't have the means to help feed the malnourished children.

We stayed a week in a stone-age village that has avoided Christianity. The people grow their root vegetables and penis gourds, raise their pigs, laugh, and are very playful with us. The women even told us through our interpreter their minor problems with their spouses, and it is amazing how similar all of us are. They complained, "He doesn't stay with the children," "He is too bossy," etc. At first it is very strange to see these three-feet or longer, decorated gourds resting on the men's and boy's testicles with the rest of the body naked except for the leaf or twigs covering the anus so that no bad spirit can enter the body through that orifice. Women wear skirts made of reeds. All of the people smear themselves with smelly pig fat, paint their bodies, and wear elaborate wigs plus head-dresses.

Sometimes they are so carried away with singing and dancing that they go on all night. These villages have an age-old custom that a couple cannot have sex from the birth of a child until the child can walk well enough to join the tribe, so woman have a child only every three years. You must visit these villages with someone who speaks the village language and is an accepted friend. If you are physically able, a local guide will take you on a trek so far into the jungle that you will meet groups who have almost never before seen a white person. Go as soon as possible, while there still are primitive people. You can find tours on internet or simply fly into the capital and ask for a personal guide. I have what I consider a brilliant suggestion. Go to two of the most different places imaginable: one year Irian Jaya and the next year Iceland.

Because of the terrible cruelty of the government I wouldn't consider visiting **Burma** today, though I loved it when I went thirty years ago.

Singapore and **Hong Kong** are bores, but I'll bet you will find something interesting if you have to stay there awhile. An Indian friend, who now lives in Singapore, says, "Yes, it is uninteresting and a dictatorship, but the country functions. The water turns on, it is clean, and everything happens on time. It is heaven to India's hell."

I prefer **India**. You need lots of time and more than one trip to see

India even superficially. Bob and I took three trips to different parts of India on our own, after teaching in Bombay. There was no religious warfare in Srinigar then, so one year we were able to live on a houseboat on a beautiful lake surrounded by mountains, rode sleds in the snow, and Bob fished for trout in local rivers. I fulfilled a childhood dream by visiting the Shalimar gardens; "Pale hands I love beside the Shalimar" was a song my mother sang. My fourth trip was in southern India, which also has beautiful ruins, temples, and scenery. Traveling alone is difficult. Trains are mobbed, tourist agencies poor, and even crossing a street seems perilous in cities where you have to dodge motorcycles, cars, buses, bicycles, camels, and cows. I advise a tour group for the first trip,

Galapagos. Don't miss it! Best of the best for sea animals and rare birds. A furred seal and I played together, splashing each other.

Spend time in **Ecuador**, too. See the Andes, Indians who still wear native dress, and the wonderful native markets.

Chile. Take a trip from Chile to Argentina across the Andes. The Andes are incredible. Visit Torres del Paine in the southern tip of Chile, with its incredible ice and rock formations. On the way take a short boat trip to see ice floes, fjords, and penguins.

In **Italy**, go to the usual splendid places off-season to avoid crowds. Don't skip **Sicily**, with its Greek ruins, medieval cathedrals, beaches, fuming Mt. Etna, and wonderfully friendly people.

Spain, like Italy, is unique in the variety of its appeal. I apologize for writing only of Barcelona, a couple of beach towns, and my stay with friends. I love the Alhambra, Seville, Cordoba, Segovia, and dozens of other places. Off the tourist circuit in little mountain towns, Spain is an inexpensive country where you may want to spend weeks or months.

Wild Animals in Africa, I only went once, with six good friends who planned the trip with an agent who is a specialist. I don't feel competent to say which places are both safe and special now. But that one time! It is still as vivid as yesterday: Mother lions snoozing in the sun with their young, not ten feet from us; male hippos battling ferociously; lovely giraffes eating delicately and never making a sound; huge herds of elephants, and much more. Lions ignored us as they crept alongside our open jeep, stalking prey; their eyes transparent, they seemed not to notice us at all. There is no experience more fascinating than a big game jungle.

How will you choose your own special places, your:

Far-away places with strange-sounding names
Far-away over the sea.
Those far-away places with strange-sounding names
Are calling, calling to me.

I started choosing long ago. In childhood, my choices were imaginary. When I was in bed for months with rheumatic fever and then, almost immediately, whooping cough, I was still too young to read, so each night my father read to me from his old collection of OZ books. That was the beginning of my fascination for travel. Dorothy was a bore, because she was always trying to get back to her dull Kansas. I wouldn't have gone back on a bet. In fact, I spent my sick days touring OZ in fantasy. I played games with the Munchkins, lived in the palace with Ozma, roamed the forests with the Cowardly Lion, and discovered a new city, pure blue, made of a jewel found nowhere else. People didn't have to wear special glasses as in the Emerald City. This blue was real. It was my city and I named it Bluest Ever.

On another adventure, the Cowardly Lion and I led the OZ army through huge underground tunnels that ended eventually in the Nome King's kingdom. This time the King was friendly. The tunnels were exciting and we were very proud to have found a way to avoid the poison desert. I didn't talk about any of this to my father; I had already learned the joy of solo travel. My imaginary trips helped keep pain and boredom at bay.

A few years later, healthy and literate, I read Richard Halliburton's books over and over again, I wanted to do everything he had done, swim the Hellespont and the Panama Canal, spend a night on the Acropolis, run from the Marathon battlefield to Athens, visit the Taj Mahal. I also read and reread Peter Freuchen, and believed I would spend a year in an igloo in Greenland and travel by dogsled. Before I finished junior high school, I had mapped out a seven-year trip around the world.

I began studying Spanish in college and in 1943 spent the summer as a waitress on the S.S. North American, a cruise ship between Chicago and Buffalo. I saved all my tips, a bit over $500, and took a bus to Mexico, where I lived six months until my visa expired. I watched Diego Rivera paint his murals in the National Palace, and was one of the first tourists to see the Aztec murals of swimmers and butterflies which had recently been unearthed. I studied at the National University, though I rarely understood the professors' lectures. I had a Mexican lover whose family lived in the mountains east of Mexico City, and when we visited them we rode horses and he let me wear his pair of pistols and cowboy belt. I cried on the bus back to Illinois, and promised myself I would return to a life of traveling as soon as I had the money.

Instead I did what was expected, graduated from college, married, and had a family. (P.S: I do not regret this the tiniest bit.) I got my first passport in 1972, when Bob and I began doing psychotherapy workshops in other countries. Our firm rule: whenever we worked a week abroad, we would spend at least a week traveling in that country. Now widowed with my "children" in their fifties, I have become a homeless old soul who lives abroad except when I need the damned hip surgery.

How about you? Did you begin to dream of travel or did you actually travel when you were young? Did you have relatives who talked about their homelands? Or are you just beginning to wonder about travel? What would be for you splendid travel adventures? You can plan trips by reading travel books and the travel sections of Sunday newspapers, using internet, or asking friends and travel agents.

Or you can ask yourself. Sit back, be comfortable, close your eyes, and return to your past. Remember any early history of wanting to see new places. Don't hurry your exploration. Usually, we tend to forget our dreams or make them unimportant; instead, let yourself become fascinated with what you discover.

If you weren't much of a reader, remember countries in movies and television. Casablanca? Remember songs, and places you were told about in school. Do this for perhaps half an hour for several days. If you are as old as I am, you'll remember listening on the radio to princesses Elizabeth and Margaret saying goodnight to British children during World War II. Did you want to see England when the war was over? Now remember any places you have thought of visiting recently. Did any of my travels turn you on? When you have built a list of specific places, look up them up on the internet and read about them. My favorite method is to go to a book store that has comfortable chairs and sells coffee. I settle down and browse through every book pertaining to the place I want to see. I look for new ideas. For example, if Greece excites you, the Lonely Planet has descriptions of interesting Greek islands that are not over-run with tourists. I take notes and, before I set out, I buy one of the books.

Are you considering short or long vacations? If you are working and only have a couple of weeks a year, the answer is obvious. Remember the young Japanese woman who crossed the world to see Starry Night? Perhaps you have plenty of time, but you are a Dorothy, who likes to travel, but loves home most of all? Do you keep yourself stuck at home with a cute dog like Dorothy's Toto? She could take Toto to OZ, but not to real countries without lots of difficulties. A short trip is most interesting if you don't crowd it, or if you choose a tour. If you are a city lover, London, Paris, Edinburgh, Amsterdam, Barcelona, Venice, Florence, and others can keep you entranced for a week or two. So can a tiny mountain town or seaside resort.

Do you want to travel alone or with family, friends, or tour groups? Ask yourself if you enjoy your own company. If not, going alone may be difficult. Another important question: do you especially want to meet locals when you travel? If so, traveling alone works best. Almost everywhere, people speak English (except at the subway in the Ukraine. But notice that nothing terrible happened). You'll meet people in cafes, on park benches, or sitting next to you in the theater. If you belong to international groups such as Kiwanis, Elks, or professional associations, write them that you are coming. When asked, "Where are you from?" I find it easiest either to say, "I am American and detest our government" or "I am from Vancouver." Everybody likes Canadians. If you speak the local language, do go alone and practice making friends. It's a fine adventure.

Traveling by tour is much less adventuresome and you will meet fewer locals (except for those rounded up by tour companies to lecture to the group), but it is much easier. This summer, with my hip hurting and my walker a necessary nuisance, I truly enjoyed the tours I took. There are fascinating tours, economical or elegant, to all parts of the globe.

Perhaps what you really want is to be treated like royalty for a week or two. There are books written just for you. They describe the one hundred finest hotels, spa centers, luxury tours, or special cruises. Travel agents will be happy to make suggestions. For my husband's final trip, when he was in a wheel chair and on oxygen, we took a luxury cruise, in a stateroom with our own private balcony, from San Francisco to Alaska, and it was a beautiful trip.

How to make every trip a splendid, even brilliant vacation:

So much depends on how you color your experiences. Think serendipity. How lucky there was no flight to all the Central American countries, because instead I got to snorkel in San Blas! If the Alps are fogged in, as they almost always are when I am there, have fun in the darling little towns or visit the spas. Or leave. I did not enjoy being stuck in Chamonix for day after day of bad weather, and Paris was so close! Unlike tours, where you are locked in for the entire trip, or an all-inclusive resort vacation, you have the option of moving on. No matter how bad the weather in Honolulu, somewhere within a half hour flight the sun is shining. If you don't enjoy where you are, ask the locals where to go. If everything goes wrong, if the equivalent of the Khmer Rouge are shooting up the place, do your best to take care of yourself as you think, "What a great story this will be when I get home!" Life is how you define it. Define your trip as brilliant and do everything in your power to make it so. That isn't really very different from life everywhere. You make your life joyful, pleasant, sad, infuriating, fearful, anxiety-filled, or boring. Vacations are a good way to practice excitement or the pleasure of calmness. Give yourself a splendid trip and a splendid life.

Keep a diary, take photos, and buy postcards. Include in your diary the names of towns that you would otherwise forget. You can relive your brilliant vacation, just as you can relive your splendid life, whenever you choose. Why else do you suppose I have written this book? I relive my adventures as I write.

ADDENDUM

Passports. Be sure your passport is good for at least a year, because some countries require this. It must have sufficient empty pages for the seals and stamps from other countries.

Leave your passport, driver's license, credit cards, and extra cash in a safe, locked place. When you must have them with you, carry them around your neck or in a fanny pack that cannot easily be cut or unlocked. Carry in your inexpensive purse, wallet, or just in pockets whatever amount of money you need that day and are willing to have stolen; muggings occur in San Francisco and New York, just as in Barcelona and Rio. If you are dripping jewelry and carrying an expensive purse, take a taxi. If you are wandering about an unknown city alone, dress inconspicuously.

Credit cards. I buy airplane tickets with my American Express platinum card, because it guarantees my return flight in case of a medical emergency or death, and in major cities American Express offices will sell you national money and/or dollars. Mastercard and Visa are acceptable almost everywhere, whereas American Express is not. You should have your photo on your cards. I use ATM everywhere except Cuba. Nowadays, take euros to Cuba.

Itinerary. Leave copies with friends and family, plus known hotels and phone numbers. Keep your itinerary up to date by email.

Packing. I've written about packing before. Carry as little as possible. When you need to look dressy for several days, try one dress, two scarves, a dressy pair of slacks, a jacket that harmonizes with the dress and slacks, a sweater and a couple of blouses that can be used with both dress and slacks. For ordinary travel, I prefer to dress like the people on the street, except that all my clothes must be wrinkle-proof and machine washable. In warm climates my clothes are light weight and I add swimming suits and shorts. In cold weather I add thermal underwear and a coat. I put my medicines and vitamins in marked sandwich bags to eliminate the weight of bottles. I take a notebook, pens, and a maximum of three books, which I exchange in used book stores. My one luxury is my own small feather pillow.

Sometimes, like right now in Mexico, I carry my laptop to use as a typewriter only. Internet cafes do the trick.

Miscellaneous hints for making traveling easier:
Get reserved bus seats on the shady side. Carry a sweater in case of over air-conditioning.

Always carry a card with the name and address of your hotel in English and in the language of the country. Each time you go exploring around the city, take a map on which you mark your destinations. This is for you! Don't expect locals to read maps that are printed in English. Also carry a daily card with your destinations and any places you change buses or trains, written in the language of the country. Someone in your hotel will write this for you. When you are ambling, pick out a local landmark near where you are staying, to serve as home base. A particular church, statue, or park, for instance.

Be respectful. Apologize for not knowing the local language.

Tip well. (I was a waitress, so I know the importance of tips.)

Don't tell marketplace merchants that you can't afford their merchandise. They know you are richer than they can even imagine. You came by plane, and an inexpensive hotel room costs more for one day than they earn in a week or a month. It's okay to say, "Too much," or "No, thank you," and smile. If you find something you really like, buy it. It may not appear again anywhere.

Don't question locals about their politics, if they differ from yours. There are today five Cuban professional men who were railroaded into prison for life in Miami. All Cubans in Cuba know and care about these men, so don't try to tell them that our government is in any way superior to theirs. The same applies everywhere. Don't go to convert. Go to learn and enjoy.

WISH ME LUCK

Wish me luck as you wave me good-bye.
Cheerio, here I go on my way.
Give me a smile I can keep for awhile,
In my heart while I'm away.
Till we meet once again you and I,
Wish me luck as you wave me good-bye.
             - Gracie Fields

About the author:

Mary Goulding MSW began in early childhood imagining herself traveling through OZ, and never stopped loving the idea and then the reality of being in new countries.

She and her late husband, Robert L. Goulding MD, developed **Redecision therapy**, a brief, effective form of psychotherapy which they taught internationally and at their famous Western Institute For Group And Family Therapy, in California. Mary continues to lecture at psychotherapy conferences and occasionally still gives teaching workshops to professional audiences.

Mary finished this book in time for her eightieth birthday. She describes people she has met and places she has experienced, and uses her teaching skills to help you make your own splendid travel adventures.

EXPLORE THE WORLD ALONE
by Mary Goulding
Additional copies may be ordered from

CHANDRA BOOKS
PO BOX 650
AROMAS CA 95004

Send check or money order:
$12 plus $5 postage and handling in the United States.
Mexico or Canada (US dollars only) $12 plus $6 postage and handling
Overseas: (US dollars only) $12 plus $13 airmail postage and handling

Name_____
Address_____
—

Name_____
Address_____
—

If this is a gift please add your name and address

_____

_____

Message on gift card/s

_____

_____

$3 off postage and handling for each additional book sent to the same
address
Number of books ____

HOW TRAVEL SPLENDIDLY ...
A MEMOIR OF PEOPLE AND PLACES